The Quick Reference Guide to Your Child's Health:
Birth to Age Five

The Quick Reference Guide to Your Child's Health

Birth to Age Five

Alia Y. Antoon, M.D.
and
Denise M. Tompkins, R.N.

LOWELL HOUSE

LOS ANGELES

NTC/Contemporary Publishing Group

The purpose of this book is to educate. It is sold with the understanding that the publisher and author shall have neither liability nor responsibility for any injury caused or alleged to be caused directly or indirectly by the information contained in this book. While every effort has been made to ensure its accuracy, the book's contents should not be construed as medical advice. Each person's health needs are unique. To obtain recommendations appropriate to your particular situation, please consult a qualified health care provider.

Library of Congress Cataloging-in-Publication Data

Antoon, Alia Y.
 The quick reference guide to your child's health : birth to age five / by Alia Y. Antoon and Denise M. Tompkins.
    p.   cm.
 Includes bibliographical references.
 ISBN 0-7373-0492-8 (pbk.)
 1. Pediatrics—Popular works. 2. Infants—Care and hygiene—Popular works. 3. Children—Care and hygiene—Popular works. I. Tompkins, Denise M. II. Title.

RJ61.A58 2000
618.92—dc21   00-058631

Published by Lowell House
A division of NTC/Contemporary Publishing Group, Inc.
4255 West Touhy Avenue, Lincolnwood, Illinois 60712, U.S.A.

Managing Director and Publisher: Jack Artenstein
Executive Editor: Peter Hoffman
Director of Publishing Services: Rena Cooperman
Managing Editor: Jama Carter
Editor: Claudia McCowan
Project Editor: Carmela Carvajal

Design by Nancy Freeborn
Illustrations by Ilene Robinette Studio

Printed in the United States of America
International Standard Book Number: 0-7373-0492-8
00 01 02 03 04 DHD 18 17 16 15 14 13 12 11 10 9 8 7 6 5 4 3 2 1

Dedication

To my sons, Austin and Brendan, for giving me greater dimension and knowledge about the care of children.

—ALIA Y. ANTOON, M.D.

I would like to dedicate this book to my three children, Megan, Ryan, and Cate, who have taught me volumes about child care, and to my husband Ron for his unending support, understanding, and encouragement throughout this project. I would also like to thank the staff of the Boston Shriners Burns Institute from 1975 to 1992 for everything that they taught me about the care of sick children, and the staff at the Boston Children's School and The Learning Project Elementary School, for everything they taught me about normal children's behaviors. I'd also like to thank Dr. Antoon for being a great pediatrician for my three children and teaching me to always trust my instincts as a mother who truly can tell when my children need health care.

—DENISE M. TOMPKINS, R.N.

Acknowledgments

We would like to offer a special thank you to Stephanie O'Brien, Walter Cahners, and Howard Speicher for all of their help, encouragement, and practical reviews of different aspects of the book. Thanks also to our editor at Lowell House, Linda Hudson Perigo, for her wonderful enthusiasm and guidance. Many personal and professional thanks to Dr. Ronald Tompkins, Chief of Staff at the Shriners Hospitals for Children, Boston, for his constant interest and moral support throughout the project. And a final thanks to Dr. David Chedekel for introducing us to Jack Artenstein and giving us the opportunity to work with the Lowell House team.

Contents

Chapter Three: Common Childhood Illnesses and Diagnoses   101

Chapter Four: Common Injuries   179

Chapter Seven: Behavior and Developmental Issues   **251**

Foreword

Neither academic degrees nor business success can prepare one for being a parent; you only come to realize this the first night that your child is sick. My husband and I are parents of two-year-old Katie and ten-month-old Michael, and many times during these past two years we've relied upon Alia and Denise, longtime colleagues and friends. Alia Antoon, M.D., is an outstanding Harvard pediatrician who is well known and respected for her commonsense approach to pediatric medical problems and child rearing. Denise Tompkins, R.N., is a highly experienced pediatric nurse who lectures worldwide on pediatric nursing issues and injury prevention. Both are working "supermoms" with lovely, healthy, well-adjusted children to prove it.

A Quick Reference Guide to Your Child's Health: Birth to Age Five will help you sort out your children's medical needs and start them on the road to recovery. This book is rich with practical information that is just not found as readily anywhere else. There is basic advice commonly given to parents by pediatricians during regular well-baby visits, as well as information on newborn care, nutrition, behavior, and development. Most important, the book addresses the kinds of questions that go through your mind when you are pacing back and forth in the middle of the night with a crying baby (or two) in your arms. How can I make this poor child more comfortable? Should I take his temperature, and which thermometer should I use? How serious is a "serious" fever? Should I call the doctor right now or can it wait until morning? Should we rush to the hospital? What happens if she goes into seizure? What is this rash? And what exactly was that hand, foot, and mouth disease I heard the neighborhood kids had? Should I line up alternative child care for tomorrow, or phone the office and cancel my appointments now? "Honey, get out that book and look up fever again, would you?!"

Alia and Denise have provided a tremendous service to today's busy parents by giving us answers that are clear, concise, and readily understood. This is the medical "instruction manual" that should come with all new babies when they are born. It should be required reading for concerned parents, nannies, and others responsible for the care of small children.

—COLLEEN M. RYAN, M.D., F.A.C.S.
Assistant Professor of Surgery, Harvard Medical School;
Associate Surgeon, Massachusetts General Hospital,
Shriners Burns Hospital, Boston Unit; Working Mom

CHAPTER ONE

Fundamentals of Child Health

INTRODUCTION

Parents provide a basic framework for making certain their child is as healthy as possible. This includes a well-balanced diet, regular exercise, sufficient sleep, a safe environment, and regular medical checkups. Your child's health care needs, growth pattern, and developmental milestones are intimately connected. Your job is to provide the structure and environment to enable a healthy child to flourish. When your child does get sick, you can often help him feel better by being on top of the problem and treating his symptoms with the help of your child's doctor. This book will give you:

- practical advice about how to handle common childhood symptoms, injuries, and illnesses.
- fundamental information about caring for a newborn baby.
- basic information about healthy children and how to tell when they are sick.
- what to do in an emergency.
- an overview of developmental and behavioral issues.

CHOOSING A DOCTOR FOR YOUR CHILD

Your first task is to set up a system of primary health care for your child. Primary health care involves treating and preventing common health problems through routine checkups. These visits will give you an opportunity to discuss your child's progress and any matters of concern. Regular checkups will ensure that minor problems are noticed before they become serious problems. There are many choices for obtaining primary health care and a primary health care provider for your child.

In general, a good way to choose a primary health care provider for your child is to talk to friends, neighbors, and relatives to gather recommendations. Your personal doctor or clinic may also give you a recommendation. "M.D." stands for medical doctor and means that a doctor has graduated from an accredited medical school and has registered with the state board of medicine. A pediatrician is a doctor who has specialized in the care of children and has taken further training to be certified by the American Board of Pediatrics. Family physicians or general practitioners (GP's) are also qualified to care for children, and some people prefer that the same doctor take care of the whole family. You can call your state medical society to research a doctor's credentials or look them up in your local library in the *American Medical Directory* or the *Directory of Medical Specialists*. Many hospitals also offer a referral list of doctors that are affiliated with their hospital.

The primary places where you can get a regular checkup (primary health care) for your child include: a private medical practice, a neighborhood or community health clinic, a public health clinic, or a health maintenance organization (HMO). Opting for a private medical practice means that you choose a doctor and go to her office for checkups, immunizations, and routine laboratory tests. This physician usually works with an office nurse or pediatric nurse practitioner. He may work by himself or in a group practice that lets other doctors in the same group rotate coverage for sick children when the office is closed.

Neighborhood and community health clinics are often available in cities and are usually associated with a hospital. They are often called well-baby clinics and are staffed by primary health care teams that include doctors, nurses, and other health professionals. You may not always see the same person when you bring your child to the clinic, but all the members of the

> **Ways to Obtain Primary Health Care**
>
> - Private medical practice with a pediatrician or family practitioner
> - Neighborhood or community health center or clinic
> - Public health clinic
> - Health maintenance organization (HMO)

health care team will work together to benefit your child's health care. These clinics are usually open for long hours during the day and early evening but usually are not available for twenty-four-hour coverage. Public health clinics are similar to neighborhood and community health clinics except that their hours and services are usually more limited. They are often found in cities and rural areas and provide select free health care services for children. Check with the public health department in your city or county to determine what is available in your area.

HMO's are prepaid medical insurance plans that provide a variety of health care services through their own clinics and doctors. They have a lot of rules governing how you access health care, and you have to follow their protocols. With many HMO's it is very important that you become a vocal advocate for your child. Always be prepared with all the information you can gather about your child's problems so that you can articulate your child's needs. Always read your health care plan carefully and ask a lot of questions to learn exactly how it operates.

When choosing your child's health provider care it is also important to consider the practical aspects. These may include:

- Is the office or clinic conveniently located? Is it near public transportation? Does it have parking?
- Are the hours suited to your family's schedule? Are night or weekend hours important to you, and are they available?
- What happens when the office or clinic is closed? How do you access medical care after hours?
- Is it hard to get an appointment? How long do you have to wait?
- What are the fees?

Before making a final choice regarding regular health care for your child, you should schedule an appointment and talk with the doctor or key person in the clinic or health care service. You want to be sure you can easily ask questions and that you and your family are comfortable with both the doctor and his group practice or clinic. Once you have chosen a primary health care provider for your child, you can work on a long and trusting relationship to help keep your child as happy and healthy as possible.

GUIDE TO WELL-BABY/CHILD CHECKUPS

Babies and young children spend a lot of time having routine well-baby checkups as well as calls and visits for illness. Before your baby is discharged from the hospital, he will receive the first of many complete physical exams. This is done either by your pediatrician or one employed by the hospital. At that time your baby will also receive his first immunization, the hepatitis-B shot. The schedule of future checkups for routine well-baby care will center around your baby's growth, developmental needs, and immunization schedule.

Because you know your child better than anyone else, your involvement in his health care is critical. It's your job to speak up for your child, ask questions about anything you don't understand, or voice any concerns you may have. It may be helpful to go to each checkup with a list of questions in hand.

Every time you take your child for a well-baby checkup, he will be measured for length, head circumference, and weight. These growth parameters give your baby's doctor a good idea of how he is progressing. The exact numbers are not important. Your doctor is looking at the trend of your baby's overall growth pattern. Many times your doctor will chart your baby's weight, length, and head circumference on a special growth chart. These forms have normal growth patterns for children at different ages. A sample of this growth chart is contained in Appendix B.

Your doctor will also look at your child's skin, listen to her heart and lungs, look in her ears, palpate her abdomen, and check her reflexes. He will also discuss diet and nutrition as well as check on what new things your child has learned to do, such as rolling over, sitting up, crawling, and so on. During her first five years, your child is changing rapidly, and each change builds upon previous ones. Your child's health care provider will be monitoring your child's trends in these areas and discovering what the normal pattern for your child will be. Each physical exam adds to the baseline data of what is normal and healthy for your child. Charts and tables for normal patterns are only guidelines, so remember that your doctor will work with you to develop specific guidelines and expectations for your unique and wonderful child.

Basic Health Exam for Infants and Young Children

- Weight, length, and head circumference measurements
- Immunization update as needed
- Skin assessment
- Heart and lung auscultation
- Ear and throat check
- Abdominal exam
- Reflex check
- Developmental assessment for motor skills, language development, and intellectual skills

Developmental milestones, another measure of continued learning in the areas of motor activities, language development, and intellectual and emotional skills, are discussed in chapter 7.

Immunizations

Another key element for keeping your child healthy is to keep her immunizations up to date. The purpose of immunizations is to protect individuals and communities from the most severe infectious diseases. An immunization works by introducing a very mild form of the infection to a person through a vaccine so that the body can develop immunity without actually contracting the disease. Modern immunizations and vaccinations have brought infectious diseases such as polio, diphtheria, pertussis (whooping cough), tetanus, measles, mumps, and rubella under control. (See appendix C, Routine Immunization Schedule.) In fact, smallpox (once the cause of many childhood deaths) has

Table 1.1

Guidelines For Well-Baby/Child Checkups	
Age	**Procedures for Checkup**
Newborn	Physical exam including developmental assessment and hearing screen. Baseline measurement for length, weight, and head circumference. Review umbilical cord care/hygiene and circumcision care if applicable. Infant car seat needed for transport home. Report any fevers immediately. Immunization: Hepatitis-B (1).
1 month	Physical exam including developmental assessment and hearing screen. Growth assessment with length, weight, and head circumference. Report any fevers immediately. Feeding reviewed. Immunization: Hepatitis-B (2).
2 months	Physical exam including developmental assessment and hearing screen. Growth assessment with length, weight, and head circumference. Discuss need for vitamins, iron, and fluoride supplements. Check visual and hearing acuity. Immunizations: DPT (1), Polio (1), Hib (1).
4 months	Physical exam including developmental assessment and hearing screen. Growth assessment with length, weight, and head circumference. Discuss contagious disease if in a day care setting. Between four to six months, introduce baby cereal. Immunizations: DPT (2), Polio (2), Hib (2).
6 months	Physical exam including developmental assessment and hearing screen. Growth assessment with length, weight, and head circumference. Discuss baby cereal and baby food. Introduce only one new food at a time to note allergy or intolerance. Review teething. Deciduous teeth start at six months. Start using toothbrush. Immunizations: Hepatitis-B (3), DPT (3), Polio (3), Hib (3).

Table 1.1 *continued*

Age	Procedures for Checkup
9 months	Physical exam including developmental assessment and hearing screen. Growth assessment with length, weight, and head circumference. Review childproofing your house before baby is mobile.
12 months	Physical exam including developmental assessment and hearing screen. Growth assessment with length, weight, and head circumference. TB test and blood test for lead levels and anemia. Discuss feeding and weaning from bottle. Start whole milk. Immunizations: Chicken Pox (Varicella).
15 months	Physical exam including developmental assessment and hearing screen. Growth assessment with length, weight, and head circumference. May switch vitamin and fluoride drops to chewable tablets. Begin more table food. Cut in small pieces to prevent choking. Immunizations: MMR (1), Hib (4).
18 months	Physical exam including developmental assessment and hearing screen. Growth assessment with length, weight, and head circumference. Immunization: DPT (4).
2 years	Physical exam including developmental assessment and hearing screen. Growth assessment with length, weight, and head circumference. Discuss toilet training readiness.
2½ years	Physical exam including developmental assessment and hearing screen. Growth assessment with length, weight, and head circumference. Discuss falls and first aid.
3 years	Physical exam including developmental assessment and hearing screen. Growth assessment with height, weight, and head circumference. Blood pressure taken. Take for first dental visit.

Age	Procedures for Checkup
4 years	Physical exam including developmental assessment and hearing screen.
	Growth assessment with height, weight, and head circumference.
	Blood pressure taken; vision screen done for color and acuity.
	Hearing discussed; test may be ordered if any question of hearing loss or frequent ear infections.
	Discuss bike helmet even with tricycle or training wheels.
5 years	Physical exam including developmental assessment and hearing screen.
	Growth assessment with height, weight, and head circumference.
	Vision and hearing screen in preparation for formal school.
	Completion of school health forms. (Keep copy at home for immunization reference and camp.)
	TB skin test and blood test for lead and anemia.
	Discuss transition from car seat to car seat belt according to height, weight, and age.
	Immunizations: DPT (5), Polio (4), MMR (2).

been eradicated worldwide because of successful vaccination programs. New immunization programs have begun for haemophilus influenza-B (which protects the body against several diseases, especially meningitis, epiglottitis, and pneumonia), chicken pox, and hepatitis-B. Many immunizations require a booster dose to continue maximum immunity throughout your child's life. Influenza immunization (flu shot) and an annual pneumonia immunization are also available each year. Because of their short protection periods (about one year), they are usually given only to children who are considered high risk. Children at high risk for influenza or pneumonia include children with chronic cardiovascular or pulmonary disease, immunosuppression, diabetes, HIV or AIDS, kidney disease, or abnormal hemoglobin diseases. Talk to your child's doctor if you think your child is at risk and would benefit from these vaccines.

Measurements

Head circumference, length, weight, physical exams, immunizations, diet, and developmental milestones are all part of your child's well-baby checkups. Table 1.1 describes in general terms what will happen at each well-baby checkup from birth until the age of five. This is meant as a general guide; your doctor may choose a slightly different age for certain medical tests and immunizations or a slightly different time interval between visits, but this should give you a general idea of what to expect and when to expect it.

DIET

A well-balanced, nutritious diet forms the basis of good health. Good nutrition supplies the body with energy for physical activity and is essential for growth. It is important to eat well both to prevent illness and recover from illness. During the first five years of life your child will experience a multitude of dietary changes both in terms of type of food and amount of food eaten.

The first diet choice for your newborn is whether to breast-feed, formula feed, or some combination of the two. It's important for you to know that your baby can grow and develop normally—whichever method you choose. For the first four to six months of your baby's life, this will be your child's source of nutrition. See chapter 6 for in-depth information about feeding newborns. Once you have established a feeding pattern, talk to your baby's doctor about giving supplemental vitamins, iron, and fluoride.

Babies and young children basically eat and drink when they're hungry and thirsty. You can control the quality and types of food offered, but your baby will control the quantity. During the first year, babies generally drink three ounces of formula or breast milk for each pound of body weight spread out over twenty-four hours. Keep your baby on breast milk or formula until he is close to twelve months old. If you have chosen to feed your baby milk formula, make sure that it is high in iron. You can start to introduce solid foods to your baby's diet at four to six months of age. You know your baby is ready to start eating solid foods when he:

> **Sample Formula/Breast Milk requirement for a fifteen-pound baby:**
>
> Three ounces per pound x 15 = 45 ounces over a 24-hour period

- Can sit up and hold his head up by himself.
- Weighs at least double his birth weight.
- Will open his mouth for a spoon.
- Is four to six months old.

Start solid foods by feeding your baby a small amount of baby rice cereal. Do not put baby cereal or any food in a bottle as it can cause choking. Rice cereal is the easiest to digest. Place a small amount on a baby spoon or small spoon. She may spit it out at first. This is normal. It takes time for your baby to get used to any new taste and texture as well as the mechanics of getting food off a spoon. Also, be prepared for a mess! After rice cereal, try clear fruit juices like apple juice and white grape juice. Then go to a few pureed fruits and vegetables or commercially prepared baby foods. Read all labels carefully on commercially prepared items because excess sugar, salt, and starch are often added. These items will not improve your baby's nutrition and may get him used to tastes that might best be avoided. Be sure to add only one new food at a time. Wait three to five days before adding a new one in order to watch out for potential food allergies. Symptoms of a potential food allergy may include a skin rash, runny nose, itchy and watery eyes, vomiting or diarrhea, or a breathing problem.

Also at about six months, you may want to start your baby drinking from a cup. Start by letting her hold a plastic cup to get used to it. Drinking from a cup is a new skill and takes practice. We recommend starting with a "tippy cup" or one with a spill-proof lid. Use breast milk or formula for her first drinks so that she can learn the new skill with a familiar taste. Once able to drink successfully from a cup, you may want to introduce fruit juice in a cup. At this age, limit fruit juices to no more than eight ounces a day so that your child will have an appetite for other foods. As your child learns to use a cup and eat solid foods, she may begin to breast-feed less often or take fewer bottles.

At about eight months of age, your baby will be able to try "finger foods" that she can pick up and eat herself. Good finger foods include pieces of cheese, soft-cooked vegetables, Cheerios-type cereal, or a special teething cookie. Give her a small amount at a time and let her feed herself while you are watching. Never leave your child alone while he is eating.

When your baby is twelve months old, you can begin to introduce cow's milk. Stay with whole milk until your child is at least three years of age. The extra fat in whole milk is essential for brain development. Also at around twelve months, encourage your child to use a bottle less and the cup more. Slowly decrease the number of bottles and increase the number of cups per day. The evening bottle is typically the hardest to give up.

After the first year, your baby's appetite, rate of weight gain, and growth will begin to slow down. At this time, he will also begin to eat many of the foods the rest of the family eats, and you should aim to include your baby in family meals. Just be sure to cut everything into very small pieces. Avoid foods that can cause choking such as hot dogs, grapes, carrots, popcorn, nuts, raisins, chunky peanut butter, and any other small hard foods. If you do serve small, round items like hot dogs and carrots that could block your child's airway if inhaled accidentally, cut them into fourths or in a half-moon shape to avoid this potential hazard.

To keep your child growing well and healthy, offer a variety of foods from each food group every day. A balanced diet for a one- to two-year-old child should include:

- Three servings from the milk group.
- Two servings from the meat group.
- Four servings from the fruit and vegetable group.
- Four servings from the bread and grain group.

Don't worry if your child doesn't get these exact amounts every day. Children are notorious for peculiar eating habits. Chart eating patterns over one week to see if he is getting a well-balanced diet—and remember to continue giving your child a multivitamin. Many children do not eat large meals and need a healthy snack between meals to keep their energy up and their dispositions sunny. Nutritious snack foods should include fresh fruits, applesauce, small chunks of cheese, yogurt, rice cakes, crackers, creamy peanut butter, pretzels, graham crackers, and frozen juice pops. Be careful at this time not to introduce too much extra sugar into your child's diet with pre-packaged, processed snack foods. Too much sugar may not only result in tooth decay, but in bad lifetime eating habits as well.

These general nutrition requirements will continue for the two to five year old, but the portions will increase. Continue to read labels carefully and avoid processed foods that add sugar, salt, and starch. Over the course of a week, she will get all the nutrition needed to grow and develop. Many children at this age go through some sort of "food fad" during which she will become extremely fussy about how a food is prepared or limit her diet to certain foods only. It is very common for a child to start rejecting a wide range of foods that she previously had eaten. The best way to cope with this situation is to basically ignore it. Continue to offer a highly nutritious selection of foods each day but do not be upset if your child refuses. If you try to force your child to eat these other foods, you will only cause conflict. There is little danger your child will develop a specific nutritional deficiency. A child can remain healthy for a surprisingly long period of time on a limited diet. A child who senses that her parents are anxious about eating may refuse food as a means of getting attention. Remain calm and unconcerned if this occurs. Continue to give her multivitamins regularly, make sure she gets plenty of fluids to drink, and make sure she is gaining weight normally.

THE IMPORTANCE OF FLUIDS

The earth is comprised of 70 percent water. Human beings are also approximately two-thirds water. *Proper hydration is essential to good health.* Always make sure that your child drinks plenty of liquids. Whenever your child is sick, increase the amount of fluids he drinks because illness increases fluid loss. This may lead to further problems including:

- higher fever.
- thicker mucus or "phlegm" that will clog the child's respiratory passage, starting at the nose and potentially proceeding to the lungs.
- major fluid and body mineral losses through vomiting or diarrhea.

Fluid replacement and maintenance is necessary because a sick child is losing extra fluids during his illness and he needs to replace those as well as keep up his normal requirements. Once a child is six months old, she needs to have approximately thirty-two ounces or one quart of liquids each day. A child with a fever needs to drink at least two more ounces of fluid for each pound of body weight per day. This should be increased to at least three ounces of fluid per pound of body weight per day if he is vomiting or has diarrhea. Sick children often do not feel like eating and drinking. Your child can survive without much food when sick; it is very important, however, for him to drink as much as possible to replace fluids lost due to sweating, vomiting, and diarrhea. While your child is awake you must constantly try to administer fluids. The *key technique* is to offer *small amounts of liquids at frequent time intervals*. Be creative and also use the illness as a time to offer treats.

> *You should not force your child to eat; however, it is important to make sure he drinks plenty of fluids.*

Tips for giving fluids to sick children:

- Soda that is allowed to go flat is tolerated better than fruit juice.
- Make flavored water or ice cubes.
- Consider diluting their favorite liquid. Fruit juices or even milk or formula can be diluted so that your child can tolerate it better and take in more liquids. You might start with one quarter of the juice or milk, and three quarters water. As they feel better, advance to one half liquid and one half water, then three quarters liquid and one quarter water, to finally full strength again.
- Give frequent small amounts of liquids. Every half hour works best. To entice your child to drink, you might use a huge special glass or a tiny play teacup filled to the brim. Some children like to drink liquids with a teaspoon, or they may like to use a medicine dropper or syringe to squirt liquids into their mouth. Special flexible straws may also help encourage fluid intake for a sick child.
- Popsicles and ice chips also count as liquids, as well as soup and Jell-O. You can make your own ice pops out of any liquid your child likes. It could be their

favorite fruit juice or even frozen soda. If you don't have the ice-pop forms just use your ice cube tray and make flavored cubes.

- Use an oral electrolyte solution if your child (over one month old) has severe vomiting or diarrhea. It is absorbed quickly and is useful to keep your child hydrated in these circumstances. Common commercial oral electrolyte solutions for children under the age of one year are Pedialyte, Ricelyte, and Kao Lectrolyte. They are also available as a generic product at larger drug-stores. You do not need a prescription for them, and they can usually be found with infant formula. Children over one year old may continue to use the oral electrolyte products for severe vomiting or diarrhea, but you may also use one of the sports electrolyte drinks like Gatorade or SportAde, which are available in most grocery stores. As your child improves you can gradually add diluted juice, milk, or formula. You can even make flavored ice pops from the oral electrolyte solutions.

It usually doesn't matter if the liquids are hot or cold unless your child has a very high fever. In that case, cold liquids may help to reduce the fever.

EXERCISE AND PHYSICAL ACTIVITY

Regular exercise is good for everyone, even babies. Exercise strengthens the heart and lungs and helps keep the body fit. The first thing a baby may learn is how to hold her head up. Babies love to grab and shake objects and kick their feet, and play can encourage these activities. Place toys just out of her reach so that she has to stretch and reach for them. Help your baby clap her hands or stamp her feet to exercise her limbs.

Children love to move and run around, and young children get a lot of exercise from play. Exercise will help to shape your child's body and her sense of self. It also gives your child coordination and balance, speed and flexibility. Group activities help teach cooperation. Try rolling a ball for your child to catch or help her with a pull toy. Take your toddler to the playground and on frequent walks. Don't confine her to the stroller. Buy her a toy stroller or another pull-or-push toy and let her walk alongside you. Young children love repetitive activities so encourage some that also provide exercise. As your child gets older, she may become more social and coordinated and better able to follow rules. Teach your child games that involve movement such as hide and seek or freeze tag. A four or five year old can start with hopscotch, jump rope, and T-Ball. Some communities offer a "half-kick" soccer program for three to five year olds that gives them directed running with friends. Young children also enjoy climbing structures at playgrounds, swings, and riding tricycles. Encourage your child to wear a toddler bike helmet when riding her tricycle. This will establish a good habit for wearing protective gear in sports activities as she grows older. Many children develop sedentary lifestyles from watching television or playing video games all day. Encourage your child to spend more time outdoors in active play.

YOUR CHILD'S TEMPERATURE

Your child's body temperature is one of the measurements you can use to determine if she is sick. In children, normal body temperature ranges from 98.6°F (36°C) to 100.4°F (38°C). A child's body temperature may also fluctuate with her activity level and the time of day. It is often lower in the morning after a night's sleep and higher in the afternoon after a day's activity. It will also be higher after a vigorous physical workout.

*Fever is usually a sign that
your child's body is fighting off infection.*

A hot forehead or flushed cheeks may be the first sign that your child has an elevated temperature, but you must take her temperature with an appropriate thermometer to be sure. Doctors will usually call body temperature a fever when the body temperature registers higher than 100.4°F (38°C) rectally, 99.7°F (37.6°C) orally, or 99°F (37°C) axillary (the armpit). Fever by itself is not dangerous. It is usually a sign that the body is fighting off an infection. What is more important is how your child looks and feels. A child can be very ill without a fever or quite healthy with one. And the degree of fever doesn't always reflect the extent of the child's illness, either. Certain childhood illnesses such as Roseola are known to cause a very high fever like 104°F, taken rectally. Your child's fever may also increase if she is dehydrated. This means she has not ingested enough fluids. Dehydration will often occur due to your child throwing up or having diarrhea. A low body temperature or hypothermia develops if the body temperature falls below 95°F (35°C).

Measurement of Body Temperature

You must measure your baby's body temperature with a thermometer. There are many types of thermometers available today. The most common are *mercury, digital, and liquid crystal thermometers.* You should choose the one that you are most comfortable with and are able to use accurately. Be sure to keep more than one thermometer in the house in case you misplace one, it breaks, or a battery dies. The liquid crystal thermometers tell only if your child is warm. They may change color or register a number on a scale. You can use them to determine if your child is getting a fever, but you will also have to take your child's temperature with the more accurate digital or mercury thermometer for a true measurement so that you can track the course of your child's fever.

The *most accurate* thermometers are the *mercury* and *digital thermometers*. Mercury thermometers are the old-fashioned glass thermometers where the mercury forms a thick silver line down the middle to register the body temperature. Some people find them hard to read at first so you may want to practice on yourself. They are fairly inexpensive and come as rectal, oral, or armpit thermometers.

A rectal thermometer has a round bulbous tip; oral thermometers have a ¼-inch slender tip. The oral thermometer may also be used under the armpit to take an axillary temperature. Special axillary thermometers are also available with a short stem to fit under the armpit. Digital thermometers cost approximately $7 to $10. They are quick and they will measure an accurate body temperature in thirty seconds to one minute. After two years these thermometers may need new batteries, and you can tell the batteries are getting low when it takes the thermometer longer to register a temperature. The ear probes are expensive, often in the $50 range; but they are very fast, registering an accurate body temperature in approximately fifteen seconds or less. Ear probe thermometers are sometimes hard to use in children less than two years old whose ear canals may be too small for the thermometer tip to fit into properly. They are also difficult to position in fidgety babies. Although the liquid crystal thermometers are not as accurate, they are extremely easy to use. They are often useful with squirmy babies to let you know when their temperature is going up and you need to monitor it. Liquid crystal thermometers come as a disk or strip to place on the child's forehead and also as a special pacifier. They usually work in about fifteen seconds. The prices vary, but they usually can be found for under $10.

> **When Is Body Temperature a Fever?**
>
> Rectal: 100.4°
>
> Axillary: 99°

Taking a Rectal Temperature

Use a rectal thermometer with a round bulbous tip. (See Figure 1.1.) A rectal temperature will usually measure higher than an oral or armpit temperature because it is further in the body. It also will give a temperature reading faster than the other methods.

- For a mercury thermometer, shake the thermometer down to under 96.8°F (36°C). For a digital thermometer, turn it on per instructions.
- Lubricate the end of the thermometer with petroleum jelly or some other emollient cream.

Figure 1.1: Rectal Thermometer

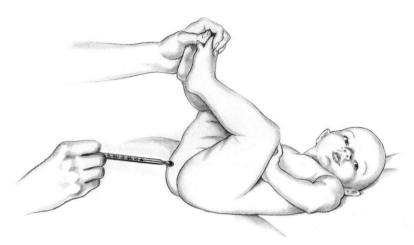

Figure 1.2: Taking A Rectal Temperature

- Position your child so that you can easily see the rectum. This may mean laying him on his side, on his back, or on his belly. For infants and toddlers, it is usually easier to lay them down on their bellies in your lap. This also helps you to hold them still. (See Figure 1.2.)

- Gently insert the thermometer approximately one-half inch into the rectum.

- Leave mercury thermometers in approximately three minutes until the silver line stops rising. Digital thermometers usually beep when they have registered an accurate temperature.

- To read a mercury thermometer, gently roll the cylinder until you can see the top of the silver column. A digital thermometer will give a numeric readout.

- Wash the thermometer tip with warm, soapy water; rinse and dry well; then store in case.

Converting Farenheit (F°) to Celsius (C°)
98.6°F = 37.0°C
99.5°F = 37.5°C
100.1°F = 37.8°C
100.4°F = 38.0°C
101.0°F = 38.3°C
102.0°F = 38.9°C
103.0°F = 39.5°C
104.0°F = 40.0°C
105.0°F = 40.6°C

Taking an Oral Temperature

Oral temperatures should be taken in children who are at least five years old and able to keep their mouths closed. If you are using a glass mercury thermometer to measure an oral temperature, be sure the child understands that he cannot bite the thermometer. Some digital oral thermometers come with a plastic biter "sleeve" which makes them easier and safer to use in young children. The child should not have had anything to eat or drink for fifteen minutes prior to using an oral thermometer because the temperature of food or drink in the mouth could influence its reading. Use an oral thermometer with a slim tip. (See Figure 1.3.)

Figure 1.3: Oral Thermometer

- For a mercury thermometer, shake the thermometer down to under 96.8°F (36°C). For a digital thermometer, turn it on per the instructions.
- Place the oral thermometer under your child's tongue and have your child close her mouth.
- Leave a mercury thermometer in place for three minutes. The digital thermometer will beep when an accurate temperature has registered, usually in thirty seconds to one minute.
- Your child should not have anything to eat or drink for fifteen minutes prior to taking an oral temperature to insure accuracy.
- Wash the thermometer tip with warm, soapy water; rinse and dry well; then store in case.

Taking an Axillary Temperature

If you are taking an axillary temperature, we recommend using a digital thermometer because a mercury thermometer has to be left in place too long for most children to have to hold still. Use an oral thermometer or special axillary thermometer to take an axillary temperature. Measurement of an axillary temperature is less accurate when increased perspiration is present.

- Shake a mercury thermometer down to under 96.8°F (36°C) or turn a digital thermometer on per the instructions.
- Place the thermometer under your child's dry armpit. Mercury thermometers have to be left in place for four to six minutes. Digital thermometers will beep when they are ready and usually have a readout in under one minute.

- Wash the thermometer tip with warm, soapy water; rinse and dry well; then store in case.

SUPPLIES FOR YOUR BABY'S ILLNESS

There are some basic supplies and nonprescription (over-the-counter) items that you should keep at home for your child's home health care. After your child has had a few illnesses, you will know which supplies are more helpful and should always keep a larger supply of these items on hand. You can find most over-the-counter medicines that need to be swallowed in a *liquid, capsule,* or *chewable tablet.* Some are also available in a *rectal suppository* that is quite useful when the child is throwing up or very resistant to swallowing medicine. Choose the best form of medicine for your child based on your child's age, personal preference, and illness.

We have compiled a checklist of basic items, but please modify it and add to it as you see fit. We also recommend that you keep a fully stocked first aid kit, and have included specific recommendations in chapter 4 under Basics of First Aid. Talk to your pharmacist about new products and items as they become available. When possible, we have used the generic name of a medicine and in parentheses listed some of the common trade names as well. Most of the time the generic product will be just as useful and probably cost less, too.

Checklist of Commonly Used Supplies

Medicines

- *Fever-reducing medicine:* Acetaminophen (Tylenol, Tempra) and Ibuprofen (Children's Advil or Motrin). Acetaminophen is available in drops for infants, liquid for toddlers, chewable tablets in regular and junior strength, caplets, and adult tablets. Acetaminophen is also available as a rectal suppository for those times when your child has a fever and is also throwing up. Fever-reducing suppositories are also useful for children who may suffer febrile convulsions when they get a fever. Usually, you must ask the pharmacist for the suppositories. You do not need a prescription for them, but they are usually kept with the prescription medicines. (For more about febrile convulsions, see page 50.) Ibuprofen is also available as a liquid for children over two years of age, in chewable tablets, and caplets. As your child grows you might want to change the preparation so that they can get the required amount in as easy a form as possible. Their correct dose will also change along with their weight. (Please refer to the chart in Appendix D for the proper dose of medicine according to your child's weight or ask your pharmacist or doctor for a dosage chart by weight.)
- *Allergy and rash medicine:* Diphenhydramine (Benadryl).

- *Ipecac Syrup* to induce vomiting if needed after ingestion of poison. Call your local poison control center first. (You should not induce vomiting of any poisonous substance.)
- *Antacid.*
- *Decongestant.*
- *Cough medicine.*
- *Topical antibiotic cream.*
- *Topical antifungal cream.*

Medical Supplies

- *Oral electrolyte solution* (Pedialyte, Ricelyte, Kao Lectrolyte or generic brand; Kao Lectrolyte is available in a powder and has a longer shelf life) for children under age one. (Older children may use Gatorade or other sports drinks.)
- *Ointments and creams.* These should include antibiotic ointment like Bacitracin or triple antibiotic ointment, antifungal cream like Lotrimen, steroid cream such as 0.5 percent hydrocortisone cream, zinc oxide, and petroleum jelly.
- *Saline nose drops* (like Ocean) and a *nasal bulb syringe* to help clear nose during a cold for infants and young children who cannot blow their own nose.
- *Cool air humidifier* and/or vaporizer.
- *Thermometers* both rectal and oral.
- *Bandage materials.* This includes a box of Band-Aids in all sizes, gauze bandage square (large enough to cover a big scrape, four inches by four inches), gauze bandage roll to wrap around an extremity, surgical tape, triangular bandage (at least eighteen inches wide) to make a sling, and an elastic rolled (ace) bandage.
- *Hydrogen peroxide* (in a tightly covered bottle) or a small bar of antiseptic soap.
- *Calamine lotion.*
- *Measuring aids* to give medicines. This would include a dropper, a calibrated medicine spoon, an oral syringe (without a needle), and a dosage medicine cup.
- Rubbing alcohol.

Household Supplies

- Baking soda to use in bath to decrease itching.
- Karo syrup to help with constipation.
- Ice pack or bag of small frozen vegetables like peas or corn (to use as an ice pack).
- Soap to clean wounds. Liquid soap is often easier to use.

- Blunt edge tweezers to remove splinters or tics.
- Scissors.
- Safety pins.
- Flashlight.
- Sun screen.
- Jell-O and Popsicles, or containers to make ice pops from fruit juice. This will help to keep your child hydrated when sick.

USING OVER-THE-COUNTER REMEDIES

There are many over-the-counter, nonprescription remedies available today. However, deciding which preparations are best for your children can be very confusing. Many preparations have different ingredients and different purposes. In general, most of the over-the-counter medicines will relieve or prevent symptoms; however, they will not cure the underlying problem or illness. They may also ease the severity of a particular symptom. Always remember that they are still medicines and you must *be careful about the type and amount of medicine* that you give to your child. Just like prescription medicines, *the proper dose of an over-the-counter medicine depends upon how much your child weighs.*

Table 1.2 lists common symptoms (in alphabetical order) that may be relieved with common over-the-counter medicines available for children. Because many products have multiple ingredients that serve different purposes, we have limited our table to the principal ingredient for a principal symptom. Generic names are used with suggestions of brand products that contain only the specific generic product.

The areas of cold/cough products and decongestants and antihistamines are the most confusing. The rows of available cold medicines can easily confuse even the most educated consumer. Many manufacturers have a whole line of products with the same root name, but they contain many different ingredients. For example, there is Pediacare-1, 2, and 3 as well as Pediacare Chewable Cold Tablets, and Pediacare Infant's Cold Relief drops. The ingredients of each are different. Children's Nyquil has different medicines than regular Nyquil; it is not just a different dose. Also, many of these products should not be used by children under age two or under age six. Always read the labels very carefully and check with your doctor or pharmacist for specific questions.

The exact dose for each over-the-counter medicine depends upon your child's weight, just the same as prescription medicines. Doses for acetaminophen and ibuprofen are in Appendix D. For other over-the-counter medicines, check the package information or call your doctor. *Remember to change your child's dose as his weight changes.* Read all labels carefully and use this guide for reference. For more information see specific symptoms and diagnoses.

Table 1.2

Guide for Over-the-Counter Remedies

Symptoms	Generic Name	Action	Brand Names
Aches and Pains	Acetaminophen (a-seat-a-mee'noe-fen)	Relieves pain by inhibiting the substances in the body that send pain signals to the brain. It doesn't eliminate the pain but only the pain sensation. Also reduces fever. Lasts four to six hours. Dose is based on child's weight.	Liquiprin Panadol Tempra Tylenol
	Ibuprofen (eye-byoo'proe-fen)	Relieves pain sensation as above and works as an anti-inflammatory medicine. Also reduces fever. Lasts six to eight hours. Dose is based on child's weight.	Children's Advil Children's Motrin
Allergy*	Diphenhydramine (die-fen-hye'dra-meen)	Relieves allergic symptoms of nasal congestion and itching. Also causes dry mouth and is one of the most sedating antihistamines. Suppresses the cough reflex by a direct effect on the medulla of the brain. Also works as a topical anesthetic to relieve throat pain due to irritation from repeated coughing. Dose is based on child's weight.	Benadryl Benylin Cough Syrup
	Brompheniramine Maleate (brome-fen ir'a-meen mal-ee'ate)	Also used for relief of seasonal and perennial allergy symptoms. Causes less drowsiness than other antihistamines. Dose is based on child's weight.	Dimetapp Chewable Tablets Dimetapp Elixir
	Tripolidine Hydrochloride (trip-oe'li-deen)	Interferes with histamine production and prevents further development of allergic symptoms of runny nose, watery eyes, etc. Dose is based on child's weight.	Actidil

Symptoms	Generic Name	Action	Brand Names
Colic/Gas/ Tummy Pain	Simethicone (si-meth'i-cone)	Works to break up gas bubbles that cause pain in the gastrointestinal system.	Flatulex Mylicon Infant Drops Phazyme
Congestion**	Pseudoephedrine (soo-doe-e-fed'rin)	Helps to decrease excess mucus by temporarily shrinking mucous membranes. May cause excitability in children. Read labels; many decongestants should not be used in children under age six. Check with your doctor. Dose is based on child's weight.	Children's Sudafed Liquid Pediacare Infant Drops Sudafed Children's Chewables
Constipation***	Mineral oil	Softens stool and lubricates GI tract.	Agoral Plain Mineral Oil
	Malt Soup Extract	Natural barley malt; promotes soft, easily passed stools.	Maltsuprex
	Glycerine Suppositories (glis-e'rin)	Stool softener that stimulates the rectum to contract and expel stool.	Glycerine liquid Glycerine suppositories for children (suppositories are only effective if the stool is not hard or dry; useful only in the early stages of constipation).
	Magnesium hydroxide	Draws water into the gut, increasing pressure and intestinal mobility.	Phillips Milk of Magnesia
Cough, Dry and Hacking	Dextromethorphan (dex-troe-meth-or'fan)	Used to suppress the cough reflex when the respiratory tract or lungs are irritated. Also used when a nonproductive cough interferes with sleep. Dose is based on child's weight. Do not use for children under age two.	Benylin DM Pediatric Cough Formula Cremacoat-1 Delsym Pediacare-1 St. Joseph Cough Syrup for Children

Table 1.2 (*continued*)

Symptoms	Generic Name	Action	Brand Names
Cough, Dry and Hacking (*continued*)	Diphenhydramine (die-fen-hye'dra-meen)	Suppresses cough reflex by direct effect on the cough center in the brain. Also has a topical anesthetic effect to relieve throat pain due to coughing. Also an antihistamine (see allergy) with a very potent sedating effect. Dose is based on child's weight.	Benadryl Benylin Cough Syrup
Cough, Productive and Wet	Guaifenesin (gwye-fen'e-sin)	Expectorant; helps the body to expel mucus. Helps liquify mucus to make it less thick and easier to spit out. This removes blockage of the respiratory tract due to mucous secretions. Dose is based on child's weight.	Cremacoat-2 Glycotuss Robitussin
Diaper Rash/ Irritation	Petroleum Jelly	Forms a protective barrier against moisture and irritants; moisturizes skin.	Vaseline Petroleum Jelly
	Zinc Oxide	Also forms a protective barrier, and the zinc may help promote healing.	Balmex Desitin Johnson and Johnson Baby Cream
	Clotrimazole (kloe-tri'ma-zal)	Antifungal cream used to treat diaper rash that is complicated by a fungus such as yeast. Fungal infections often involve cracked, peeling, and inflamed skin. See your doctor about specific concerns.	Lotrimen
Ear Wax	Carbamide peroxide 6.5% (kar'ba-mide per-ox'ide)	Helps soften and dissolve ear wax; gently relieves pressure and pain caused by ear wax.	Auro Ear Drops Debrox Ear Drops by Murine May also use half strength hydrogen peroxide. (equal volume water and hydrogen peroxide)

Symptoms	Generic Name	Action	Brand Names
Fever	Acetaminophen (a-seat-a-mee'noe-fen)	Reduces fever (and relieves pain). Lasts four to six hours. Dose is dependent on your child's weight; see chart in Appendix D.	Acephen (suppository) Liquiprin Panadol Tempra Tylenol
	Ibuprofen (eye-byoo'proe-fen)	Reduces fever (and relieves pain due to inflammation). Lasts six to eight hours. Dose is based on child's weight.	Childen's Advil Children's Motrin
Nasal Irritation/ Congestion	Sodium Chloride drops	Restores moisture to provide relief for dry, crusted, and inflamed nasal passages caused by low humidity, colds, minor nosebleeds, and allergies. Also useful to thin out thick mucous secretions due to colds and flu.	Ayr Saline Nasal Drops or Mist NaSal drops or spray Ocean Mist
Superficial Skin Infection	Bacitracin (bass-i-tray'sin)	After cleaning a superficial cut or scrape, this antibiotic ointment will interfere with the growth of many types of bacteria.	Bacitracin ointment
	Polymixin B, Bacitracin, Neomycin (pol-ee-mix'in, bass-i-tray'sin, nee-oh-mye'sin)	To help prevent bacterial infection of minor cuts and abrasions; aids healing.	Neosporin Triple Antibiotic ointment
	Tolnaftate (tole-naf'tate)	Used to treat fungal infections such as Athlete's Foot. Fungal infections involve cracked, peeling, inflamed, and itchy skin. The antifungal creams and lotions will soothe, decrease itch, and promote healing. See your doctor if you are not sure which treatment to use.	Desinex Fungatin Micatin Tinactin

Table 1.2 (*continued*)

Symptoms	Generic Name	Action	Brand Names
Swimmer's Ear	Boric Acid 2.75% in isopropyl alcohol	Used for the prevention of inflammation of the outer ear canal that occurs when water remains in the ear after swimming or bathing.	Auro-Dri SwimEar
	Acetic Acid 1.0% with Burrow's Solution 10% and Boric Acid 1.0% (a-seat'ic)	Acetic acid and boric acid together limit microorganisms and help to maintain the ear canal in its normal acid state.	Star Otic

* These medicines all fall into the category of antihistamines. They prevent the release of histamine that causes the allergic symptoms of nasal congestion; itchy, watery eyes; and runny nose. *They will not reverse symptoms* already present.

** Many decongestants are combined with antihistamines in the hope that the excitability effect of decongestants is offset by the sedative effect of the antihistamines. (See Allergy.) Be careful and read labels.

*** Laxatives, bowel stimulants, and bulk products should not be given to children unless directed by a physician.

TIPS ON GIVING MEDICINES TO CHILDREN

Giving medicines to children may be confusing as you try to figure out the correct medicine, the correct amount, and how to ensure your child's safety as you administer it. Most medicines you give to your children will be some type of oral preparation including liquids, chewable tablets, caplets, and capsules. You may also have to give your child medicines that come as rectal suppositories, topical skin creams, eyedrops or ointment, and eardrops. Proper technique and positioning will ensure the medicine is given safely and effectively.

Oral Medicines

Oral medicines include all medicines your child will take by mouth. Liquid medicines for young children come in a syrup, elixir, or suspension. Syrup medicines come in a sugary liquid that helps them to taste better. Elixir medicines come in an alcohol-based liquid that helps to dissolve certain medicines. The percentage of alcohol will vary, so please read the label carefully before giving it to your child. A suspension is used for certain powdered medicines to help maintain a uniform concentration, and these are most commonly antibiotics. In suspensions, the medicine may settle at the bottom of the bottle so be sure to shake it well before pouring the correct dose for your child. Many of these different medicines, however, still have an unpleasant taste, and sometimes the flavor just may not appeal to your child. There may be different preparations and flavors available for the same medicine, so read the labels and talk to your doctor and pharmacist about this. For example, liquid fever-reducing medicines come in cherry, grape, orange, and bubble-gum flavors. Generic and brand name antibiotics also come in different flavors—though you might have to shop around to find them. Some medicines also come in chewable tablet form that some older children find more pleasant to take than liquid. (See Table 1.2.)

Try to administer medicine by itself.

In general, give medicine by itself. If you must mix it in something to make it more tasty, use the smallest amount possible in order to ensure that your child finishes the mixture and receives the proper dose of medicine. Some parents like to mix medicine in cola syrup or applesauce. Always consult your doctor or pharmacist regarding how specific medicines are likely to combine with foods and liquids. For example, some medicines should not be mixed in dairy products because it can affect absorption of the drug. Another trick, if you are using a liquid, is to wet the dispensing spoon, dip it in table sugar, and then add the medicine. The sugar will disguise the medicine taste while keeping the amount your child has to swallow small.

There are also many aids available for measuring the correct amount of medicine (dose) prior to giving it to your child. Some common ones include:

- Nurser or special nipple dispenser.
- Oral medicine dropper.
- Oral syringe.
- Calibrated spoon.
- Dosage medicine cup.

The first four can usually be found among the baby supplies in your pharmacy, and dosage medicine cups are often included with liquid medicines. Be sure to ask your pharmacist for help to find any other type of medicine dispenser for children.

It's important that you believe in a specific medication because your belief system will be transmitted to your child. Be honest when describing the medicine to him and be positive as you explain that the medicine will help him feel better. Most of the time your child will be cooperative, but nearly everyone is faced at one time or other with a child who simply refuses to take medicine. Children are never given medicine without a reason, so it is very important that they do take the full dose that has been prescribed. Be firm in your approach but never punish your child for being uncooperative. Remember, if he is taking medicine he is probably sick. And, finally, a promise of a reward afterward may also help the medicine go down just that much easier.

Occasionally, a child may resist physically. In this case, there is no alternative but to be forceful and hold your child down even with the help of another adult. If you encounter a lot of resistance on a regular basis, talk to your doctor. One hint may be to ask someone else to help as some children may be more willing with the second parent or another adult present. Determine what works best for you. But take heart: usually, giving medicines to children becomes easier as they get older.

Tips for Giving Oral Medicines to Babies

- Get someone else to help. Babies are squirmy, and it is often helpful if another person can hold the baby while you concentrate on getting the proper dose of the medicine in them. If you are on your own, place the baby in an infant seat so that you have two free hands. You might also tuck a receiving blanket around the baby's arms to help hold him steady.

- Position your baby so that his head is raised slightly, either in your arms or in an infant seat. *Never lie a baby flat to give medicine because he can inhale it into his lungs.*

- Use a medicine dropper, syringe, or special medicine spoon to measure out the proper dose to allow you to give it with just one hand. (You may need the other hand to steady your baby.)

- Put only a little bit of the medicine in his mouth at a time. If you are using an oral medicine dropper or oral syringe, aim for the side of his mouth to prevent gagging.

- Lightly stroke the front of your child's throat to stimulate him to swallow.

- Give a pacifier or bottle after the medicine to promote swallowing.

- Do not mix the medicine in your baby's bottle or a cup with other liquid because you won't be able to make sure she takes the entire dose of medicine.

- If your baby spits out the medicine, hold his mouth open and use a dropper or syringe to place the medicine by the rear gum and cheek. Hold his mouth gently but firmly closed until he swallows.

Tips for Giving Oral Medicines to Older Children

- Give an accurate dose of medicine in the smallest amount possible.

- Have your child's favorite drink ready to follow the medicine. Do not add the medicine to the drink because it will sink to the bottom or stick to the side of a bottle or cup and you can't be certain that she will get the full dose. If you must mix it, add it to a small amount of flavored syrup in a medicine dosage cup.

- Ask your child to hold his nose while he drinks the medicine so that he doesn't smell it and taste it quite as strongly.

- Use a medicine dropper or syringe and let the child squirt it in himself. (Be sure to buy one that is large enough to hold one dose for an older child. Your pharmacist can help with this.)

- Use a calibrated spoon dipped in water and then coated with sugar before you add the medicine.

- Have your child brush his teeth immediately after taking liquid medicine to prevent syrup from sticking to his teeth and prolonging the taste.

- Sometimes with an older child, a bribe may be helpful to ensure cooperation in taking medicine. It may be a small one like a drink of a favorite soft drink after each dose, or a bigger prize that can be "bought" with the empty medicine bottle when the entire course of medicine is complete.

- Teach your child to swallow small tablets as early as age four or five. They are more practical to give at school or when traveling, and it may save you a lot of hassle later.

Non-Oral Medicines

Tips for Giving Medicines Using a Rectal Suppository

- Make sure the suppository is child-size and check the dose indicated on the label.

- Wash your hands before and after administering the suppository.

- Have your child lie on his side with his knees bent toward his chest.

- Coat the suppository with a water soluble gel like petroleum jelly (Vaseline or K-Y jelly).

- Spread his buttocks and insert the suppository One-half to one inch beyond the rectal opening. For a child three or younger, use your pinkie to insert the suppository. For an older child, use your index finger.

- Hold your child's buttocks together for about one minute after insertion so the medicine can be absorbed before your child can push it out.

Tips for Applying a Topical Skin Medicine

- Wash your hands before and after applying a cream or ointment medicine to the skin.
- Gently wash and dry the affected area on your child.
- Smooth a single layer of the medicine starting at the center or the top of the affected area and apply in one direction—not back and forth.
- You may use a cotton-tipped swab (Q-tip) or plain gauze if the skin is broken.
- Trim your child's nails or consider using mittens on a baby or young child to prevent scratching.
- For a spray, have your child turn his face away, aim the nozzle four to six inches from the affected skin area, and apply from the center out or top to bottom in short spurts.

Tips for Using Nose Drops or Spray

- Wash your hands before and after application.
- Remove mucus by gently using a nasal aspirator or cotton-tipped applicator (Q-tip).
- For drops: Have your child lie down and slowly insert required number of drops in each nostril. Have him lie still for ten seconds afterward, then sniff two to three times.
- For spray: Have your child sit with his head tilted back slightly or place a baby in an infant seat. Insert the spray and have him gently inhale (if old enough) while you squeeze the spray. Continue to squeeze as you remove the spray.

Tips for Using Eyedrops or Ointment

- Wash your hands before and after applying eye medicine.
- Drops or ointment are usually more comfortable if they are at room temperature.
- Have your child lie down and tilt his head back slightly.
- Gently pull down his lower lid to form a small pocket.
- Insert the drops or squeeze a thin line of ointment into the pocket.
- Have your child close his eyes for about thirty seconds so that the medicine can be absorbed.
- Try to keep him from rubbing his eyes.

Tips for Administering Eardrops:

- Wash your hands before and after administering the eardrops.

- Make sure that the eardrops are stored at room temperature. Cold drops can cause dizziness or vomiting. If the drops are cold, roll the bottle back and forth between your hands to warm it. Do not immerse the bottle in hot water or put in the microwave—this will make the drops too hot.

- Have your child lie on his side with the ear that needs drops facing up.

- Gently pull the outer ear back.

- Squeeze the dropper so that the liquid drips slowly into the ear canal.

- Don't let the dropper enter the ear canal.

- Place a small cotton ball in the outer ear and have your child sit quietly for about five minutes until the drops are absorbed.

DEALING WITH COMMON CHILDHOOD ILLNESSES

Sometimes you need to seek medical attention for your child, but other times you can treat your child's health problems yourself. In order to make these decisions, you need to acquire a basic understanding of your child's health and the fundamental *problem-solving* techniques that can help you care for your child when she is sick.

A *contagious disease* is a viral, bacterial, or fungal illness that can be passed from one person to another. As your baby becomes exposed to contagious illnesses, you will become aware of the incubation period and contagious period for each. The *incubation period* is the time interval between exposure to infection and the onset of symptoms. He may not become ill with every illness he is exposed to; this often depends upon his immune system and susceptibility at the time. I have had one child home sick with a strep throat and two others healthy and at school or day care at the same time. The *contagious period* is the time during which a sick child's illness may be passed on to others. Some day care centers and nursery schools will not allow your child back into a group setting until she is no longer contagious. Check with your doctor regarding the specific contagious period for your child's illness. See Table 1.3 for more information on some of the most common contagious diseases.

Colds and accompanying fevers account for over half of all routine childhood infections. Having colds is an unavoidable part of growing up, and children may get as many as five to eight colds per year. (Even adults average four colds per year.) Colds are not caused by poor diet, lack of vitamins, bad weather, or wet feet. A cold is a viral infection, and the main reason your child is susceptible to them is that she is constantly

Table 1.3

Quick Reference to Contagious Diseases				
Illness	**Definition**	**Symptoms**	**Incubation Time**	**Contagious Time**
Bronchiolitis	Inflammation of the small air passages by a respiratory syncytial virus that causes them to narrow.	Difficulty breathing and wheezing.	2–8 days	Start of cough until 7 days.
Cold	Upper respiratory, viral infection that enters the body through the nose and mouth.	Sneezing, fever, runny nose or blocked nasal passages, cough, sore throat, aching muscles, irritability.	2–5 days	Start of runny nose until fever is gone.
Cough	Protective reflex caused by irritation of the air-way or lungs, often mucus.	Cough is often symptom of a viral or bacterial infection or an allergy.	2–5 days	Start of cough until fever is gone.
Diarrhea (bacterial, viral, or travelers)	Frequent liquid or loose bowel movement.	fever and "the runs."	1–5 days for viral; bacterial and travelers depend on the causative organism.	Until bowel movements are formed (not runny) and fever is gone.
Fifth Disease	Viral disease caused by Parovirus B19 with a 3-stage rash known as erythema infectiosum.	Fever, coldlike symptoms, pink rash on cheeks and ears that deepens to a "slapped cheek" rash, fol-lowed by a lacy, bumpy rash on trunk and extremities.	4–21 days	7 days before the rash (once the rash appears, it is no longer contagious).
Hand, Foot, and Mouth Disease	Viral infection caused by Coxsackie A virus.	Fever; small, round, clear blisters inside the mouth, on the soles of the feet, palms of the hands, and between fingers and toes. (Some children also get a body rash.)	3–6 days	Start of mouth ulcers until fever is gone, usually 1 week.
Head lice	Small parasites that attach themselves to human hair and skin.	Intense itching in the scalp and sometimes a rash (from the bites) or swollen glands in the neck.	7 days for eggs (nits) to hatch	Start of itch until treatment.

Illness	Definition	Symptoms	Incubation Time	Contagious Time
Impetigo	Superficial bacterial skin infection usually caused by *streptococcus* or *staphylococcus*.	Itchy rash with small red bumps that turn to blisters with a cloudy fluid which then break and crust over with yellowish-brown scabs that look like brown sugar.	2–5 days for staph; 7–10 days for strep	Start of rash until 24 to 48 hours on oral antibiotic treatment.
Pinkeye or Conjunctivitis (with pus)	Common viral or bacterial infection in the mucous membrane of the eye.	Redness, irritation, and purulent (pus-filled) drainage from the eye; possibly fever and cold symptoms.	2–7 days	Start of pus until 24 to 48 hours on antibiotic eye drops or ointment.
Roseola	Short-term viral illness, usually affecting children under age 2.	High fever (103°F to 106°F rectally) for three to four days followed by total body rash.	5–15 days, average 10 days.	Start of fever until the rash is gone.
Scarlet Fever	Illness caused by *streptococcal* bacteria associated with sore throat or skin infection.	Fever, bright red rash with a sandpapery feel, sore throat, and strawberry-red patches on a furry-looking tongue. Sometimes also belly pain and swollen lymph glands in the neck.	1–7 days (average 3 days)	Start of fever or rash until 48 hours on antibiotic.
Sore throat (strep or viral)	Pain, discomfort, or raw feeling of the throat, especially after swallowing.	Fever, sore throat, swelling of lymph glands in the neck. Some children also complain of belly pain.	2–5 days	If strep, start of sore throat until 48 hours on antibiotic. If viral, start of sore throat until fever is gone.

exposed to new viruses. The number of colds increases during the cold winter months when children and adults spend more time indoors. Most children shed germs during the first days of their illness, often before they even look sick or have symptoms. Exposure to respiratory infections, therefore, is unavoidable in enclosed group settings such as supermarkets, nursery schools, and day care centers.

Ear infections may also be related to colds. They occur when mucous secretions block off the passage connecting the middle ear to the back of the throat (the eustachian tubes). The number of colds your child experiences decreases as she gets older and her immune system builds up a good antibody supply to combat various viruses. The number of ear infections your child contracts also decreases as she gets older. This is because the eustachian tubes grow with age, and mucous secretions do not become trapped as frequently.

In addition, two or three times per year most children experience stomach and intestinal ailments accompanied by vomiting and/or diarrhea usually caused by viruses. Some children are particularly worrisome to their parents because they tend to get high fevers with most of their colds or contract frequent viral gastroenteritis with diarrhea or vomiting. In general, if your child is vigorous and gaining weight, you don't have to worry about these common illnesses. You can treat the symptoms, prevent them from getting worse, and help your child pass more comfortably through this rite of passage.

How to Reduce Infectious Illnesses

- Wash your hands frequently and teach your children proper hand washing. Frequent hand washing helps prevent the spread of respiratory and gastrointestinal (diarrhea and vomiting) illnesses.
- Teach your child to keep his hands away from his face and mouth (to prevent spread of infections from surfaces he has touched).
- Cook meat and eggs thoroughly to kill bacteria.
- Clean all kitchen surfaces frequently with a disinfectant such as Lysol or Clorox Kitchen Disinfectant.
- Don't expose your child to secondhand smoke.
- Make sure your child eats a well-balanced diet and gets plenty of fresh air and outdoor exercise.
- Limit exposure of newborns and young babies to large crowds in enclosed places whenever possible. (Colds and other viruses present more complications in babies under-one year of age.)
- Keep your child's immunizations up-to-date.

Guidelines for Calling Your Doctor

During the next routine visit to your child's doctor, inquire about her policy regarding when to call the office. Many practices have written information for parents listing emergency telephone numbers, guidelines regarding when to call the doctor, and instructions for common health problems. Many busy offices have nurse practitioners available to answer routine questions and see your child for routine childhood infections on a more timely basis, so find out how you should relate to this professional.

It is a judgment call whether to phone after hours or wait until the next day. A sick child is always distressing, and the situation can exacerbate if you cannot decide whether or not to call your doctor. If you are unsure, it is always better to make the phone call and get your doctor's advice. If your child has been getting sicker, it is probably best to evaluate her condition just before bedtime and then give your doctor a call if you are worried. This may prevent panic and stress at 2 A.M. It is also important to have the number of your local drugstore (preferably one that is open twenty-four hours), hospital, and ambulance or emergency transport system handy. At the same time, if you have stocked your first-aid and medicine chest with basic supplies and have a set of guidelines to follow for basic symptoms, you may be able to handle easily the many times your child will get mildly ill and not be feeling well.

What to Have Ready When You Call Your Doctor

You want to have your information organized when you call your child's doctor. This will allow the doctor to gather all essential information during the initial call so that she will have a complete picture of your child's condition. Start the conversation by stating the *name, sex, and age* of your child. Tell *when the symptoms first started* and *why they are worrisome* to you. Also describe any actions you have taken to relieve symptoms and the result. Then have the following pertinent information available:

- Recent body *temperature* and how you took it (oral, axillary, rectal, ear probe). It is important to take your child's temperature even if she doesn't feel warm. The doctor will want to verify this.
- Description of *current symptoms*. Be very specific.
- Precise *time frame* regarding how long your child has had the symptoms.
- Name and phone number of your *pharmacy*.
- List of *current medicines* the child is taking and when she took her last dose.
- List of over-the-counter pediatric medicines you have available at home.
- Pencil and paper to write down instructions.

- Phone number of your local hospital emergency room and emergency transport system.

Depending upon the exact nature of your child's complaint, other information such as food recently eaten, frequency of bowel movements, or diarrhea may be necessary. If it is not an emergency, look up your child's problem before calling the doctor and write down specific information. The doctor may prescribe a medicine over the phone, but often she may wait until your child can be seen. Medicines such as antibiotics may mask the true problem or affect subsequent laboratory findings, so it may be important to sort out the problem before giving any new medicine. An exception may be fever-reducing medicines such as *acetaminophen* and *ibuprofen*. Before you finish your telephone conversation, ask if it is necessary to call the doctor back and under what circumstances.

EXAMINATION OF A SICK CHILD BY A DOCTOR

When your child is sick and you take him to your doctor or clinic, your doctor will conduct a systems assessment to try to figure out what is wrong. The doctor will first get a sense from you of how your child looks compared to normal and how sick you think he is. The doctor will then check your child's temperature, breathing, pulse, and assess his state of alertness and hydration. With the use of a small flashlight and a tongue depressor, the doctor will examine your child's *throat and mouth,* looking for redness, inflammation, or swelling. An *otoscope* (consisting of a light and magnifying glass) will help the doctor look in your child's *ears (including outer ear and eardrum)* as she checks for evidence of infection. The otoscope itself is not sharp and does not hurt. However, if your child does have an ear infection, any touching of areas around the ear may be tender and painful. The doctor will also check your child's *lymph glands* along his jaw, armpit, and groin for any signs of swelling that may indicate infection. She will also use a *stethoscope* to listen to your child's *heart and lungs.* Abnormal sounds in the heart or lungs may indicate an infection or illness. Finally, your doctor will gently press your child's *abdomen* to check for any swelling of internal organs that may indicate an illness.

HOW TO DRESS A SICK CHILD

Sick children should be dressed comfortably in either pajamas or a T-shirt and comfortable shorts or pants. If your child has a fever, he should be dressed in as little clothing as possible; you do not want a lot of heavy clothes or blankets to keep body heat in and temperature up. He should stay in a room that is draft-free with a constant temperature. The room should not be hot. If it is comfortable for you it should be comfortable for your child. There is no need to keep a sick child in bed if they feel like being up and about. Within reason, let him dictate his activity level.

WHEN TO SEND YOUR CHILD BACK TO NURSERY SCHOOL OR DAY CARE

There are two key points to consider here. You want to make sure your child is well on the road to recovery after illness and won't suffer a relapse—and you want to prevent the rampant spread of infectious illness to others. This is often a tough problem when both parents work outside the home and no one is available to stay home and help your child recover fully. There are some "sick child" day care facilities available but unfortunately they are rare and expensive.

Use the following key criteria to determine when your child is ready to return to day care or nursery school:

- Fever is gone.
- Sleep has returned to near normal.
- She is able to eat and retain a regular diet.
- If an antibiotic is required for a bacterial infection, your child must also have taken the medicine for at least forty-eight hours in addition to the other criteria.

In the case of the common cold, it is *not* necessary to keep your child home until the virus has passed and all symptoms have resolved. Your day care or nursery school may also have a list of criteria stating when your child can return after an illness.

Common Symptoms

ABDOMINAL PAIN

Definition

Your child complains of a tummy ache or holds his belly and cries. You first need to figure out, as closely as possible, the exact nature of the pain and any associated symptoms. A bad stomachache may be a sign of a real emergency, or it may be nothing serious at all. Abdominal pain is best described by its location, quality of the pain, and related symptoms.

Location

Different areas of pain may be associated with specific problems. This is extremely difficult to diagnose in young children, but try your best to get the child to point to the specific area that hurts. Abdominal pain or discomfort is located between the bottom of the rib cage and the groin crease. You may start by finding out if the pain is above or below the belly button and if it is on a particular side. Older children may be more articulate about their pain. With babies and small children, let your sense of what is bothering them guide you.

Quality of Pain

How does the pain feel? Some adjectives to help you include:

- Sharp and knifelike.
- Dull and achy.
- Hot as fire.
- Steady, never stops hurting, and remains about the same.

- Gets worse when your child does something, for example: move, jump, eat, breathe, bend over.
- Gets better when your child does something.
- Just gets worse all the time.
- Intermittent; pain comes and goes.
- Crampy.
- Maybe just rumbly like Winnie the Pooh.

Related Symptoms

Young children often can't distinguish abdominal pain from nausea and may complain of a tummy ache just prior to an episode of vomiting or diarrhea. In general, look for these type of symptoms:

- Fever or any increase in body temperature.
- Vomiting; note the frequency and description of what your child is throwing up (food particles, green or yellow color, dry heaves, etc.).
- Diarrhea; note the frequency and description of the bowel movements (all liquid, color, unusually foul smelling).
- Constipation; note last bowel movement and description.
- History of an accident or fall, or your child being hit in the abdomen.
- Complaint of a sore throat or difficulty swallowing.

What to Do

- Locate the pain.
- Help your child describe the quality of the pain and its frequency.
- Look for other symptoms (diarrhea, vomiting, sore throat, fever, etc.).
- Take temperature.
- Think of possible causes, for example, eating different food, having returned recently from a trip overseas, contact with another person who you know is sick, a recent fall or playground accident, etc.
- Make sure your child has not swallowed any harmful substance.
- Figure out when your child had her last bowel movement and describe what it was like (hard, loose, diarrhea, etc.).
- Write down what your child has eaten in the last twenty-four hours.

When to Call Your Doctor

Immediately

- Your child looks very, very sick or sicker than usual.
- Pain makes your child either speechless, unable to stop crying, or unable to move. (A baby or young child may draw his legs into his chest and cry inconsolably.)
- Pain is localized in the lower abdomen, regardless of which side, and remains there for one hour without change.
- Any blood in your child's bowel movement or if it has a dark, tarry or mahogany color. (Be aware that severe diarrhea or constipation may also cause some bleeding.)
- Bile or green color in the vomit.
- Persistent, uncontrollable vomiting.
- Pain is associated with an accident or some kind of recent impact to the abdomen.
- Your child walks bent over or holding her abdominal area.
- Your child lies down and refuses to walk.
- You suspect possible poison or drug ingestion.

In the Near Future

- Pain lasts longer than twenty-four hours.
- Temperature is greater than 101°F rectally for more than twenty-four hours.
- Pain keeps returning.
- Vomiting or diarrhea lasts for more than twelve hours.
- You notice swelling in his genital area or pain in that location.
- Pain when your child urinates.

Home Care Tips

If you don't have to call your doctor immediately, you have more time to sort things out, but watch your child carefully and record his progress so that you have an accurate record to report to your doctor. In the meantime:

- Give small sips of clear liquids as tolerated and advance his diet slowly. Be sure he stays hydrated.

- Treat fevers with acetaminophen and ibuprofen at the appropriate dosage according to your child's weight. (See dosage chart in Appendix D.)
- Evaluate your child for changes every two hours and call your pediatrician regarding any drastic change, especially if your child suddenly looks very sick or if his pain changes suddenly.
- Do not give any medicine for pain unless instructed to do so by your child's doctor. Medicine could irritate the stomach lining and worsen the pain.
- Encourage your child to lie down and rest until she's feeling better.
- Treat diarrhea, vomiting, fever, and other symptoms. Monitor for dehydration.

Additional Information

Locating abdominal pain on a child is very difficult, but if you can get your child to point to a specific area the information will prove very useful. For example, the appendix and liver are more to the right side, the spleen is on the left, the stomach is fairly central. The pain may be throughout the belly. This is common with stomach flu, vomiting, and diarrhea or even constipation.

Viral gastroenteritis or stomach flu is the most common cause of abdominal pain when associated with vomiting and/or diarrhea, especially when other family members or other children in nursery school, day care, or play group have similar symptoms. *Food poisoning* is a form of gastroenteritis caused by eating contaminated food.

Some children complain of a stomachache no matter where something on their body hurts. Sometimes a stomachache and a fever, usually associated with a headache, are the first symptoms of a strep throat. The stomach may hurt because the lymph nodes in the groin are swollen due to infection. If there is strep going around at your child's nursery school, day care center, or neighborhood, mention this to your child's doctor. He may want to obtain a throat culture to check for strep. Similar abdominal pain may also occur with pneumonia.

Appendicitis causes sharp, knifelike pain in the center of the belly which then moves to the lower-right side. The belly is often painful to touch even with your hand. It is usually associated with nausea, vomiting, and fever. In children under three years of age, it is very difficult to make this diagnosis, and you should be in contact with your pediatrician with all available information.

Intussusception is a rare finding that results when one portion of the bowel telescopes over the other, causing obstruction. The obstruction causes spasms of severe pain at fifteen- to twenty-minute intervals. The child will appear extremely ill during the spasms but show marked improvement in between. Any pattern like this should be reported immediately to your pediatrician.

Don't rule out diet as a cause. *Lactose* and other forms of carbohydrate intolerance may also cause recurrent abdominal pain. The symptoms may be related to the amount ingested or may appear after very small amounts are taken. *Lactose intolerance* or cow milk allergy may be suspected if there is a family history or colic in early infancy. Apple juice drinkers frequently complain of cramps, gas, and loose stools. The symptoms will often disappear when the drink is removed from the diet. Children who drink large amounts of soda may be *fructose intolerant,* and this causes abdominal pain. Another less common food intolerance is gluten. Gluten is the protein found in wheat or rye. This is known as *celiac disease.* Abdominal pain may be a symptom of celiac disease when accompanied by abdominal distension, decreased appetite, generalized irritability, and greasy, bulky, foul-smelling diarrhea. Celiac disease may also prevent a child from achieving adequate weight gain and eventually affect normal growth. The symptoms for any of these digestive intolerances will disappear when the food or drink is removed from the diet. See the section on Allergies and Sensitivities to Food (page 104) for a description regarding how to keep a diet history and conduct an elimination diet to find the offending food or drink.

See Related Areas

Allergies and Sensitivities to Food, Constipation, Dehydration, Diarrhea, Fever, Food Poisoning, Gastroenteritis, Pneumonia, Scarlet Fever, Sore Throat, Urinary Tract Infection.

ALLERGIES

Definition

Allergic reactivity is the normal ability of the body's immune system to reject foreign substances. In some individuals this response is more dramatic and pronounced, and we say they have "allergies." Individuals may have an allergic response to:

- Things they inhale.
- Foods they eat.
- Medications.
- Things they touch or that come in contact with their skin.

Children can be allergic to more than one substance at a time, and sometimes these allergies develop as the child grows. Allergies tend to run in families, with some children outgrowing them and others retaining an allergy for a lifetime. Regardless of the individual pattern, it is usually the parents who figure out the specifics of allergies in children.

What to Do

- If you think your child has allergies, be extremely vigilant in watching them to help determine what the allergen might be.
- Keep a diary of activities, places, and types of food and medicines your child ingests, and all the symptoms you observe.
- Work with your child's doctor to reduce or eliminate allergic reactions once you figure out what your child is allergic to.

When to Call Your Doctor

Immediately

- Call your doctor for *all* severe allergic reactions.
- Wheezing or trouble breathing.
- Cold clammy skin.
- Loss of consciousness.
- Swelling and itchy rash all over.

In the Near Future

- You think your child has allergies.
- You need help treating the symptoms.
- The allergies seem to be changing.

Home Care Tips

- Treat the symptoms.
- Use careful observational skills.
- Try to anticipate your child's needs in terms of environment.
- Have your child wear identification, such as a Medi-Alert bracelet, at all times if he has had a severe reaction in the past.
- Make sure all his caretakers are aware of his allergies, know how to avoid them, and know how to treat them if there is a problem.
- See specific allergies for individual details.

Additional Information

Allergies to something inhaled are fairly common. When it causes irritation to the nasal passages, the medical term for this type of allergy is *allergic rhinitis*. It is also commonly known as *hay fever* and is usually observed in children over the age of three. *Allergic rhinitis is characterized by:*

- A runny nose with a thin, watery discharge.
- Sometimes red or irritated eyes.
- Mouth breathing.
- Sneezing and tearing.
- Headache.
- Fatigue or tiredness.

Food and/or drug allergies may have a number of different symptoms including:

- Rash/hives and itching.
- Swollen lips and mouth.
- Wheezing.
- Vomiting.
- Change in bowel movements, usually diarrhea.
- Tummy pain sometimes experienced after eating a particular food.

In order to better understand allergies, we present information in three categories: allergic rhinitis/hay fever, allergies to food, and allergies to medications or drugs. Asthma is presented separately. Sometimes a reaction to an insect bite or sting is also considered an allergy.

See Related Areas

Allergic Rhinitis/Hay Fever; Allergies and Sensitivities to Food; Allergies to Medicine; Asthma; Colds or Upper Respiratory Infections; Eczema; Food Poisoning; Headache; Hives; Immunization Reactions; Poison Ivy, Oak, and Sumac; Rashes; Stings—Insect; Stings—Jellyfish. *See also related areas in chapter 5 "Emergency Situations."*

BOILS

Definition

A boil is a localized infection of the skin causing a large, tender, red lump, usually one-half to one inch in diameter. Boils are caused by a bacterial infection, usually around a hair follicle or foreign substance. *Staphylococcus* is usually the bacteria involved. After a week, the center of the boil becomes soft and may start draining pus. This relieves the pain.

Although boils may occur anywhere on the body, they are more commonly found on the buttocks, upper back, face, and neck. Boils are very common skin infections among children and with proper care usually resolve in a week or so.

What to Do

- Wash area with warm, soapy water.
- Apply warm, moist compresses to affected area three to four times a day.
- Follow Home Care Tips.

When to Call Your Doctor

- Your child has more than one boil or they seem to be spreading.
- The boil is tender, not draining, and you notice red streaks spreading out from the center of the boil.
- Your child has a fever.
- Boils are present on the face.
- The boil is in a sensitive place such as the armpit or buttocks (especially if a child is still in diapers).
- A drained boil does not seem to be healing after three days.

Home Care Tips

- Keep the boil area clean. Continue washing with warm, soapy water even after it has burst. Use a topical antibiotic ointment if there is a break in the skin.
- Continue to apply warm, moist compresses three to four times a day until it is healed. A warm face cloth usually works well, and it will feel soothing to your child.
- Sometimes a boil can be brought to a head quickly by soaking it frequently in a saltwater solution. You can make a saltwater solution by dissolving one teaspoon of table salt in one quart of boiling water and then cooling the water to room temperature. *Be sure to cool the solution to room temperature* before using it on your child.
- Wash your hands and have your child wash his hands frequently.
- *Do not squeeze the boil,* even when it comes to a head. Squeezing may spread the infection to the surrounding area. You may apply slight pressure once it starts draining to further ease drainage.
- If the boil is in a place where clothing might rub it, cover it with a gauze pad to prevent friction and irritation.

- If the boil drains or if you notice a break in the skin, wash the area two times a day and apply an antibiotic ointment to the area until it is healed.
- Keep your child's towel and face cloth separate from other members of the family.

Additional Information

Although a boil may look unsightly, it is rarely a serious problem. It can, however, be very painful, especially if it develops over a bony area and the skin is stretched tight. The best way to prevent boils is proper daily hygiene. If your child seems to develop boils, you may want to use an antibacterial soap regularly. In addition, be sure to treat all skin irritations promptly and completely.

See Related Areas

Bites—Animal, Bites—Human, Bites—Insect and Tick, Eczema, Impetigo, Rashes.

COLD SORES/FEVER BLISTERS

Definition

Cold sores and fever blisters are common names for the infection caused by the virus called herpes simplex. They are tiny blisters that form around the nostrils and mouth area. The herpes simplex virus lives permanently in the nerve endings of some adults and children. The first attack usually takes the form of mouth sores and may be confused with canker sores. Subsequent attacks occur when children are run-down and take the form of blisters. Your child may report a tingling sensation up to twenty-four hours before the cold sore appears. The virus seems to be activated by:

- Tiredness.
- Stress.
- Rise in skin temperature, perhaps caused by a cold, or going in and out of the sun.
- Injury to the mouth.

What to Do

- Try to prevent your child from touching any blisters.
- Keep your child's hands clean.
- Use Home Care Tips to alleviate discomfort.

When to Call Your Doctor

- Any sores near your child's eye.
- The cold sore becomes redder and develops pus in its center, or you suspect infection.
- Recurrent cold sores; your doctor may prescribe an antiviral cream to help contain the infection.

Home Care Tips

- Lip blisters heal by themselves. Try to keep your child from touching the blisters or picking at the scabs.
- Adjust her diet so she can still eat and drink when the blisters are painful. Soft or pureed foods, popsicles, and ice cream may be easier to eat.
- Be sure your child gets plenty of fluids. Sometimes young children may refuse to drink because it hurts the blisters.
- Make sure your child uses his own facecloth and towel to prevent infecting other family members.
- Encourage frequent hand washing.
- Sometimes a fever may accompany the cold sore. Treat fever symptoms for your child's comfort. (See Fever.)
- Don't let your child kiss other children. The virus can spread this way.
- If your child tends to develop cold sores after exposure to sunlight, use lip sun block and sun block on the face whenever he plays in the sun.
- Try applying hydrogen peroxide to cold sores to help them dry up. Do not use hydrogen peroxide near your child's eyes
- Apply a soothing cream such as Vaseline to keep the cold sore moist while the virus runs its course.
- Phenol and camphor preparations may provide some relief, especially if they are applied at the first sign of a cold sore.

Additional Information

Often before a blister appears, a spot on the lips will tingle and swell. The blisters usually last seven to ten days and then dry and form scabs. Before the blisters become scabs, they may itch and burn.

See Related Areas

Canker Sores, Fever, Rashes, Sore Throat.

CONSTIPATION

Definition

Most constipation in children is related to diet or from waiting too long to use the bathroom. Constipation in children is usually not serious; however, it is uncomfortable. Look for these common symptoms:

- Hard pebble-like bowel movements.
- Pain, crying, or discomfort with bowel movements.
- Appearance of blood on diaper or underwear, or bright red streaks in the stool.
- Change in the frequency and consistency of bowel movements.

What to Do

Home Care Tips will usually correct the problem.

When to Call Your Doctor

Immediately

- Abdominal pain for more than two hours.
- Bleeding from the anus.
- No bowel movement for more than five days.
- Extremely painful bowel movements.

In the Near Future

- Recurrent abdominal pain.
- Pain with every bowel movement.
- Tear or cut around the anus.
- Soiling on the underpants or diaper between bowel movements.
- Periodic trouble with constipation for more than four weeks.
- Constipation associated with toilet training.
- Constipation for any newborn less than one month old.

Home Care Tips

Treatment for constipation is aimed at softening bowel movements to make them easier to pass. This is best done by giving plenty of fluids and changing your child's diet to include increased fruits and vegetables. Never use laxatives or enemas unless your doctor advises it. The basic measures to improve constipation include:

- Have your child drink plenty of water and fluids, especially in hot weather or when they have an infection.
- For infants younger than twelve months, add a teaspoon of regular table sugar to their formula bottle once a day until bowel movements become soft.
- For babies over twelve months old, add fruit juices such as apple, pear, or prune juice to their diet.
- For children older than the age of two you may discourage cow's milk, cheese, bananas, and applesauce because they are constipating.
- For children over age two, give one teaspoon of Karo syrup twice a day until bowel movements return to normal.
- Feed your child foods with fiber. Babies six months old and older can have whole-wheat baby cereals. Older children can get fiber from fruits, vegetables, and whole-wheat breads and cereals. Fruits and vegetables high in fiber include peas, beans, broccoli, apricots, pears, figs, and prunes.
- Include as many natural, unprocessed foods in your child's diet as possible.
- Be supportive during toilet training and develop good toilet habits early. Don't leave your child sitting on the toilet for long periods of time, as he may get the impression he must perform in order to win your approval.

Additional Information

Children's bowel movements have many different patterns. Don't expect every child to have a bowel movement every day. Some children may normally go only once every three or four days but have a soft bowel movement. This is not constipation. A change in the bowel pattern that includes the consistency of the bowel movement as well as the number of days between movements represents the most important sign of constipation.

Diet is a major factor in constipation and should be the first thing to consider. For children age two and older, excessive intake of cow's milk may contribute to constipation. Increase intake of water and fruit juices. Eating foods low in fiber and taking vitamin supplements high in iron may also contribute to the problem.

When a child is being toilet trained, he may also get constipated from trying to hold bowel movements. This can happen either because he doesn't want to lose a part of himself or as a control issue between the child and parent or caretaker. Some children are also afraid of the toilet flushing. Sometimes during toilet training, parents become preoccupied with regular bowel movements for their child. This will sometimes lead to the child holding back his bowel movements as a weapon in the battle of wills. A general guide is that if your child is happy and healthy and does not have any pain when he has a bowel movement, and if his bowel movements are not hard little pebbles, he is not constipated. If your toddler becomes constipated while you are trying to toilet train him, put him back in diapers and eliminate all pressure. Try toilet training again in a month's time.

Occasionally, when your child is sick with fever or vomiting, his bowel movements may become temporarily hard and dry. This is not constipation. His body is compensating for the loss of fluids from the fever or vomiting by absorbing more water from his bowel movements. Everything will return to normal when his illness has passed. Encourage him to drink plenty of fluids and eat lots of fruits and vegetables when he is feeling better. His bowel movements will return to a normal pattern in less than a week.

If your child is soiling his underpants when he has already been toilet trained, you may think he has diarrhea. It might well be diarrhea, but it may also be due to constipation and a condition called *encopresis*. Encopresis refers to the syndrome of "soiling" of your child's underpants with liquid bowel movements after he has been toilet trained; it is related to chronic constipation. Chronic constipation may lead to hard stools getting stuck in the intestine; loose, watery bowel movements resembling diarrhea may leak around this blockage. Often, the child will not know that he has leaked. If you suspect this is happening to your child, talk it over with your doctor and set up a treatment plan. It is very important to attend to this problem as soon as you recognize it. Once symptoms have continued for weeks or months, you need an aggressive plan to change your child's bowel habits. Under your doctor's supervision, a trial period of laxatives may be tried to break the pattern.

Occasional constipation is not a problem. It usually can be relieved by adjusting the diet and by drinking an increased amount of water and fruit juices. Chronic constipation is more serious and can develop into other problems—particularly as your child gets older. Blood in your child's bowel movements can be a sign of a more serious illness and should always be reported to your child's doctor.

See Related Areas
Abdominal Pain, Dehydration, Diarrhea.

CONVULSIONS OR SEIZURES

Definition
A seizure is a temporary disturbance of brain function, usually caused by an area of irritation in the brain. There are many forms of convulsions and many different causes. Some of the common symptoms include:

- Stiffening of the neck muscles.
- Rhythmic jerking of the arms and/or legs.
- Staring into space.
- Eyes rolling.
- Loss of consciousness.
- Loss of bladder and/or bowel control.
- Drooling.
- When the seizure is over, your child may be in a confused state and may fall asleep.

Epilepsy is a disorder of the electrical impulses in the brain, characterized by attacks of seizures. The word *epilepsy* actually means "recurrent seizures." A major seizure is called a *Grand Mal Seizure* and usually lasts from two to five minutes. *Petit Mal Seizures* are small and brief and may only be a short episode of decreased awareness or an episode of staring off into space.

The vast majority of seizures in children under three years of age occur during sudden onset of high fever, usually caused by a viral infection. These are called *Febrile Seizures* and occur in 2 to 5 percent of normal, healthy children. Febrile Seizures usually occur between the ages of six months and three years and in general do not have any long-term effects. Once your child has had a seizure associated with a high fever, it is likely to happen again when she has another high fever. Children usually outgrow the tendency for febrile seizures after age three. It is thought that the tendency to have febrile seizures runs in a family. Seizures may also be caused by meningitis, encephalitis, and occasionally, low blood sugar in a child with diabetes.

Seizures may occur when there is disruption in the brain's normal electrical impulses. This electrical misfiring may be caused by poisons, infection, reactions to drugs, snake bites, and vaccinations. Even breath holding may cause a seizure, though this is rare.

What to Do

- Keep calm and don't panic.
- Make sure his air passage remains open:
  - Roll the child on his side to allow saliva to drain from his mouth;
  - Clear his mouth of vomit or any liquids to facilitate easy breathing;
  - Gently pull down his jaw and extend his head backward to open his airway.
- As soon as the jerky movements have stopped, turn your child on his side to keep his airway open.

- If he has stopped breathing (this is rare), start using rescue breathing techniques (CPR) and have someone call for emergency help.
- Do not give any medicines, food, or liquids by mouth during a seizure.
- Remove hard or dangerous objects, including furniture, from the immediate area.
- Ease your child to the ground and place him in the middle of the floor, if possible, and near a telephone in case you need help.
- Stay with your child to make sure he doesn't hurt himself or stop breathing.
- Let the seizure run its course, don't try to stop any of the jerking movements, and don't try to open his mouth if his teeth are clenched.
- Try to keep your child's fever down when he is ill.

When to Call Your Doctor

Immediately

- A child's first seizure.
- Seizure doesn't end after two or three minutes.
- Difficulty breathing.
- Child does not become his usual awake and alert self after the seizure is over.
- Child is confused, delirious, or difficult to arouse.
- Child has a fever and is showing behavioral changes, vomiting, headache, or stiff neck.

In the Near Future

- Child has a fever and you are unable to keep it below 102°F rectally.
- There is an episode of staring or unusual movement of his face, tongue, or mouth.
- Child has a history of epilepsy, and you are unable to get him to take his anti-seizure medication.
- Increase in the frequency of seizures.

Home Care Tips

If your child's seizure *is caused by a sudden onset of high fever,* you must focus on cooling him and bringing the fever down as soon as the seizure is over.

- Dress your child in light, loose clothing when ill to avoid overheating.

- Discuss using fever-reducing suppositories with your doctor instead of oral (by mouth) preparations if your child has a tendency to have febrile seizures.

- Sponge your child with tepid water whenever she gets warm. Make sure your child does not shiver.

- After a febrile seizure, focus on cooling your child and bringing your child's fever down as soon as possible.

If your child is known to have a seizure disorder and he is already on anti-seizure medication, *it is essential to ensure that he is getting the medication regularly* and that the dose of medication is appropriate for his weight.

- Treating epilepsy essentially means preventing seizures. Many children with epilepsy respond well to the use of special medications called anticonvulsants.

- Make sure your child receives his seizure medication on the exact schedule prescribed. Make sure he actually swallows all of his medication.

- An incorrect dose of anticonvulsant medicine can produce side effects such as sleepiness, dizziness, coordination problems, and nausea.

- Anticonvulsant medicines should be monitored regularly by your doctor with periodic blood tests and physical exams. The dose will have to be updated periodically to match your child's weight.

- Whenever your child is sick, remind your doctor that he is on seizure medication so that your doctor can assess whether your child is still getting the appropriate dose of medication throughout the illness—particularly when vomiting or diarrhea is present.

- Be aware of sudden weight gains/losses and growth spurts. The seizure medication may need to be adjusted. Your doctor can inform you about getting your child's blood level tested to prove that he is getting the correct therapeutic dose.

- Sometimes medication needs to be changed, and some children may need to take more than one kind of anti-seizure medication.

Additional Information

Proper classification and treatment of seizures depends upon an accurate and detailed account of the sequence of events leading up to, and during, the spell. As soon as possible after the spell, you should write down all the information you can remember about the event. This will enable your doctor to diagnose and treat your child properly.

Most seizures or convulsions are not life threatening and will stop spontaneously.

For all first seizures, your child should be seen by a doctor as soon as possible.

A parent should not drive alone—even if the seizure has stopped—because a recurrence of the seizure while in transit could be dangerous. Also, you are probably too nervous to drive safely. Therefore, arrange for a neighbor to take you and your child to the doctor, or call for an ambulance.

Many children fall into a deep sleep after a febrile seizure. As long as they are breathing comfortably there is nothing to worry about; let them sleep it off. Do not cover her with a blanket; remember to keep her cool. Doctors used to think that febrile seizures occurred only with high fevers. We now know that each child has an individual set point for body temperature, and a febrile seizure can occur at a lower point. Most often, however, febrile seizures occur with a sudden rise of body temperature. This quick increase in temperature seems to be the trigger for the seizure.

Several conditions may resemble seizures, and these will be discussed by your doctor. They may include: sleep disturbances, breath-holding spells, shuddering spells, staring spells, and pseudo-seizures. Any activity that suggests the possibility of a seizure should be discussed with your doctor.

Be sure to inform your child's nursery school or day care that he has epilepsy. They should be fully informed about the condition and told what to do if a seizure occurs in school.

See Related Areas

Allergies, Fainting, Fever, Headache, Neck Pain.

COUGH

Definition

A cough is a protective reflex caused by an irritation of the airway or lungs, that prevents mucus or pus from accumulating. A cough itself is usually a symptom of another problem and not a medical condition. Most coughs are caused by viral infections of the throat and windpipe. A cough is also a protective mechanism if a child inhales food or a foreign object into her airway; coughing will help to dislodge the object. Other causes of coughing in children include croup, bronchitis, and inhaling irritants such as smoke and air pollutants. Finally, in some children a chronic cough may be a sign of asthma.

What to Do

- Use the *Heimlich Maneuver* if you suspect that food or a foreign object is blocking his airway.
- Look for related symptoms such as a runny nose, sore throat, or fever.
- Give your child plenty of fluids, especially water.
- Listen for and describe the sound of your child's cough. For example, croup sounds like a barking seal; allergies may cause a dry, hacking cough; postnasal drip causes a wet, rumble-like sounding cough that is worse at night when your child is lying down and when he first wakes up in the morning.

When to Call Your Doctor

Immediately

- Sudden onset of violent coughing that could possibly be associated with food or a foreign object blocking the airway.
- Trouble breathing or blueness of nails and lips.
- Coughing spasms that cause choking, fainting, or the lips to turn blue.
- Blood coughed up in the mucus.

In the Near Future

- Croupy, "barking seal"–type cough.
- Wheezing or increase in breathing rate.
- Fever for more than seventy-two hours.
- Your child is younger than six months of age.
- Coughing causes vomiting three or more times.
- Cough interferes with sleep.
- Cough lasts longer than a week.

Home Care Tips

The best treatments are geared to the exact cause of the cough. Home care methods will relieve irritation but they won't make it go away. The cough won't stop until the cause is found and treated. Coughs associated with colds will generally have to run their course. A cold will usually last ten days to two weeks, and, in some cases, the cough may linger another two weeks.

- Give your child plenty of fluids. Water is nature's best cough medicine. It loosens and thins mucus and soothes an irritated throat.

- Warm, clear liquids like tea and chicken broth are helpful.

- Use a cool mist humidifier in your child's room. Be sure to clean it frequently because vaporizers and humidifiers can be a breeding ground for bacteria if not cleaned regularly.

- Steam may also help reduce irritation at the back of the throat. Have an older child take a shower. For a younger child or baby, run a hot shower in a closed bathroom until it is good and steamy. Sit with your child in the steamy room for ten to fifteen minutes. It is also sometimes helpful to take a child from a steamy bathroom to a cold doorway.

- Raise the head of your child's bed to promote drainage and decrease abdominal pressure on the lungs. This works best if a pillow or wedge is placed under the mattress, not under the child's head. For children under age two, use a car seat or upright infant seat for sleeping.

- Check with your child's doctor about using cough medicines and antihistamines and which brands she would recommend if appropriate. Cough suppressants may make your child sound better; however, they will interfere with your child's ability to cough up mucus and may lead to worse problems.

- If a severe cough interferes with sleep, a cough suppressant containing dextromethorphan can be used for children over one year of age.

- You can make your own cough medicine for children over one year old by mixing equal parts honey and lemon juice. This will soothe an irritated throat.

- For children three years of age and older, cough drops or lemon hard candies may also ease coughing. (Small hard candies and cough drops are a choking hazard for younger children, so be sure your child is not running around while sucking on such objects.)

- If your child is vomiting with hard coughing, reduce the amount of each feeding. Give smaller amounts in more frequent feedings. Cough-induced vomiting is more common with a full stomach.

- When your child has a cough in cold weather, have him wear a neck warmer or scarf over his nose and mouth. Cold air aggravates a cough, and using a neck warmer or scarf will warm the air he breathes.

- Do not smoke or expose your child to secondhand smoke.

- Avoid chemical fumes and other air pollutants that could damage the lungs and cause your child to cough.

- Be careful with small objects around children under age three; they could be inhaled and cause breathing and choking problems—especially small parts on toys, paper clips, pins, coins, beads, buttons, etc. Also be careful of deflated balloons and plastic bags.

- Do not give young children peanuts or popcorn. The oil in these foods is especially damaging to the lungs if they are accidentally inhaled. This will often happen if the child is running around while eating snack food.
- For children under age three, be careful to cut round or cylindrical foods like hot dogs, grapes, and cherries in half so that if they are accidentally inhaled into the airway, they will not block your child's airway and cause choking. Other foods that may prove a choking hazard include: hard candies and lollipops; carrots, celery, and other hard fruits and vegetables that may snap off into small pieces; raisins; and sticky spoonfuls of peanut butter.
- LEARN THE HEIMLICH MANEUVER.

Additional Information

Encourage your child to be active. This will strengthen breathing muscles and improve his chances of fighting infections when they occur. Provide opportunities for outdoor activities such as bike riding. Also make sure that your growing child drinks lots of water.

If your child's sleep is interrupted by continual coughing, your doctor may recommend a cough suppressant so that your child can get needed rest. Dextromethorphan is a common cough suppressant found in nonprescription cough medicines. It is usually indicated by the initials "DM" on the label. Check the label for proper dosage according to your child's weight or check with your doctor. There are other, stronger cough suppressant medicines that require a doctor's prescription. Do not use any cough medicine if your child is under one year of age unless you check with your doctor first.

Expectorant cough medicines work by increasing the production of fluids in the respiratory tract. This helps to thin and loosen mucus so that your child can cough it up. Guaifenesin is the key ingredient to look for on a cough expectorant label. Guaifenesin can cause drowsiness, so follow the label for the correct dosage according to your child's weight.

Coughing due to whooping cough or pertussis has a characteristic "whoop" sound that occurs upon inhalation after a bout of coughing. The child may have a history of a recent cold with runny nose, appear ill, have his color change with coughing, and throw up following a coughing spasm. Despite immunizations, whooping cough is still present in many communities. Immunized older children may have modified symptoms of whooping cough that resemble bronchitis.

Coughing associated with postnasal drip is usually loose and has a rumbling sound. It is worse at night when your child lies down. Use of a decongestant or antihistamine for these symptoms may provide some relief.

Frequently, coughing associated with a lower respiratory infection is a persistent, short, crisp cough that gets worse when your child lies on his stomach. This cough is present all day, may get worse at night, and typically worsens after physical exertion or exercise. Lower respiratory infections include bronchitis, bronchiolitis, and pneumonia; they are more likely to be accompanied by fever and wheezing with the cough.

See Related Areas

Allergies, Asthma, Bronchitis, Bronchiolitis, Colds, Croup, Dehydration, Fever, Headache, Pneumonia, Sore Throat.

DEHYDRATION

Definition

Dehydration is excessive loss of body fluids that may result from excessive vomiting, diarrhea, lack of adequate fluid intake, or high fever in children. The body needs a certain amount of water to maintain the proper chemical balance in the body and to help get rid of waste. When your child is sick, extra fluids, over and above his normal requirements, must be taken in order to avoid dehydration. Common symptoms include:

- Dry mouth and cracked lips.
- Extreme drowsiness or a very sleepy child.
- Concentrated urine as evidenced by ammonia smell and dark amber color.
- No urine output or dry diapers for six to eight hours.
- Crying without tears.
- Sunken eyes and for an infant under eighteen months sunken *fontanelle* (the soft spot at the top of the head).
- Rapid heartbeat or pulse.

Many children will begin to exhibit some of these symptoms when sick. Although dehydration is usually associated with vomiting, diarrhea, and high fever, it also can occur with respiratory illnesses when extra fluids are lost through rapid breathing and increased mouth breathing. You can often prevent any serious complications by always giving a large quantity of fluids whenever your child becomes ill. If you find you are unable to give fluids to your child because of vomiting or any other reason, call your doctor immediately.

What to Do

- Whenever your child is ill, immediately gear up to increase the amount of fluids he drinks.

- When your child is vomiting or has diarrhea, always try to reduce fever with tepid sponging and fever-reducing medicines to decrease risk of dehydration.
- For bottle-fed babies, you may dilute the formula to half strength and give frequent feedings (every two hours) to increase fluid intake. Breast-fed babies should nurse every two hours.
- Carefully observe your child for signs of increasing dehydration and seek medical advice whenever things seem to be getting worse rather than better.

When to Call Your Doctor

Immediately
- Infants six months of age and under with vomiting or diarrhea two or more times within twenty-four hours.
- Child of any age with extreme drowsiness and inability to wake easily.
- No urine for eight hours or crying without tears.
- Sunken eyes and/or fontanelle.

In the Near Future
- Vomiting or diarrhea for more than twenty-four hours.
- You are unable to get your child to drink liquids.
- Drowsiness is increasing, or he is becoming extremely irritable.
- You are worried about dehydration.

Home Care Tips

Children with mild to moderate dehydration can usually be treated successfully at home without worry of possible after-effects. Children with severe dehydration require prompt medical attention and possibly hospitalization. Do not worry if your child needs to be hospitalized; sometimes there is nothing you can do at home to maintain your child's fluid intake, and intravenous feeding of fluids will be necessary. This is more often necessary in children three years of age and younger. For mild and moderate dehydration, giving fluids is the most important thing you can do. A child normally requires about one quart of liquids each day; when she is sick, however, you need to give that same quart of fluids plus two to three extra ounces for each pound of body weight per day. If you suspect dehydration may be a potential problem, or if your child has vomiting and diarrhea with fever, start these home care measures immediately.

- Give your child clear fluids continuously. You may have to give small amounts every hour. (Water alone is not enough.)

- Try to overhydrate your child. (Unless there is a known medical condition for your child that requires limiting fluids. In this case, seek medical attention immediately.)

- Monitor his body temperature and try to reduce any temperature greater than 101°F taken rectally, by using tepid sponging and fever-reducing medicines.

- Keep track of your child's toilet patterns, and in babies monitor diapers for urine output. Children should pass urine at least once every six to eight hours while they are awake. Also watch for tears when he cries. If there are no tears, he is not drinking enough liquids, and this is an early sign of dehydration.

- Have your child get plenty of rest.

- If your child's fluid intake is decreasing, switch to one of the oral electrolyte solutions, such as Pedialyte or Ricelyte, available at drug stores without a prescription. These special solutions are clear, bland solutions that contain exactly the right combination of body salts and calories for children. They are quickly absorbed by your child's digestive system and work very well to prevent dehydration and correct mild dehydration. Follow the directions for proper use. They are available flavored or unflavored, in liquid or powdered form, or ready to be put in the freezer as an ice pop. For children under age three, always keep oral electrolyte solution on hand for these emergencies and check the expiration dates frequently.

- Call your doctor to discuss your child's condition whenever you are worried.

- Write down what your child is drinking and when he passes urine so that you have good information to follow his progress.

Additional Information

Diarrhea continues to be the major cause of dehydration worldwide. In the United States, death from dehydration is rare. However, outside the U.S., dehydration as a complication of diarrhea is a major cause of death in infants and young children.

The rate of metabolism for infants and young children is usually high, and they normally require large amounts of fluids. When excessive amounts of fluids are lost through vomiting, diarrhea, or the sweating that accompanies a fever, a child's metabolism will be impaired. The body chemistry that carefully balances body salts such as sodium, potassium, and calcium as well as magnesium becomes upset and these essential nutrients are washed away along with the fluids. This may also dangerously lower the volume of blood circulating throughout the body. Dehydration can be very serious and should always be treated immediately.

See Related Areas

Abdominal Pain, Asthma, Colds, Croup, Diarrhea, Fever, Gastroenteritis, Vomiting.

DIARRHEA

Definition

Diarrhea is defined as frequent liquid or loose bowel movements or stools. These frequent or loose bowel movements may be caused by an irritation or infection in the intestines and are usually light brown or green in color. Common causes include a viral or bacterial infection, a parasite, or diet change. Food allergy, intolerance to a particular food, or too many antibiotics—especially amoxicillin—may also cause diarrhea. Babies who are breast-fed usually have yellow, mushy bowel movements; they may have them after each feeding and as often as ten times a day. This is not considered diarrhea.

Diarrhea connected with a stomach flu (viral gastroenteritis) is common in children. It is usually accompanied by a fever, runny nose, and sometimes a sore throat. Vomiting may also be present. Abdominal cramps may come and go, often occurring just before the onset of diarrhea.

What to Do

- Check temperature.
- For severe diarrhea, eliminate all solid foods and milk for twenty-four hours. Increase intake of liquids. (Children can go several days without solid foods as long as they are drinking plenty of liquids.)
- For breast-fed babies, continue frequent nursing and give an oral electrolyte solution between feedings.
- When diarrhea is mild, reduce solid food to applesauce, bananas, rice, toast, and half-strength milk (except breast milk) for twenty-four hours and make sure the child drinks plenty of fluids.
- Prevent dehydration. Make sure your child drinks lots and lots of clear liquids. Offer something to drink every hour when your child is awake, even if you have to feed her liquids in a teaspoon. Or revert back to a bottle for small children already weaned from the bottle.
- Consider adding an oral electrolyte solution such as Pedialyte or Ricelyte if the diarrhea continues for more than twelve hours. Oral electrolyte solutions are more easily absorbed and will help prevent dehydration.
- Observe your child's behavior between episodes of diarrhea to assess the degree of illness.

When to Call Your Doctor

Immediately

- Severe belly cramps for more than a half hour that don't seem to go away after a bout of diarrhea. A baby or young child with belly pain will draw their legs into their chest and cry inconsolably.
- Blood in the bowel movements.
- High fever, over 101°F taken rectally, and your child is looking very sick.
- Your child is also vomiting and can't hold anything down.
- Baby less than one month old has had three or more large diarrhea bowel movements.
- Baby less than one year old has had eight diarrhea bowel movements in the last twelve hours.
- Your child has not urinated for six hours, and crying does not produce tears.

In the Near Future

- Diarrhea increases in frequency or amount after twelve hours.
- Diarrhea and vomiting are both getting progressively worse with more than twelve episodes of diarrhea and vomiting in twenty-four hours.
- Diarrhea does not start to improve and lessen in twenty-four hours after taking clear liquids, or is not completely gone after four days.
- Mucus in the stool.
- Child is taking medication, especially an antibiotic, even if it is one that she has previously taken with no problems.
- Outbreak of diarrhea in your child's day care or nursery school.

Home Care Tips

- Treatment of diarrhea in children is aimed at preventing excessive body-fluid loss (dehydration). This is especially important if the child is also vomiting. Dehydration can occur quickly in babies and small children. Signs of dehydration are decreased urination and crying without tears.
- Give your child plenty of clear liquids to prevent dehydration. Give as much liquid as your child wants. (Avoid full-strength fruit juices with diarrhea; mix equal volume fruit juice and water.)
- A minimum twenty-four-hour guideline for a liquids-only diet is: 1½ quarts a day for infants, and 3 quarts a day for children ages one through five.

- Use oral electrolyte solutions if diarrhea persists for more than one day. Oral electrolyte solutions such as Pedialyte or Ricelyte are available without a prescription in your drugstore. They are particularly useful to prevent dehydration for children under age two because they are absorbed quickly. Oral electrolyte solutions come in plain or fruit flavors and also are packaged ready to be frozen as ice pops. You can also make your own clear liquid solution by mixing five teaspoons of sugar and a half teaspoon of salt with four cups (one quart) of water.

- Water alone is not enough for children with diarrhea. For children older than two years of age, give other clear liquids as well such as sport drinks, clear broth, flat or defizzed soda like cola or ginger ale, weak tea with sugar, Popsicles, and Jell-O. (Don't give red Jell-O because you may mistake it for blood in the stool.) These liquids can be mixed half liquid and half water at first.

- Give the liquids at close to room temperature. Very hot or very cold liquids may stimulate the colon and cause more diarrhea. Also avoid giving apple juice because it sometimes worsens diarrhea in children.

- If your child has a hard time drinking liquids, try ice chips or Popsicles.

- Do not give your child any anti-diarrhea medicine unless you are directed to use a particular medicine by her doctor.

- When the diarrhea is improving you can begin feeding your baby (older than four months) or your child the *BRATT diet*. These letters stand for *Bananas, Rice, Applesauce, Tea* (diluted), and *Toast*. These foods tend to be easily digestible and should be the first foods you give your child after a bout of diarrhea.

- Once the diarrhea has stopped, feed your child small amounts of soft food such as mashed potatoes and crackers. Starchy foods are absorbed better. It's also a good idea to stay away from milk and dairy products for another day or so in older children. Babies on formula should be started back on formula after twenty-four hours. Continue the oral electrolyte solution between feedings. You may want to start first with half strength formula and go slowly. To make half-strength formula, pour equal amounts of formula and water into her bottle. Gradually increase the formula and decrease the water until you are back to her normal feeding.

- Soy formula may prove useful if regular formula is not tolerated after severe diarrhea. After a few days you should be able to return to your child's regular formula.

- Avoid raw fruits and vegetables and any high-fiber food that causes loose bowel movements until your child's bowel movements have returned to normal.

Additional Information

Frequent hand washing is extremely important when anyone has diarrhea. This is particularly important to prevent the spread of infection that is causing the diarrhea. Teach your child proper hand washing after going to the bathroom and before eating to prevent bacteria and foreign substances from finding their way into your child's system.

Most cases of simple diarrhea are caused by viruses. Other microorganisms that can cause diarrhea include bacteria, fungi, and protozoa. Your child can pick these up from other children or from contaminated food and water. Food poisoning causes diarrhea very quickly, usually within six hours after eating. Milk allergy or food sensitivity can also cause diarrhea.

Bulky, greasy, foul-smelling diarrhea may also be a symptom of celiac disease. *Celiac disease* involves the body's inability to digest gluten. Gluten is the protein found in wheat or rye. Symptoms of celiac disease usually occur after the child has been eating food with gluten in it for at least six months. It is usually noticed by the age of two. Common symptoms include poor appetite, chronic irritability, and characteristic foul-smelling diarrhea and abdominal distension. This condition can also cause a child not to gain weight adequately and eventually slow her growth. Treatment is aimed at eliminating gluten from your child's diet.

Occasionally, small, watery stools similar to diarrhea may be caused by constipation. This is called spurious, or false diarrhea. Hard, dry stools may accumulate in the bowel causing a blockage. A small amount of loose, liquid stool leaks around the blockage and trickles out resembling diarrhea.

See Related Areas

Abdominal Pain, Allergies, Constipation, Dehydration, Fever, Food Poisoning, Gastroenteritis.

EYE IRRITATION/PAIN

Definition

Eye irritation can cause redness, discomfort, tearing, pain, and/or discharge. You will probably first notice your child rubbing her eyes. She may complain that her eyes are itchy or that she has a grainy feeling in them. Many sources of irritation will cause tearing while pain may indicate the presence of a foreign body in the eye or an eye injury.

Colds and sore throats produce some sort of eye drainage that can become thick, causing the eyelid to crust over. Eye irritation can also occur due to an allergy or irritant such as chlorine from a swimming pool. If the skin around the eyelids becomes red, swollen, hard to the touch and tender, this might indicate a skin infection.

A foreign object in your child's eye, such as metal, glass, or small stones, will cause sharp knifelike pain that seems to shoot right back through your child's head. The same type of pain can be caused by a corneal scratch or abrasion (usually when something such as a fingernail or tree branch touches the eye).

What to Do

- Keep the eye clean.
- Rinse the eye frequently with plenty of water.
- Apply any eyedrops or ointments ordered by your doctor.
- If you suspect that a small foreign object is in your child's eye—such as dust, sand, an eyelash, or hair—see the Tips below.
- If a chemical has splashed into your child's eye, rinse the eye well with tap water for at least fifteen minutes and then call your doctor for advice. (Be sure to protect your child's unhurt eye from any fluids injuring it during rinsing.)
- Follow Home Care Tips for eye irritations.

When to Call Your Doctor

- Severe eye pain.
- A foreign body is not easily removed.
- A foreign body has stabbed your child's eye—call 911.
- A discharge from the eye contains pus.
- Baby is under one month old.
- Skin around eye is red and swollen.
- Some toxic substance or chemical splashed into your child's eye.
- A high-speed object, even a Little League baseball, hits your child in the eye.
- Your child complains of blurred or double vision.
- Eyes do not improve as a result of Home Care Tips.

Tips to Remove Small Irritants from Your Child's Eye

This includes dust, sand, eyelashes, or hairs.

DO NOT USE THESE TECHNIQUES TO REMOVE ANY ABRASIVE OR LARGE ITEM: SEEK MEDICAL ASSISTANCE.

- Pull down the lower lid and look carefully. Try to wipe away a small dust or dirt article with a cotton ball or tissue. (See Figure 2.1a.)

- Rinse your child's eye with running tap water or hold her eye open and pour tap water in from a small cup. (See Figure 2.1b.)

- You can also try to pull the outer corner of your child's eye a few quick times to see if you can dislodge the item.

- If there is a sharp object in your child's eye or if his eye was stabbed and he sustained a puncture wound, do not try to remove the item yourself. Get professional medical help.

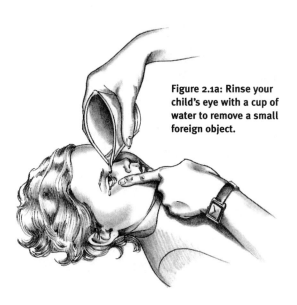

Figure 2.1a: Rinse your child's eye with a cup of water to remove a small foreign object.

Figure 2.1b: Use a cotton ball or tissue to remove a small foreign object. Always wipe from the center of the face outward.

Home Care Tips

- Gently clean your child's eye every two hours while she is awake. Wet a clean cotton ball with warm water and gently wash from the inner to outer corner of the eye. Be sure to wash your hands thoroughly with soap and water beforehand.

- As the eye starts to improve you can decrease the frequency of cleaning to every four, then every six hours.

- If your doctor has ordered eyedrops, pull the lower lid down and gently place the drops in the lower lid.

- Make sure your child uses her own towel and facecloth to prevent the spread of any infection.

- If an allergy or irritant caused your child's eye irritation, try to avoid the irritant. If chlorine is irritating to your child's eyes, get swimming goggles to protect them.

- Try an over-the-counter antihistamine such as diphenhydramine to relieve itching at night and help your child sleep.

- Your doctor may order special medicine to be administered orally if the eye irritation is due to allergies.

Additional Information

Sometimes newborn babies get a *blocked tear duct.* Although drainage or discharge can reoccur until the duct opens permanently, this condition is not serious, and home treatment will usually help. Massage the tear duct at the inner eye corner by applying a little pressure with a warm, moist cotton ball. Then wipe the discharge from the eye with a fresh cotton ball soaked in warm water, and apply a thin layer of petroleum jelly over the eyelashes. Your doctor may also prescribe an antibiotic cream for you to apply until the tear duct opens permanently.

Eye injuries such as a cut or puncture require immediate emergency-room treatment. Severe eye pain also needs to be treated as an emergency.

See Related Areas

Allergies, Colds, Conjunctivitis, Earache/Infection, Facial Injuries, Fever, Puncture Wounds, Rashes, Sore Throat.

FEVER

Definition

Fever is not a disease; rather, it is a symptom—and the *body's normal response to infection.* Most fevers in children are caused by viral illnesses; some are caused by bacteria.

Children are usually considered to have a fever when their temperature measures 100.4°F (38.0°C) or higher, taken rectally—or with an oral temperature greater than 99.7°F (37.6°C). Note that it is normal for body temperature to fluctuate throughout the day; it is usually at its lowest in the morning (after a night's sleep) and at its highest in the afternoon and evening (after a day's activity). It is more important how your child looks and feels than how high her temperature is. Rectal temperature readings are usually more accurate and read a degree higher than oral temperature readings. Axillary (armpit) temperature readings are a degree lower than oral temperature readings and are the least accurate.

Occasionally, children under age three will develop convulsions due to sudden onset of a high fever. These are called *febrile convulsions*. Usually occurring in 2 to 5 percent of normal, healthy children between the ages of six months and three years, they generally have no long-term effects.

What to Do

- Give a fever-reducing medicine such as acetaminophen or ibuprofen for fevers greater than 101°F taken rectally.
- Remove excess clothing; dress your child lightly.
- Encourage her to drink a lot of cool liquids.
- Look for other symptoms such as rash, pain, pulling on ear, stomach upset, or inability to be comforted.
- Settle your child to rest.

When to Call Your Doctor

Immediately

- Fever over 103°F rectally, over 102°F orally, or over 101°F axillary.
- Baby is under six months old.
- Your child has a convulsion or seizure.
- Wheezing or trouble breathing.
- Severe pain.
- Stiff neck or unable to touch her chin to her neck.
- Purple spots/rash.
- Immunization given in the last forty-eight hours.
- Your child is difficult to awaken or seems confused.
- Your child is unable to swallow anything.
- Your child is crying excessively or is irritable and difficult to console.

In the Near Future

- Vomiting or diarrhea with the fever.
- Frequent urination or pain, crying, or burning with urination.
- Ear pain.
- Severe sore throat.

- Child has a fever longer than seventy-two hours.
- Recurrent fever.

Home Care Tips

Remember that fever is a symptom—not a disease. Treatment is aimed at making your child comfortable and discovering if there are any other symptoms that combined with the fever will provide a clue to the illness. Most fevers in children are caused by a viral infection, and sometimes a fever may be its only symptom. Give fever-reducing medicine for fevers greater than 101°F rectally. Be sure to give the dose appropriate for your child's age and weight. Acetaminophen can be given every four to six hours and ibuprofen every six to eight hours. (See Appendix D, Dosage Charts for Common Over-the-Counter Medicines.)

- If your child tends to have febrile seizures, discuss using fever-reducing suppositories with your doctor.
- Bathe or sponge your child with lukewarm—not cold—water until the temperature drops to 102°F rectally. If your child starts shivering, add a little warm water to provide a gradual cooling effect. (DO NOT use rubbing alcohol. Although it will cool her fast, the fever will also return quickly. The alcohol may also be absorbed through the skin.) Afterward, dry her skin briskly with a towel. The brisk rubbing will promote skin capillary circulation and heat loss.
- Give lots of cool liquids. Offer her frequent drinks in small amounts. Ice chips and Popsicles are also useful. If your child does not feel like eating solid food, do not force her, but provide any liquid she desires. Babies and young children may want milk and that is okay, too. Good hydration replaces sweat and improves heat loss through the skin.
- Dress your child lightly. A T-shirt and shorts or light pajamas is fine for around the house. Extra clothes will keep heat in. Remember: overheated babies cannot undress themselves.
- Encourage rest; activity can increase body temperature. Your child does not have to lie in bed unless she feels like it, but quiet activities, games, reading, and perhaps watching television can encourage rest.

Additional Information

If your child develops a fever within two weeks of traveling outside the country, tell your doctor where you were. Your child may have caught a disease that is so rare in this country your doctor may not otherwise suspect it.

Don't expect the doctor to give your child an antibiotic every time she has a fever. Most fevers are caused by a virus, and an antibiotic will work only on a bacterial infection. There is even controversy over whether all fevers should be treated. Fevers turn on the body's immune system and are one of the body's protective mechanisms. Low-grade fevers (usually 101°F or lower by rectal measurement) only need to be treated if they cause discomfort.

The degree of body temperature is not the sole indication of how sick your child may be. It is more important how your child looks and feels than the temperature's exact reading.

Over-the-Counter Information

Most fever-reducing medicines are available without a prescription and usually come in infant drops, liquid, caplets, and chewable tablets in child and junior doses. (See Table 2.1.) Acetaminophen is available in a suppository for use when your child has a fever accompanied by vomiting.

Acetaminophen suppositories do not require a prescription; however, they are usually kept in a refrigerator behind the pharmacist's counter with the prescription medicines so you may have to ask for them.

Table 2.1

Fever-reducing Medicines			
Generic Name	**Action**	**Dose**	**Brand Names**
Acetaminophen	Reduces fever (and relieves pain). Lasts four to six hours	Depends on child's weight. See Dosage Chart (Appendix D).	Acephen (suppository) Liquiprin Panadol Tempra Tylenol
Ibuprofen	Reduces fever (and relieves pain due to inflammation) Lasts six to eight hours	Depends on child's weight and age. See Dosage Chart (Appendix D).	Children's Advil Children's Motrin

NOTE: It is usually okay to alternate using acetaminophen and ibuprofen for fever control. For example, give Motrin at 3 P.M., Tylenol at 6 P.M., and Motrin at 9 P.M. Give the ibuprofen before bedtime because it has a longer effect and your child will get more sleep.

See Related Areas

Abdominal Pain, Cold, Convulsions or Seizures, Cough, Dehydration, Earache/Infection, Gastroenteritis, Headache, Pneumonia, Rash, Roseola, Scarlet Fever, Sore Throat, Swollen Lymph Nodes, Vomiting.

HEADACHE

Definition

Headaches, more common in older, schoolaged children, adolescents, and adults, can be described as pain or discomfort in the scalp or forehead region. (The face and ears are usually excluded.)

In younger children, a headache may be a symptom of allergies or a common infection such as an earache, sore throat, sinus infection, toothache, or tooth abscess. Some children also get headaches when hungry or depressed.

Migraine headaches usually occur on one side of the head and are accompanied by nausea, vomiting, sensitivity to light, and belly pain. They come on quickly, and children often complain of a transient visual disturbance or "aura" before the headache begins. Migraine headaches usually run in families and rarely occur in children under five years of age.

A headache is a more serious problem when it is associated with head trauma, a fall, or convulsions.

What to Do

- For minor headaches, give acetaminophen or ibuprofen for the pain and use Home Care Tips.
- Check temperature for fever and possible infection.
- Look for other symptoms.
- Provide rest in a quiet, dark room.

When to Call Your Doctor

Immediately

- Stiff neck or inability to touch the chin to the chest.
- Traumatic head injury or fall.
- Persistent vomiting.
- Confusion, speech or vision disturbance, or marked behavior changes.
- Pupils are of unequal size.

- Severe pain that continues for several hours and is not relieved by pain medicine.
- Severe headache for any child under age five.

In the Near Future

- Headache lasts longer than forty-eight hours.
- Headache wakes up child from sleep.
- Fever over 101°F rectally.
- Other signs of infection such as ear pain, rash, or sore throat.
- Recurrent headaches.

Home Care Tips

The main goal for treatment of minor headaches is to minimize pain and return your child to his regular routine. Treatment generally includes use of over-the-counter pain medicine, rest, and relaxation.

- Administer acetaminophen or ibuprofen in proper dose for child's weight. In some cases, it is useful to alternate the two medicines. For example, give Tylenol followed three hours later by Children's Motrin, followed three hours later by Tylenol, followed three hours later by Children's Advil or Motrin, etc. (Tylenol may be given every four hours; Children's Advil or Motrin may be given every six hours.)
- Have your child rest in a quiet, dark room with his eyes closed. A cool washcloth over his forehead and eyes is also helpful.
- Give your child a warm, relaxing bath.
- Massage your child's head and temples.
- Give plenty of cool liquids to drink.
- Make sure your child eats well and gets snacks between meals so that hunger doesn't play a role in headaches.

Additional Information

Headaches are rarely caused by brain tumors.

Carbon monoxide poisoning can also cause a headache. Carbon monoxide is an odorless, colorless, and tasteless gas. It frequently reaches dangerous levels as a result of malfunctioning fuel-burning appliances, improperly maintained water and space heaters, cars idling in a closed garage, and blocked or poorly vented chimneys. If you suspect carbon monoxide poisoning, take your child to the doctor immediately.

Severe headache is a common sign of *lead poisoning*. Lead poisoning is a condition caused by swallowing lead particles or breathing lead-laden dust. Children are most often poisoned by lead dust and lead paint found in older homes. Have your home tested for lead by a licensed inspector. If you rent, ask your landlord for a copy of the lead inspection report. Lead can also be found in painted toys, furniture, and playground equipment made before 1978. Lead poisoning is very dangerous to young children, and children of any age may inadvertently ingest dust from old paint chips. Lead poisoning can cause permanent damage to your child's brain and kidneys. Even small amounts of lead poisoning can cause learning and behavior problems. Talk to your doctor about lead testing for your child.

See Related Areas

Abdominal Pain, Earache/Infection, Fever, Head Injury, Meningitis, Neck Pain, Rashes, Sore Throat.

HIVES

Definition

Hives are an itchy, noncontagious skin rash, characterized by red, raised patches of skin and swelling, that develops as an allergic reaction to food, medicines, insect stings or bites, sun exposure, and viral infections. Hives may also be related to emotional stress or a more serious systemic disease. However, the cause of hives often is not found. They usually come and stay for three to four days and then disappear.

What to Do

- Use an over-the-counter antihistamine such as diphenhydramine for severe itching.
- Follow Home Care Tips.

When to Call Your Doctor

- Difficulty or rapid breathing.
- Swelling is occurring in the face, mouth, tongue, or neck region.
- Your child complains of abdominal pain.
- Your child starts acting quite sick.
- To help you find the substance that is causing the hives.

Home Care Tips

- An antihistamine will reduce the number of hives and decrease itching. Diphenhydramine or Benadryl is available over the counter. You should administer the medicine regularly until the hives are gone. It will cause some sleepiness in your child so be sure to give the dose that is appropriate for your child's weight.

- Soak affected areas in cool water (tub) or apply cold compresses to relieve the itch and swelling.

- You can also apply calamine lotion to soothe the itch.

- Consult your child's doctor to determine the cause of the hives, if possible.

- Avoid exposure to hive-inducing situations and substances.

- If the hives are associated with insect bites, change your child's sheets and clothes regularly. Have your child wear an insect repellent when outdoors.

- If the hives are related to sun exposure (solar hives), be sure that your child applies a sunscreen everyday—even in winter—before going outside to play.

Additional Information

A child's medical history may help your doctor to identify the possible cause. If your child has reoccurring episodes of hives, keep a diary of her activities, diet, and any medicines she has taken. The best way to prevent hives is to avoid contact with the substance or situation causing them.

Some common pediatric antibiotics such as amoxicillin may cause a rash. An allergic antibiotic rash often appears as hives and commonly begins during the first four to five days of taking the medicine.

See Related Areas

Allergies, Allergies and Sensitivities to Food, Allergies to Medicine, Rashes, Stings, Sunburn.

IMMUNIZATION REACTIONS

Definition

Your child may occasionally feel ill or out of sorts after receiving a routine immunization. The most common reactions are non–life threatening and include pain at the injection site and a low-grade fever. *Severe reactions usually start within twenty minutes of an injection and last up to two hours.*

Some vaccinations are made using cells from chicken eggs, and some children are highly allergic to the proteins in these eggs. If your child does have an egg allergy or if you have a family history of egg allergies, we strongly recommend that you report this to your child's doctor before any vaccinations are given.

DTP and DT

The diphtheria, tetanus, and pertussis (whooping cough) vaccinations are usually given together in an injection called a DTP. For a few children, the physician may decide to give only the diphtheria and tetanus vaccination, called a DT. Pain, tenderness, and swelling at the injection site occur in about half of all children who receive it, and the reaction usually lasts only twenty-four to forty-eight hours. Less than half of all children may also get a fever for twenty-four to forty-eight hours. Mild drowsiness, poor appetite, and fretfulness have also been reported.

Hib

The haemophilus influenza-B vaccine, abbreviated Hib, results in a sore injection site or fever in only 1.5 percent of children.

Hepatitis-B

Hepatitis-B gives a sore injection site in about one-third of all children, and fever in about 3 percent.

Measles, Mumps, and Rubella

Measles, mumps, and rubella are given as a triple vaccine, MMR, in one injection. A side effect could result from any one of them. The measles vaccine results in a fever for about 10 percent of all children and a rash in seven to ten days following the injection in 5 percent of all children. This mild, pink rash will appear mostly on your child's trunk. Mumps and rubella usually result only in pain at the injection site.

Polio

The oral polio vaccination (OPV), developed by Dr. Albert B. Sabin, uses the live polio virus and may cause a severe reaction in children having compromised immune systems. The American Academy of Pediatrics now recommends giving the injectable polio vaccine (IPV), developed by Dr. Jonas Salk, for the first two doses. Discuss this with your doctor.

Chicken Pox

The chicken pox vaccination may result in pain or swelling at the injection site for one to two days. Sometimes a fever will develop seventeen to twenty-eight days after the vaccination and last for one to three days. There is a possibility your child could develop Reye's syndrome (please see the Selected Glossary) if he takes aspirin around the time of the vaccination.

***Never give aspirin for fever or pain for at least six weeks
after receiving the chicken pox vaccination.***

Sometimes a chicken pox–like rash may develop at the injection site or become scattered across the body within five to twenty-eight days after the vaccine. It usually lasts only a few days and is probably not contagious.

What to Do

- Call your doctor or local emergency medical services immediately if a severe reaction occurs.
- Use Home Care Tips for mild reactions such as pain, discomfort, and fever.

When to Call Your Doctor

Immediately

- Difficulty breathing or swallowing.
- Your child is limp, weak, or not moving.
- Your child is unresponsive or becomes difficult to awaken.
- Fever greater than 103°F taken rectally.
- High-pitched or unusual cry after DTP immunization.
- Crying constantly for three hours.

In the Near Future

- Measles vaccine rash seven to ten days after MMR.
- Redness around the injection site is greater than two inches or persists for more than forty-eight hours.
- Red streaks run from the injection site.
- Fever greater than 101°F taken rectally.
- Pain, swelling, or tenderness at the injection site lasts for more than three days.
- You notice a deep lump two to eight weeks after DTP, that feels tender to the touch.
- Chicken pox–like rash develops five to twenty-one days after the vaccination.

Home Care Tips

- For initial pain or tenderness at the injection site, apply ice to the area for twenty minutes each hour for three hours.

- Give ibuprofen (in the appropriate dosage for your child's weight) by mouth to help decrease inflammation and pain.
- For fevers greater than 102°F, give acetaminophen or ibuprofen in the appropriate dose for your child's weight.

Additional Information

If your child has a reaction to the first dose of a vaccination, the chances are that she may have a reaction to subsequent doses. Discuss this with your doctor. Be sure to mention any allergies your child may have, particularly egg allergies, before any vaccinations. Different preparations, schedules, or doses may be employed for your child. Your doctor might also recommend giving your child acetaminophen or ibuprofen as a preventive measure before the next dose.

See Related Areas

Allergies, Fever, Hives, Rashes.

LIMB PAIN

Definition

Your child complains of pain in the arms and/or legs (not associated with a fall or injury) that is brief, lasting up to fifteen minutes, or continuous, lasting from a few hours to a few days. Brief pains are usually due to *muscle spasms* or cramps, while continuous pain is usually due to *muscle strains*. Mild muscle aches also frequently occur due to a viral illness.

What to Do

- Make sure there are no broken bones.
- Check for fever.
- Review recent activities with your child.
- Ask your child to move the joint near where he has the limb pain.
- Check for any joint swelling associated with the pain.

When to Call Your Doctor

- Your child can't stand or walk.
- He can't move the joint fully, or there seems to be a lot of swelling around the joint.
- Leg pain makes your child limp.

- It is bright red around the area of pain.
- Calf pain on one side lasts more than eight hours.
- Your child seems to have muscle weakness or a tingling sensation that does not go away.
- Fever lasts more than twenty-four hours.

Home Care Tips

Most limb pain in children is due to an unnoticed muscle injury or a muscle cramp from a strenuous activity.

For Muscle Cramps

- Stretch the muscle in the direction opposite to how it is being pulled by the cramp or spasm.
- For muscle cramps in the feet or calf muscles, stretch the painful muscle by pulling the toes upward as far as they will go to break the spasm.
- Massage the painful muscle with an ice pack for twenty minutes.
- If it is a very hot day, the pain may be due to heat cramps. Give your child extra fluids in addition to an ice pack and massage.
- Give your child's feet more room to move at night by placing a pillow under the covers at the foot of the bed.
- Muscle cramps usually last from five to thirty minutes. Once they are over, the muscle quickly returns to normal.

For Muscle Strains

- Give your child acetaminophen or ibuprofen in the appropriate dosage for his weight to ease the pain.
- Massage the sore muscles with ice for twenty minutes several times during the first day.
- Use warm, moist heat or a warm bath as needed the second day. A strained muscle usually lasts for two or three days, and often the pain is worse on the second day.
- If there is a lot of stiffness, have your child relax in a hot bath for twenty minutes twice a day and gently exercise the affected muscle under water.

Additional Information

A broken bone is always a concern when there is limb pain. Watch your child to see how he is using his leg or arm. Look to see if both limbs look equal or about the same.

It often helps to compare one side of the body with the other. If he appears to have pain or difficulty moving, or if the arms or legs do not look the same, have your doctor examine him.

Muscle spasms and sprains are very common in children. Muscle spasms in the calf muscles or feet occur in one-third of children. They are sometimes referred to as *growing pains* although they have nothing to do with growth. They result from vigorous use of incompletely developed muscles and bones.

Legg-Calve-Perthes disease may begin with pain in the thigh or knee and a "painless limp" that grows worse after periods of activity and gets better after rest. It most often affects children between ages three and eleven and is more common in boys. Early diagnosis and treatment will yield the best result.

Transient mono articular synovitis of the hip joint is one of the more common causes of limping in children. It can occur at any age but is more common during ages three to eight. It is characterized by a sudden onset of pain, limping, and restriction of motion. Onset seems to follow a nonspecific respiratory infection in the past seven to fourteen days. Conservative treatment with rest and anti-inflammatory medicine is usually prescribed.

See Related Areas

Broken Bones, Fever, Sprains.

NECK PAIN

Definition

Neck pain or swelling of the neck usually occurs with infection or injury to the neck. Children who complain of neck pain or swelling often have swollen lymph nodes or "glands" related to a sore throat or other type of infection in the area of the head, mouth, and neck.

An accident or injury with neck pain requires immediate medical attention. If your child has been in an accident and has neck pain, do not move him. Wait for your emergency medical services to arrive.

What to Do

Neck Pain

- Check temperature and look for other signs of infection or for a localized cut or abrasion.
- Look for any swelling.

Neck Injury

- DO NOT move your child.
- Call an emergency medical service to ensure safe movement of your child and prevention of further injury.

When to Call Your Doctor

Immediately

- Call 911 if you suspect neck injury or trauma.
- Fever greater than 101°F rectally, and difficulty touching his chin to his chest.
- Fever and behavioral changes, especially confusion.
- Drooling, difficulty breathing, or difficulty swallowing.
- Your child has a stiff neck without any tenderness or he is unable to touch his chin to his chest.
- You notice a purple-red rash that looks like bleeding under the skin.
- Bulging fontanelle in a child under age two.
- Your child complains of extreme pain.

In the Near Future

- Your child's lymph nodes or "glands" are very tender or larger than three inches, or if the overlying skin is red.
- Fever over 101°F rectally with neck pain for more than twenty-four hours.
- Your child complains of a sore throat or ear pain.
- Neck pain lasts longer than forty-eight hours.

Home Care Tips

- Immediately immobilize an injured child who has neck pain. Cover him with a blanket. *Keep his head still.* You can roll towels or a sweatshirt and place them alongside his head to remind him to keep still, while you *call for emergency help* and assistance. Keep your child calm by offering reassurance and stroking his forehead or hand. Try not to panic.
- Treat muscle spasms with heat. Use warm soaks, a hot-water bottle, or a heating pad.
- Massage may also help.

- Administer over-the-counter pain medicine such as acetaminophen or ibuprofen in the appropriate dosage for your child.
- Most enlarged lymph nodes are due to infection. If your doctor prescribes antibiotics, be sure that your child takes the medicine until it is finished, even when he starts to feel better. Also, remember that lymph nodes may remain swollen for quite a while—weeks or even months.

Additional Information

A stiff neck is often very difficult to evaluate in a child. Children with a fever very often complain of a headache and muscle aches at the side and back of the neck. This can be very worrisome for parents, who fear the onset of meningitis. However, if a child can touch his chin to his chest with ease, meningitis is usually not a factor.

Meningitis is an inflammation of the lining membranes (meninges) of the brain and spinal cord. It usually results from a viral or bacterial infection. Viral meningitis is usually not a very serious illness. Bacterial meningitis is serious but can be treated successfully with antibiotics especially when caught early. Common symptoms of meningitis include:

- High fever, usually 102°F or higher.
- Stiff neck; child is unable to touch her chin to her chest.
- Drowsiness or extreme fatigue.
- Inability to tolerate bright light.
- Purple-red rash that looks like bleeding under the skin.
- Vomiting.
- Confusion or listlessness.
- Back pain.
- Under the age of two, the fontanelle will bulge slightly.

If you suspect meningitis, CALL YOUR DOCTOR IMMEDIATELY.

See Related Areas

Convulsions or Seizures, Earache/Infection, Fainting, Fever, Headache, Meningitis, Pneumonia, Sore Throat.

NOSEBLEED

Definition

A nosebleed is bleeding from the nose, usually from blood vessels in the nasal passage. This can be caused by hard or frequent nose blowing or sneezing, by dry air, by a blow to the nose, by picking the nose, or by a foreign object in the nose. Blood loss is usually minimal; however, it may look like a lot. The medical word for nosebleed is *epistaxis*. Nosebleeds are very common in young children (most often boys) and occur most frequently at night.

What to Do

- Remain calm and calm your child. Crying will increase blood flow.
- Pinch your child's nose and have him lean slightly forward. Continue to pinch the soft tissue of your child's nose for ten minutes to allow a clot to form. (See Figure 2.2.)
- If the nosebleed doesn't stop after pinching for ten minutes, try pinching again for ten to twenty minutes more.
- Check to be sure there is no foreign object in the nose.

When to Call Your Doctor

- Nosebleed does not stop after thirty minutes of direct pressure.
- Bleeding problems occur at other sites (for example, large bruises without trauma).
- You think there is injury to the nose.
- There is a possibility a foreign object in your child's nose that can't be dislodged by holding the good nostril and having your child blow his nose.

Figure 2.2: Pinch your child's nose just below the bony prominence to stop the bleeding. Your child should be leaning slightly forward.

- Nosebleeds are frequent: your child has had more than three nosebleeds in the past forty-eight hours.
- Your child appears ill or pale.
- Your child has a chronic medical problem such as a heart or kidney condition, or your child takes specific medication on a regular basis.

Home Care Tips

If your child has frequent nosebleeds, there are several things that you can do to minimize them.

- Lubricate your child's nostrils with a petroleum jelly, such as Vaseline, in the morning and at night.
- Use a cool air humidifier in your child's room if you live in a dry climate or if heat is very dry in winter.
- Make sure your child does not blow his nose for at least three hours after a nosebleed.
- Don't let your child put his head back during a nosebleed. This allows the blood to go into the stomach and can case irritation and vomiting.
- For recurrent and tough-to-stop nosebleeds, you can insert a gauze pad wet with decongestant nose drops. The gauze helps to apply pressure, and the nose drops help to shrink the tiny blood vessels in the nose. Continue squeezing the nose for ten minutes with the gauze pad inside.

Additional Information

In the past, frequent nosebleeds caused by fragile blood vessels in the nostril were treated by cauterizing these vessels. This is no longer a common practice and is rarely done. Humidity and local lubrication with petroleum jelly are the preferred treatments.

Sometimes nosebleeds are related to allergies such as hay fever. If this is a possibility, discuss with your doctor his thoughts on using an antihistamine to decrease nasal drainage.

Unless there is a family history of difficulty in forming clots, it's rare for a child to exhibit this complication. When it does occur, the child usually shows bleeding at other sites such as multiple bruises or bleeding from the gums.

See Related Areas

Allergies, Allergic Rhinitis/Hay Fever, Asthma, Colds or Upper Respiratory Infections, Facial Injuries.

RASHES

Definition

A rash is a visible skin irritation. Rashes come in all shapes and sizes. They may be red blotches, itchy blisters, raised bumps, lacy patterns, or patches of rough skin. Most rashes are harmless and clear up in a few days, even without treatment. A few rashes may require medical attention. Some are an allergic reaction to a food, medicine, laundry detergent, or other type of material. Some accompany fever and a viral infection. Rashes are often a symptom of an underlying problem.

What to Do

- Examine your child's skin so that you can get an accurate description of the extent and appearance of the rash.
- Look for a possible reason for a rash such as a fever, viral syndrome, new laundry detergent or food, or exposure to outdoors (possible poison plants or insect bites).
- Refer to the rash chart to see if your child's rash falls into one of the common categories. (See Table 2.2.)

When to Call Your Doctor

- You think the rash is associated with a serious illness.
- The rash appears to be associated with a medicine your child is taking.
- You notice swelling around the face, lips, or neck.
- Wheezing or difficulty breathing.
- Reddish lines or streaks coming from a rash area.
- Rash is purple, red or blood-like, and doesn't blanch when you touch it.
- Rash appears to be bleeding or bruising under the skin.
- You aren't sure what the rash means.
- You think your child has a contagious illness associated with the rash.
- Fever over 101°F rectally accompanied by a rash.
- Your child develops blisters.

Home Care Tips

A rule of thumb for rashes is: "If it is wet, dry it, and if it is dry, wet it." In general, a rash is a symptom of another problem. A condition should be diagnosed before treatment is

Table 2.2

	Common Rashes and Treatment				
Condition	Causes	Appearance	Affected Areas	Other Symptoms	What to Do
Chicken pox	Virus called varicella/herpes zoster.	Red spots, which change to small pimples that develop into small blisters that break and crust over.	Rash starts on trunk and face first, then spreads all over.	Fatigue and mild fever twenty-four hours before rash appears, sometimes flu-like symptoms, intense itching.	Cool environment. Cool baths. Discourage scratching. Fever control. Benadryl by mouth to control itch.
Cradle cap	Hormones that pass through the placenta before birth.	Scaly, crusty, white, flaky rash.	On scalp, forehead, and behind the ears.	Fine, oily scales.	Shampoo daily and brush away scabs. Use baby oil on scalp in between shampoos.
Diaper rash	Dampness and inter-action of urine with the skin that promotes fungal growth.	Small red patches or rough skin; tiny pimples.	Buttocks, thighs, lower abdomen, and genitalia.	Soreness; no itching.	Keep dry. Expose area to air when possible. Antifungal cream.
Eczema	Allergens.	Dry, red, cracked skin; sometimes blisters that ooze and crust over.	Cheeks, neck, wrist, inside of elbows, backs of knees, behind earlobes.	Moderate to intense itching (may only itch first, then rash appears hours to days later).	Keep skin moisturized with petroleum jelly. Cool environment. Loose fitting clothing.
Fifth Disease	Human parvovirus B-19.	Solid red rash on face (slapped cheek look); lacy-like rash on extremities.	Cheeks, arms and legs.	Mild disease with no other symptoms, or a slight runny nose and sore throat.	Cool environment. Fever control.
Heat rash (prickly heat)	Blocked off sweat glands.	Small red pimples; pink, blotchy rash.	Trunk, neck, and armpits.	Itching.	Cool environment. Light clothing.
Hives	Allergic reaction to food, insect bites, medicine, or other substance.	Raised red bumps with pale centers; shape, size, and location of bumps often change rapidly.	Occurs on any area; rash often changes location.	Itching—in extreme cases, swelling of the throat and difficulty breathing.	Cool environment. Benadryl HCL by mouth. May need anti-allergy injection and/or emergency care.

	Cause	Appearance	Location	Symptoms	Treatment
Impetigo	Bacterial infection of the skin.	Pus-filled blisters and red skin, or scabs on red sores.	Rash usually on arms, legs, face, and around the nose. May spread to other parts of the body.	Sometimes fever, occasional itching.	Clean all areas with soap and water. Clip fingernails. Remove scabs. Apply antibiotic ointment.
Lyme disease	Bacterial infection spread by deer tick bite(s).	Red rash that looks like a bull's eye. Fades after a couple of days.	Exposed skin areas where ticks bite: scalp, neck, armpit, and groin.	No pain or itching at the time of the bite. Fever and rash occur during the week following the bite.	Check with your doctor.
Poison Ivy, Oak, Sumac	Irritation caused by the oils of the plant touching the skin.	Red, swollen skin rash and lines of tiny blisters.	Exposed areas, often legs, arms, and hands.	Intense itching and burning.	Wash with soapy water. Apply cortisone cream or calamine lotion.
Roseola	Herpes virus type–6	Flat, rosy red rash.	Trunk	High fever two to four days before rash. Child feels only moderately ill during fever.	Cool environment. Light clothing. Increase fluid intake.
Scarlet fever	Bacterial infection (Streptococcus–Group A)	Rough, bright red rash; feels like sandpaper.	Face, neck, elbows, groin (spreads rapidly to entire body).	High fever, weakness before rash, sore throat, peeling of the skin afterward (particularly palms).	Benadryl by mouth to control itching. Fever control. May persist for weeks.
Tinea versicolor	Fungal infection.	Pink spots and patches.	Neck, upper back, shoulder, and armpits; may appear on the face.	Looks lighter in summertime; an affected area does not tan.	Antifungal cream to affected skin twice daily. Medicated shampoo. Shower after twenty minutes. Repeat daily for two weeks.

started. Use Table 2.2 to help you determine the cause of your child's rash. Refer to the specific symptom or problem for tips concerning treatment.

Additional Information

The majority of rashes in children are related to an underlying infectious illness. Many of them are viral infections and may be hard to diagnose. Consult your child's doctor for help to figure out the complicated issue of rashes in children.

See Related Areas

Allergies; Asthma; Athlete's Foot; Bites—Insect and Tick; Eczema; Chicken Pox; Fever; Fifth Disease; Frostbite; Impetigo; Stings—Insect; Stings—Jellyfish; Hand, Foot, and Mouth Disease; Head Lice; Lyme Disease; Pinworm; Poison Ivy, Oak, and Sumac; Ringworm; Roseola; Scarlet Fever; Sore Throat; Sunburn; Thrush; Warts.

SCROTUM OR GROIN SWELLING

Definition

In males, this is defined as a swelling, bulge, or lump in the groin or scrotum. In females, it can be a swelling, bulge, or lump in the groin.

Some common causes of scrotum or groin swelling include: hydrocele, hernia, and lymph nodes. A *hydrocele* is a painless sac of fluid sitting on top of the testicle. It is usually present at birth and involves both sides. Any bulge that comes and goes away completely is a *hernia*. When occurring in the groin area this is called a *femoral hernia,* while an *inguinal hernia* occurs when a loop of intestine protrudes or slides through a defect in the abdominal wall. In males, this protrusion is usually into the scrotum and in females into the labia majora. Finally, *lymph nodes* in the groin crease may become enlarged if your child has a systemic infection, rash, or local infection of the leg on the same side.

What to Do

- Check for fever.
- Ask if there is pain.
- Check for any injury or trauma.
- Apply gentle pressure to see if you can push the swelling away.

When to Call Your Doctor

- If unexplained swelling causes pain or crying.

- You notice a color change in the scrotum and pain or crying.
- Your child is vomiting with a change in the appearance of the swelling.
- You are unable to push the swelling away.

Home Care Tips

Home care can be used if the cause of the groin swelling is an inguinal hernia; once your child relaxes, the hernia usually slides back into the abdomen.

- Encourage your child to lie down with his feet slightly elevated.
- Help your child relax and play quietly to help the abdominal muscles relax so that the hernia will slide back in. You also can apply gentle pressure to see if you can push the swelling back into the abdomen. Do not try to force it back in.
- Have your child take a warm bath. If possible, have him lie down (under adult supervision at all times) in a tub of warm water to relax the abdominal muscles.

Additional Information

Most hydroceles resolve on their own with time, generally by the time your child is one year old. All inguinal and femoral hernias need to be corrected by a surgical procedure. Ask your doctor to recommend a pediatric surgeon for this.

See Related Areas

Abdominal Pain, Penis Injury, Swollen Lymph Nodes.

SORE THROAT

Definition

A sore throat is mild to moderate *pain, discomfort, or raw feeling of the throat,* especially after swallowing. It may be associated with a fever and swelling of the lymph glands in the neck. When you look in your child's throat with a flashlight, it will be bright red with or without white patches. In infants and very young children, the child might refuse to eat or will cry during feeding. In addition, some children complain of abdominal pain.

Most sore throats are caused by a virus and are part of an ongoing cold. A certain percentage of sore throats are caused by the streptococcus bacteria, commonly known as "strep throat." A streptococcal infection may also cause a fine, sandpapery rash, especially in the creases of the elbows and knees. This is known as *scarlet fever.*

What to Do

- Check temperature.
- If fever is greater than 101°F rectally, administer fever-reducing medicine and cool liquids.
- Use Home Care Tips for fever and topical relief of throat pain.

When to Call Your Doctor

Immediately

- Fever over 103°F with rash, headache, or belly pain.
- Child drooling, spitting, or having great difficulty swallowing.
- Difficulty breathing.
- Stiff neck and inability to touch chin to chest.
- Extreme pain or limitation of jaw movement.

In the Near Future

- Complaint of sore throat and known exposure to streptococcus at home, day care, or school.
- Fever greater than 101°F rectally with sore throat.
- Sore throat lasts longer than forty-eight hours.
- Signs of dehydration like dry mouth, no tears, and no urine for eight hours.

Home Care Tips

- Give your child acetaminophen and/or ibuprofen in the appropriate dose for his weight for fever and pain.
- For children over one year of age, give honey or karo syrup to soothe the throat. Avoid using expensive throat sprays as they may contain other substances that could cause a bad reaction, particularly in young children. Do not give throat lozenges, cough drops, or hard candy to children under age three because of a serious risk of choking.
- Some children respond well to gargling with warm water. This is difficult for young children to do; however, if you think your child is capable, gargling may provide some relief. Have him gargle every three to four hours while awake.
- Use a cool mist vaporizer or humidifier in the child's room. Humidified air soothes irritated respiratory membranes and helps to relieve cough and hoarseness.

- Encourage plenty of liquid drinks and soft food that is cold and easy to swallow. This is a good time for ice cream and Popsicles.
- Some children like tea with or without lemon, warm apple juice, or warm soup (chicken broth).
- Avoid secondhand smoke.

Additional Information

A throat culture is recommended whenever the streptococcus bacteria is suspected. A quick strep test can produce results in about fifteen minutes and is available in most doctors' offices. If the throat culture is positive, your child has a strep throat, and the doctor will prescribe an antibiotic—usually some form of penicillin. Your child may return to day care or nursery school when she is no longer contagious, and this should occur after she has taken the antibiotic for twenty-four hours. Because strep spreads quickly, many doctors will automatically recommend throat cultures for the entire family. Regardless, any person in your household should get a throat culture if he has a fever, sore throat, runny nose, headache, vomiting, or belly pain.

Always give the prescribed antibiotic for the recommended number of days and doses. Even if your child is feeling better, the infection may not be totally erased, and stopping the medicine too soon could lead to a relapse. It is also important to never use any leftover antibiotic from a friend or another child because it will make any subsequent throat culture inaccurate. You might also consider replacing your child's toothbrush after she has been on the antibiotic for forty-eight hours and once again after she has finished the course of antibiotics prescribed by the doctor. This may prevent reinfection.

Scarlet fever, associated with strep throat, is a red, sunburned-looking rash that appears eighteen to twenty-four hours after the onset of sore throat and fever. Upon close inspection, the redness is speckled with tiny pink dots and is almost everywhere within twenty-four hours. Scarlet fever is not the serious threat it used to be because of successful treatment with antibiotics.

See Related Areas

Abdominal Pain, Allergies, Colds, Cough, Croup, Fever, Headache, Rashes, Swollen Lymph Nodes.

SPITTING UP (REFLUX)

Definition

Spitting up is the effortless regurgitation of a small amount of stomach contents shortly after feeding. It occurs primarily in babies under one year of age and begins during a newborn's first weeks of life. It may be called reflux, *"GE reflux" (gastroesophageal reflux), "GERD" (gastroesophageal reflux disorder),* or *chalasia.* Caused usually by a weak valve at the upper end of the stomach, spitting up normally improves with age and should resolve itself completely after your baby has been walking for two to three months.

What to Do

- Evaluate your feeding techniques and use Home Care Tips.
- Monitor your baby's weight to ensure that frequent spitting up is not interfering with weight gain.

When to Call Your Doctor

- The spitting up resembles projectile vomiting.
- There is blood present in the material spit up.
- Your baby does not seem to be gaining weight.
- The spitting up causes your baby to choke.
- Your baby appears weak and listless.
- You notice a lack of bowel movements.
- Home Care Tips for feeding don't seem to work.

Home Care Tips

- Feed your baby more frequently and in smaller amounts. Start by giving him one ounce less than normal. Then feed him again in 2½ to 3 hours to be sure his stomach is empty. Make sure he still gets the same amount of food in a twenty-four-hour period.
- Burp your baby frequently during feeding in order to prevent air pockets from filling up his stomach. (Don't interrupt his feeding to burp him but take advantage of any pauses.)
- Make sure your baby always eats in an upright position. For a young baby, it might be easier to feed him in an upright infant seat so he won't slump over.
- After meals, also place her in an upright position in an infant seat or a front pack for an hour. Try not to lay her down for a nap immediately after feeding. As your baby grows older and stronger have her sit or walk after eating.
- Avoid pressure on her abdomen after feeding. Don't let people hug her tightly or play vigorously after eating.

Additional Information

If your baby is less than six weeks old and she has vomited repeatedly in a projectile fashion during or immediately after a feeding, she may have *pyloric stenosis*. This is a congenital condition that usually presents itself when your baby is four to six weeks old. The most distinctive sign is forcible projectile vomiting during or after feeding. It occurs because the muscle that links the stomach to the duodenum (pylorus muscle) thickens and narrows. This prevents the stomach contents from passing through to the intestines. A surgical procedure to widen the thickened muscle will correct the problem.

A *tracheoesophageal fistula (TEF)* is a rare abnormal connection between the trachea (windpipe) and the esophagus (foodpipe). It is usually discovered during or after a baby's first feeding when he will immediately spit up all the liquid swallowed and show breathing difficulties. A surgical repair of the problem is required.

See Related Areas

Abdominal Pain, Gastroenteritis, Vomiting.

SWOLLEN LYMPH NODES

Definition

This is often referred to as *swollen glands*. Lymph nodes are special infection-fighting tissues that often increase in size with normal childhood infections. Normal lymph nodes are less than a half inch in diameter—usually the size of a pea or a bean. You will find lymph nodes in the neck, occipital area, armpit, and groin, and generally a swollen node will be larger than the corresponding node on the opposite side of the body (See Figure 2.3.). Lymph nodes enlarge in the neck due to a cold or any infection in the mouth and throat. Those in the groin swell due to cuts, scrapes, and scratches on the leg.

What to Do

- Check your child's temperature and look for any other symptoms of illness.
- Check for local skin irritation and rash.

When to Call Your Doctor

- Your child appears extremely weak and very sick.
- A node in the neck causes difficulty in drinking or swallowing.
- The node is very tender to the touch.
- It increases in size over a few hours.

- It appears to be greater than one inch in diameter.
- Your child also has a sore throat.
- Fever is over 101°F taken rectally.

Home Care Tips

Treatment of swollen lymph nodes varies according to the cause. Most swollen lymph nodes in the neck are caused by a cold and may cause your child to complain of a sore throat. Swollen lymph nodes in the groin may also cause a stomachache because of pressure on the bowels.

Additional Information

Diagnosis of the underlying cause of swollen lymph nodes is made by a doctor after a careful physical exam and history of all your child's symptoms. The location of the swollen lymph nodes is important. Swollen lymph nodes in the neck or groin are not usually signs of a serious infection; they are usually in response to an infection in the adjacent area. If cancer is suspected, special X rays or possibly a biopsy may be performed.

See Related Areas

Abdominal Pain, Boils, Colds or Upper Respiratory Infections, Earache/Infection, Fever, Gastroenteritis, Impetigo, Neck Pain, Scarlet Fever, Sore Throat.

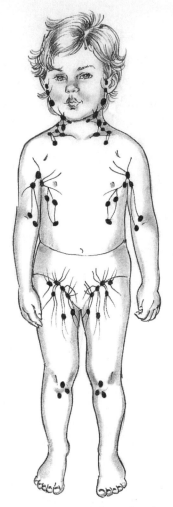

Figure 2.3: Lymph nodes, or lymph glands, are found mainly in the neck, armpits, and groin. Dots represent the location of lymph nodes in the body.

TEETHING

Definition

Teething is the term used to describe the *eruption of a baby's first teeth*. Teething may start as early as three months or as late as twelve months and continue until about age three. Symptoms include:

- Increased drooling.
- Clingy and irritable behavior.

TOOTHACHE

Definition

A toothache or tooth pain may be caused by decay and should be referred to a dentist. Even a small cavity can cause pain from hot or cold substances or contact with something sweet. If the decay reaches the inner core of a tooth, an abscess may occur. Sometimes pain in the mouth or jaw area is also caused by a canker sore or cold sore.

What to Do

- Call a pediatric dentist or your local emergency room for more severe problems.
- Use home care treatment plan to relieve symptoms.
- Encourage good dental hygiene habits at home to prevent tooth decay.
- Check for a fever if you suspect an abscess.

When to Call Your Doctor

- For referral to a dentist.
- Your child has a fever or facial swelling.
- You see a red or yellow lump on the gum line near the painful tooth.
- You are unsure what to do.

Home Care Tips

- Use acetaminophen or ibuprofen in a dose appropriate for your child's weight to relieve pain.
- Apply an ice pack to the area of the jaw that seems to be painful for twenty minutes at a time to increase comfort.
- Floss on either side of the painful tooth if you suspect food may be wedged there and thus causing pain.
- Begin good dental hygiene habits early. Use a facecloth to wash your baby's gums.
- As soon as teeth appear, buy a soft, baby/child toothbrush and brush your child's teeth every day.
- Take him to a dentist between his second and third birthday.
- Limit your child's intake of sweets. When she does eat sugary foods, encourage her to drink plenty of water afterward to wash off excess sugar. Be sure to brush her teeth soon afterward.

Additional Information

Tooth decay is the most common tooth problem in children. The best way to prevent it is to teach your child good dental hygiene and to make sure she gets sufficient fluoride, especially if you live in an area where fluoride is not added to the water. After age three, a child should see a dentist twice a year.

Nursing bottle cavities are a form of tooth decay occasionally found in infants and young children. Usually affecting the front incisors, these cavities occur most often when a child falls asleep while drinking a bottle of milk or sweet liquid or a mother's breast milk. To prevent this, avoid putting your child to sleep with a bottle or, if you must, put only water in the bottle.

Tooth decay, also known as *dental caries,* and gum disease are caused by plaque. Plaque is a thin film of saliva and food residue in which bacteria grow. The presence of sugar in the mouth helps to promote bacteria growth. You can remove this plaque by brushing your child's teeth regularly. *Fluoride* will also help to strengthen your child's teeth. You should make sure the tap water in your area has had fluoride added to it. If you use only bottled water, talk to your child's doctor about prescribing fluoride supplements. You also should buy toothpaste that has fluoride in it. Once your child starts regular dental care, she will also receive topical fluoride treatments to further help strengthen her teeth.

See Related Areas

Canker Sores, Cold Sores, Tooth Trauma.

VAGINAL PAIN/ITCHING

Definition

This occurs when your daughter complains of pain, burning, or itching in the external genitalia or vaginal area, that is not associated with urination. Most itching or discomfort in these areas in young girls is due to soap irritation of the vulva or outer vagina.

What to Do

- Check for any discharge, irritation, or redness around her vulva or vaginal opening.
- Check for fever.
- Use home care treatments.

When to Call Your Doctor

- Fever over 101°F rectally.
- Discharge, redness, or itch is present.
- You suspect sexual abuse.
- Vaginal irritation persists forty-eight hours after home care treatment.
- You are worried about a possible foreign body in her vagina.

Home Care Tips

- Avoid soaps. This includes bubble baths, bar and liquid soap in the tub, and shampoo. They most likely contain chemical irritants.
- Use only water to cleanse the vulva or baby oil to remove secretions.
- Have your daughter take a soothing baking soda, warm water bath. Add approximately two ounces of baking soda to a tub of warm water and have her soak for twenty minutes. Make sure that she spreads her legs to allow the water to cleanse the genital area. Do this four times a day for two days.

Additional Information

If the symptoms are due to soap irritation, they should clear up after two days of home care treatment. (Sometimes anal itching may be caused by pinworms, so this should also be considered.) Some antibiotics may also cause a vaginal discharge or itching.

The most common vaginal problems are due to hygiene habits. Bathing and toilet habits may be inadequate. Because the vagina and anus are so close, bacteria can spread from wiping back to front after a bowel movement. Also, colds and other infections may be spread by hand contact. *Vaginitis and vulvovaginitis* refer to an infection of a girl's external genital region. In some instances your doctor may need to prescribe a specific medicine for treatment.

Sometimes your doctor will notice adhesions of the labia minora (the inner area stuck together). This condition is called *synechia* of the vulva. This is not a serious problem but it will cause difficulties in keeping the area clean. In such cases, your doctor may prescribe an estrogen cream that usually helps release the adhesions and permits enhanced hygiene. Left untreated, synechia of the vulva may cause vulvovaginitis or urinary tract infections.

See Related Areas

Allergies, Boils, Pinworm, Rashes, Urinary Tract Infections.

VOMITING

Definition

Vomiting is the expulsion of a large portion of stomach contents through the mouth. It occurs when something causes the muscles around the stomach to contract and *"throw up"* the stomach's contents. There are many causes for vomiting in children; however, the most common is a stomach or intestinal virus known as *gastroenteritis*. This may also involve a fever and diarrhea. *Food poisoning* or eating something that irritates the stomach might also cause vomiting until the stomach is cleared of the irritant or the disagreeable food. Appendicitis, motion sickness, urinary tract infections, ear infections, and brain infections can also cause vomiting, usually without diarrhea.

Spitting up is common in infants and should not be confused with vomiting. It will decrease as your child gets older. Infant spitting up may also be caused by feeding problems or techniques.

What to Do

- Stop all solid food and offer your child clear liquids (not milk) in small amounts at frequent intervals.
- For infants, an oral electrolyte solution such as Pedialyte or Ricelyte is useful.
- Check for fever.

When to Call Your Doctor

Immediately

- Recent head or abdominal injury.
- Stiff neck and/or headache.
- Blood appears in vomited material.
- Your child does not urinate for more than six hours, or crying produces no tears.
- Abdominal pain lasts for more than four hours.
- Child is confused or difficult to wake.
- You suspect poisoning, or your child has swallowed medicine that was not intended for her.
- Child is acting very, very sick.

In the Near Future

- Vomiting continues for more than twelve hours in infants under age one or more than twenty-four hours for older children.

- Continued vomiting without diarrhea.
- Painful and frequent urination along with vomiting.
- Child is taking medication that may cause vomiting.

Home Care Tips

- When your child is vomiting, avoid solids for six to eight hours. Let the stomach rest.
- Offer room temperature clear liquids, flat or defizzed soda, Popsicles, ice chips, diluted fruit juice, and Jell-O. (Avoid red Jell-O so that you don't confuse it with blood if the child vomits.) When vomiting is severe, *oral electrolyte solutions* (available at most drugstores without a prescription) are tolerated more readily. Pedialyte and Ricelyte are two of the common brands available. Many of the big chain drugstores also carry their own generic brand of oral electrolyte solution. Consult the pharmacist if you have specific questions about one.
- Give your child frequent but small amounts of clear liquids. For example, with an infant start with one tablespoon of fluid every ten minutes, or one to two ounces every fifteen minutes for children over age one. Double the amount of fluid each hour if no more vomiting occurs.
- Continue giving liquids frequently and in small amounts even if your child is thirsty. Giving a large volume of liquids all at once may cause vomiting to continue. The stomach must rest. A *slow and steady approach works best.* Follow the doubling rule above if no more vomiting occurs within the hour.
- Give enough liquids to ensure adequate hydration. Your child should drink at least three ounces of fluid for every pound of body weight in a twenty-four-hour period. For example, a twenty-pound baby should drink at least sixty ounces of fluids in a twenty-four-hour period. You also can judge hydration by making sure your child urinates frequently (at least once every six hours when awake) and has tears when she cries. Check the diaper of an infant to make sure it is wet periodically.
- When vomiting stops for three hours, slowly expand from clear liquids to toast, dry crackers, and broth. Resume a regular diet within twenty-four hours. When your child refuses food, follow her lead. A child often instinctively knows what's best for her body.
- Be calm and sympathetic; vomiting can frighten a child. Keep a bowl or basin near your child so he doesn't have to run to a bathroom when he is nauseous. A cool washcloth placed on your child's forehead may also be soothing.

- Give your child water to rinse out her mouth after she vomits. If the taste is really foul, she may even want to brush her teeth.

- If your child also has a fever, give the fever-reducing medicine in a suppository. Acetaminophen comes as a rectal suppository. You do not need a prescription for rectal acetaminophen, but you usually have to ask the pharmacist for it. It is often stored in a refrigerator behind the prescription drug counter.

- Do not give nonprescription medicines to stop the vomiting. There is no effective one available. Diet therapy is the answer.

Additional Information

Vomiting after injury to the belly or swallowing a foreign body can indicate blockage. This requires urgent medical attention.

A common error is to give as much clear liquids as your child wants. This almost always leads to continued vomiting. It is more important to gradually increase the amount of fluids.

Some newborn babies spit up a great deal. These babies usually respond to careful attention to feeding techniques. Keep your baby in an upright position during feeding and for at least a half hour after feeding. It may be helpful to put her in an upright infant seat after feeding. Also, feed your baby more frequently using smaller amounts, and burp her often. You may occasionally hear the words *reflux* or *chalasia* when a baby spits up a great deal. Ask your doctor to explain this further if it is of concern to you. As long as your baby is gaining weight and growing, any of these feeding problems are more of an inconvenience for the parents than a problem for the child.

See Related Areas

Abdominal Pain, Constipation, Dehydration, Diarrhea, Earache/Infection, Fever, Food Poisoning, Gastroenteritis, Headache, Sore Throat, Spitting Up.

Common Childhood Illnesses and Diagnoses

ALLERGIC RHINITIS/HAY FEVER

Definition

Rhinitis usually refers to a runny nose and literally means inflammation of the lining of the nasal passages. As previously mentioned, allergic rhinitis typically exhibits the symptoms of a runny nose with a clear, watery discharge and is sometimes associated with red, watery eyes. Allergic rhinitis can be further divided into two categories:

- Seasonal allergies—caused by nonflowering, wind-pollinated plants including trees, grass, and weeds. They occur from late spring until early fall.

- Perennial allergies—caused by animal dander, house dust mites, stuffed animals, molds, smoke, cosmetics, perfume, houseplants, and flowers. They may occur anytime during the year.

With allergic rhinitis, your child's nasal membranes become swollen, inflamed, and itchy. Large amounts of mucus are produced causing nasal congestion and clogged sinuses. The common symptoms may be similar to a cold. They include:

- Runny nose with a thin, watery discharge.

- Nasal congestion and mouth breathing.

- Snoring at night.

- Wrinkling of the nose or frequent rubbing of the nose to scratch the itchy nasal passages.

- Red, itchy, teary eyes and bluish circles under the eyes.

- Headache.
- Tiredness due to allergic fatigue.
- Ears may feel clogged, and hearing may be reduced.

What to Do

- Discuss your child's symptoms with your doctor.
- Keep a written diary or log book of your child's allergic responses. Include time, place, and environment in relation to symptoms.
- Follow Home Care Tips.

The diagnosis of allergies/hay fever is based upon your child's history, symptoms, and physical examination by the doctor. Some questions for you to consider include:

- Does your child always seem to have a runny nose, congestion, and itchy nose or eyes?
- Are the symptoms worse when your child is indoors or outside?
- Can your child clear his nose by blowing it (if old enough)?
- Are the symptoms worse when your child is near animals, feathers, wool, or after going down in the basement?
- Is there anyone in your family with allergies, hay fever, asthma, or eczema?

When to Call Your Doctor

- When it is convenient.
- When your child's symptoms are not relieved by regular home care remedies.
- Your child's nasal secretions have changed to thick yellow for more than twenty-four hours.
- Your child develops sinus pain.
- Your child seems tired all the time and has difficulty keeping up with his daily schedule.

Allergic rhinitis rarely requires an emergency visit to your doctor, but you should bring your child to the doctor's office when the symptoms are present so that they may be assessed and evaluated. He will do a complete physical examination and ask for a detailed history of symptoms. Normal nasal passages are pink, but a child with allergic rhinitis may have pale, bluish membranes. It is helpful to bring a log book describing your child's symptoms and detailing when they occur.

Home Care Tips

- Identify the source of the allergy.
- Avoid or at least minimize contact with the allergic source. Unfortunately, it is often impossible to eliminate the allergic substance completely; however, it is the *amount of exposure* that produces the severity of your child's symptoms.
- Have your child rinse his face repeatedly with water to dilute the irritant.
- When possible, give your child a bath and wash her hair before bed to avoid transferring any possible irritants to her pillow or sheets.

For seasonal allergies

- Keep the windows closed.
- Use air conditioning when possible.
- Replace cooling and heating filters frequently.
- Keep your child away when mowing the lawn.
- Talk to your child's day care or preschool if outdoor activities in the spring or fall cause problems.
- Antihistamines may be used for relief of symptoms. This may be prescribed by your doctor, or she may direct you to an over-the-counter medication. Two common antihistamines are diphenhydramine (Benadryl) and brompheniramine maleate (Dimetapp). See Appendix D, Dosage Charts for Common Over-the-Counter Medicines, for more details. Watch your child for the side effect of drowsiness; should this occur, consider reducing the dosage.
- Steroid nasal sprays are also available. Talk to your doctor about the potential usefulness of these products for your child.

For perennial allergies

There are a lot of housekeeping chores that can be done to decrease the effects of these allergies.

- Damp dust daily.
- Avoid keeping items that are dust collectors like venetian blinds and "collections." (If you must keep collections such as records or CDs, try to keep them in an enclosed curio or cabinet.)
- Use synthetic pillows.
- Vacuum every three days using a vacuum with a good filtration system.
- Periodically steam-clean your carpets because dust mites are not removed by vacuuming alone.

- Wash your laundry in hot water to kill mites.
- Return your child's clean clothes quickly to his bureau so that they will not accumulate dust mites.

Additional Information

When a specific allergy-causing substance (allergen) has been identified and your child cannot avoid contact with it, a desensitization treatment may be tried. Conducted by a specialist (called an allergist), this is a series of injections of the allergen ("allergy shots") that produces an immunity. Talk to your child's doctor to discuss if this therapy is appropriate.

See Related Areas

Allergies, Asthma, Colds or Upper Respiratory Infections, Conjunctivitis, Cough, Eczema, Eye Irritation/Pain, Headache, Hives, Rashes.

ALLERGIES AND SENSITIVITIES TO FOOD

Definition

A food allergy is an unexpected reaction to something your child has eaten. Food allergies range from mild to severe, though certainly mild reactions are more common. Most reactions occur in infants as new foods are introduced, including formula and milk. Children tend to have only one food allergy at a time; it's important to introduce only one new food item at a time for all babies and children in order to monitor tolerance.

A reaction may also depend upon the amount of food ingested. Some children can tolerate a small amount of a certain food but develop a reaction when that amount is increased. Signs of food allergy typically occur within a few minutes to an hour after eating the offending food. Common symptoms of food allergies include:

- Tummy ache.
- Recurrent diarrhea.
- Rash, hives, and/or itching.
- Vomiting.
- Runny nose/allergic rhinitis.
- Swelling of the lips, tongue, or mouth.
- Mild or severe breathing difficulties.
- Wheezing or asthma.
- Eczema.

- A rare, but possibly severe reaction could cause difficulty in breathing or anaphylactic shock. This, of course, would require immediate emergency medical attention.

The most common food allergies in young children include milk, peanuts, eggs, soy, and wheat gluten. In older children, allergies to shellfish, fish, and tree nuts are also common.

What to Do

- Talk to your child's doctor.
- Keep a food diary and write down any related symptoms.
- Follow Home Care Tips.

When to Call Your Doctor

Immediately

- Wheezing or difficulty breathing (airway obstruction due to swelling).
- Signs of shock (weak rapid pulse; fast breathing; dizziness or fainting; thirst; sudden paleness; cool, clammy skin).
- Loss of consciousness.

In the Near Future

- Tummy ache, vomiting, or recurrent diarrhea unrelated to other illness.
- Any time you suspect a food allergy.

When you call your doctor, it's best to have as much information available, including a food diary and the timing of the symptoms.

Home Care Tips

- Identify the offending food. Keep a *food diary* by writing down everything your child eats and the time of day he eats it. Also write down what your child's particular symptoms are and where and when the symptoms occur.

> **A Sample Food Diary**
>
> 9:00 A.M.   Rice Krispies Cereal, Banana, Milk, Orange Juice
>
> 10:30 A.M.   Crackers and Peanut Butter
>
> 12:00 P.M.   Beef and Gravy on Toast
>
> 1:00 P.M.   Joe complains of tummy ache; small amount of smelly, watery, bowel movements.

- Until symptoms disappear, keep your child comfortable and well hydrated. Make sure he drinks plenty of clear liquids to replace any fluids lost from vomiting or diarrhea.
- Eliminate the offending food from your child's diet once it has been identified. (See elimination diet below.)
- Your child should have identification at all times or wear a Medi-Alert bracelet or necklace if she has a specifically identified food allergy.
- Teach your child and her caregivers to carefully read labels on all processed foods and to watch out for offending foods.

Although some children may tolerate small amounts of an allergen without symptoms, the best treatment is to totally avoid the offending food. If you are unsure of the offending food, make a plan with your doctor to gradually eliminate items from your child's diet. In this *elimination diet*, each item of food should be left out for a period of at least five days. Analyze what your child has eaten just before the symptoms have started. Review some of the common items that cause food allergies in children such as milk, nuts, eggs, soy, wheat, flour, and some spices. Once the offending food is removed, symptoms usually disappear within two days. It is important to maintain adequate nutrition for your child when eliminating different foods from his diet, so ask your child's doctor how you can ensure good nutritional intake for proper growth and development.

Additional Information

The best way to prevent an allergic reaction to food is to avoid eating the offending food. This may not be easy, however, because some offending foods, particularly flour, cornstarch, eggs, milk, legumes, and spices, may be hidden as ingredients in other foods. For example, look at all the ingredients listed in ketchup!

If you and your doctor have identified a specific food allergy and *your child has demonstrated a major reaction* (such as trouble breathing or shock), there is some evidence that subsequent reactions may prove worse. In this case you should obtain *emergency medical kits* from your doctor's office and keep them at home and at your child's school or day care. These kits contain special injections (such as epinephrine) that can be administered easily without medical training. They can help to relieve severe reactions.

There are other disorders that food allergies can mimic. These include irritable bowel syndrome, lactose intolerance (lactase deficiency), intestinal infections, celiac disease, pyloric stenosis, and cystic fibrosis. If there is any possibility your child may have one of these conditions, your doctor will discuss the details with you. However, you must be certain to mention a family history that might contain any of these disorders.

If your child has a documented food allergy to eggs, be sure to mention this whenever she is to receive an immunization—particularly if she is not at her regular doctor's office. Some immunizations are still prepared with egg yolk and thus may cause a bad reaction.

At least half of all children who develop a food allergy during the first year of life outgrow it by two to three years of age. Some food reactions—especially sensitivity to cow's milk or soy—are more commonly outgrown than others. Allergies to peanuts, tree nuts, fish, and shellfish often persist for life.

Food allergies are often inherited. High-risk children are those with parents or siblings with asthma, eczema, severe hay fever, or a documented food allergy. Sometimes the child is even allergic to the same food as a parent. The risk is highest if both parents are allergic to foods. The start of allergies in these children can be delayed by being careful about their diets.

If either parent is allergic, it's recommended that the mother breast-feed during the first year and that she avoid all allergic food products. If the mother cannot breast-feed, use a formula made from soy protein or protein hydrolysate (called elemental formula). It may also be helpful to delay solid foods until after six months of age.

See Related Areas

Abdominal Pain, Allergies, Asthma, Colds or Upper Respiratory Infections, Constipation, Cough, Dehydration, Diarrhea, Eczema, Food Poisoning, Gastroenteritis, Headache, Hives, Rashes.

ALLERGIES TO MEDICINE

Definition

This occurs when your child has an unexpected reaction after taking a drug or medicine. Symptoms related to a medicine allergy or sensitivity are extremely varied and truly can only be sorted out by a physician. However, the most common symptom is a very itchy rash. Other symptoms may include: fever, swelling (usually in the face, hands, or feet), and although uncommon, trouble breathing.

What to Do

- Call your doctor immediately.
- Do not give your child any more medicine until you speak to your doctor.
- Save the remainder of the medicine and the container it came in for review by your doctor.

It is important not to confuse an allergy with a known side effect. Only your doctor can do this. It is also difficult to know whether a rash that develops when a medicine is given is due to the medicine or the illness itself. In many cases, the "drug reaction" may be due to a sensitivity to the medicine's by-products and not necessarily the medicine itself.

When to Call Your Doctor

Immediately

- Wheezing or trouble breathing.
- Your child shows signs of shock (weak, rapid pulse; fast breathing; dizziness or fainting; thirst; sudden paleness; or cool, clammy skin).
- Your child develops a rash, hives, itching, or fever after taking a medicine.
- You think your child is having a "drug reaction."

Home Care Tips

Never give your child any unnecessary medicines and follow all directions for prescription medicines. Whenever you receive a prescription for your child, find out the following information:

- The name of the medicine and what it is supposed to do.
- How and when your child should take it and for how long.
- When your child should start feeling better.
- Foods, drinks, other medicines, or activities that should be avoided while your child is taking the medication.
- Any expected side effects and what to do when they occur.
- If there is any written information about the medicine that you can have to refer to.

You should also inform your child's doctor of the following:

- Names of any other medicines your child is taking—both prescription and over-the-counter medicines. Sometimes two medicines in combination can cause a different type of reaction.
- Name of any food or medicine you think your child is allergic to and what happens when she takes it. (Most medicines contain more than their active ingredient. Many contain food additives, and some liquids contain alcohol.)
- Any problems your child has had in the past with any medicines, including problems taking a specific medicine.

Additional Information

Unfortunately, it is very difficult to know whether a rash that develops after a medicine is taken is due to sensitivity to the medicine or is totally unrelated. In most cases, sensitivity to the medicine may be related to some of the by-products of the drug, and these are hard to identify. The best thing to do is to always hold off giving any further medication and call your doctor. Penicillin and sulfa-containing antibiotics are the most common prescription medicines that cause drug sensitivity in children.

See Related Areas

Abdominal Pain, Constipation, Diarrhea, Eczema, Fever, Headache, Gastroenteritis, Rashes.

ANEMIA

Definition

Anemia, a common blood disorder in infants and children, occurs due to a low proportion of red blood cells (as measured by a hematocrit) or a low proportion of the oxygen-carrying component of red blood cells (as measured by the hemoglobin). Anemia in children may be more pronounced than anemia in adults because of rapid growth patterns, especially during the first three years of life. The most common cause of anemia in children is iron deficiency related to diet.

What to Do

If you suspect your child is anemic, look for any of the following symptoms. Your child may be:

- Easily tired.
- Pale, especially at the tips of the fingers, the lips, and around the eyes.
- Dizzy on occasion.
- Eating poorly. (To check, keep a food diary of what he actually eats over a two-week period.)
- With severe anemia, your child may be short of breath and have a rapid pulse.

When to Call Your Doctor

Immediately

- If your child has shortness of breath or a rapid pulse.

In the Near Future

- If your child appears unusually tired.
- If you think your child is anemic.

Your child's doctor will usually take a diet history and do a physical examination, but a blood test for a hematocrit or hemoglobin will provide an accurate measure of the anemia. If your doctor does not think the anemia is due to a diet with a low intake of iron-rich foods, she will look for potential sources of bleeding or blood breakdown. If the cause of the anemia is uncertain, a specialist called a hematologist may be called in to consult.

Home Care Tips

- If you are bottle-feeding your baby, use a high-iron formula. If you are breast-feeding, make sure you are eating a high-iron diet or taking an iron supplement.
- For an iron deficiency, make sure your older child is eating a well-balanced diet that includes iron-rich foods such as meats, fish, poultry, spinach, raisins, dried fruit, lima beans, kidney beans, sweet potato, and iron-enriched cereals and breads.
- Make sure your child also gets plenty of vitamin C in his diet. Good sources of this vitamin include orange juice, citrus fruits, potatoes, tomatoes, cauliflower, broccoli, spinach, and cabbage.
- In addition to an iron-rich diet your doctor may prescribe iron drops such as Fer-In-Sol. She also will monitor your child's blood samples to make sure that the anemia is improving. Supplemental iron is best absorbed on an empty stomach, so you may want to give it to your child before meals. Be sure to keep all iron medicine away from small children. It is a medicine, and accidental ingestion of too much iron is dangerous.
- Continue to add iron-rich foods to your child's diet while you are giving an iron supplement. This will enable you to wean any additional iron you need to give your child.
- You may also want to restrict your child's intake of milk to no more than twenty-four ounces a day so that she will have the appetite to eat iron-rich foods.
- Be aware that giving supplemental iron medicine may cause your child's bowel movements to become almost black in color, and he may get a little constipated. Make sure that he gets plenty of fruits and vegetables to keep his bowel movements from becoming too hard.

Additional Information

Anemia should always be investigated promptly and thoroughly by a doctor. Iron deficiency is the leading cause of anemia in children between six months and two years of age. It is rarely seen in full-term infants under six months of age because the iron stores available at birth are adequate to meet the infant's needs for the first five to six months.

Iron is usually given two to three times a day and an hour before meals. It may be taken with juice, but its absorption will be decreased if given after meals. Iron can stain your child's teeth so give it through a straw or medicine dropper, if possible. Iron may also cause stomach upset. Give your child only the prescribed amounts of iron medicine. If taken in excess, iron can be dangerous.

*If your child accidentally drinks the supplemental iron medicine,
call your poison control center immediately.*

See Related Areas

Constipation, Diarrhea.

ASTHMA

Definition

Asthma is an allergic illness (often triggered by irritants such as pollens or viral respiratory infections) that affects the airway and its passages. The muscles of the small air passages going into the lungs go into spasm, constrict, and narrow the lower airway. This is often accompanied by inflammation and swelling of the airway passages and causes wheezing (a high-pitched sound from the chest, not a rattling in the back of the throat), chest tightness, cough, breathlessness, and difficulty breathing.

Asthma is a chronic disease and requires ongoing therapy and coordinated work with your child's physician. Asthma attacks vary from mild to severe, and treatment varies accordingly. It is a complex disorder that needs to be treated by a physician who can monitor your child's progress.

What to Do

During an Attack

- Keep your child calm.
- Reduce activity.
- Encourage intake of warm fluids.

- Monitor progress.
- Give medications as prescribed.

Long-term treatment goals

- Control chronic symptoms.
- Maintain normal activity levels.
- Maintain normal or near-normal lung function.
- Prevent acute attacks.
- Make sure you always have your child's medications up to date.
- Follow Home Care Tips.

When to Call Your Doctor

Immediately

- Wheezing or difficulty breathing.
- Skin, lips, or fingernail beds become blue or dusky.
- Child cannot speak because of shortness of breath.
- Increased restlessness.
- Excessive sleepiness.

In the Near Future

- Breathing is getting worse.
- Signs of dehydration (dry mouth, no tears, decreased urine or less moisture in the diapers, sleepiness, or irritability).
- No signs of improvement after twenty-four hours of treatment at home.
- Persistent fever over 101°F rectally over the last twenty-four hours.
- Difficulty sleeping.
- Change in color of mucus (phlegm) from white to yellow or green.
- Persistent cough.
- Medicines not tolerated.

Home Care Tips

Asthma often requires a combination of treatments. This includes prescription asthma medications given by mouth or inhaler, *nebulizer* treatments, and avoidance of substances that trigger an attack. (A nebulizer is a machine that mixes medicine in air so that the medicine can be inhaled into the airway passages.)

Avoid known triggers that can set off asthma attacks. These include

- An upper respiratory infection or bronchitis.
- Exposure to allergens like pollen, mold, animal dander, dust mites, and smoke.
- Eating certain foods or taking certain medicines.
- Strenuous physical activity.
- Breathing cold air.
- Emotional stress.

During an acute asthma attack

- Keep your child calm by holding or rocking him and by being reassuring and in control. Anxiety can increase the spasms in his airway.
- Encourage him to drink fluids; warm fluids seem to be more effective than cold ones. Fluids are extremely important and may be more acceptable in small sips. Don't worry if your child doesn't eat any solid food for a day or two during an attack. The liquids are more important to ensure adequate hydration.
- Keep track of whether your child is improving or getting worse.
- Give your child his prescription asthma medications. Usually the first dose is bigger, often one and a half times the follow-up dosage. Sometimes the medication is given through a nebulizer or pocket inhalant.
- For a coughing spasm, give your child (over six months of age) warm apple juice or tea. Warm fluids help to relax the airway. Do not use any cough suppressant without checking with your doctor first.

There are a few things you can do routinely to help your child control his asthma

- Have him drink plenty of liquids—at least two quarts a day—to keep his secretions loose.
- Try to determine what is triggering his asthma. Keep a diary of when attacks occur, what your child was doing, what he ate, and where he was. This will help you to eliminate irritating substances.
- Start the asthma treatments early—as soon as your child starts to cough, use only the prescription inhalant and medicine.
- Your doctor may show you how to use a Peak Flow Meter if your child is over the age of three. It measures lung function and will help you and your doctor to monitor and treat your child's asthma.
- Make a special effort to make your home—especially your child's bedroom—allergen-free.

- Wash your child's hair frequently before bed during pollen season. This will decrease the amount of irritants on the pillow during sleep when she will re-breathe them.
- Have him wear a neck warmer pulled up around his nose and mouth when he goes out in cold weather. This will allow him to breathe warmer air and decrease the problem of his airway constricting due to the cold.

There is an allergic component to asthma so it is important to remove any of these substances from your home;

- If any adults in the household smoke, discuss the importance of not exposing your child to passive smoke. This is, in fact, a good time for the adults in your household to stop smoking.
- Use plastic covers for your child's mattress and pillows to avoid dust mites that like to hide in the creases.
- Use synthetic (not feather) pillows.
- Wash mattress covers and bedclothes in hot water every week.
- Don't hang your child's clothing and bed linens outside to dry.
  Pollen can collect on them.
- Use area rugs and vacuum weekly to decrease the amount of dander, mold, and dust mites in the house.
- Avoid the use of drapes; shades are better for reducing dust.
- Evaluate the allergic potential of the family pet.
- Replace furnace and air conditioner filters frequently.

Additional Information

Asthma tends to run in families and is more likely to strike children who also have hay fever or eczema. Asthma is a physical problem, not an emotional one, although attacks can be triggered by stress, anxiety, and frustration.

If your child is in a day care or nursery school setting, make sure the adults in charge have information about your child's medicines and how to administer them in an emergency. Also try to identify potential triggers in the day care center or classroom such as hamsters, guinea pigs, or other pets as well as carpeting, dust, chalk, and plants.

See Related Areas

Allergies, Bronchiolitis, Bronchitis, Colds or Upper Respiratory Infections, Cough, Croup, Dehydration, Eczema, Fever.

ATHLETE'S FOOT

Definition

Athlete's foot is a fungal infection (occuring as a red, scaly, cracked rash) that affects the area between and underneath the toes. A more advanced case will also affect the toenails. The fungus causing Athlete's foot is very contagious, and the condition is usually contracted when your child walks barefoot in moist, wet public areas (shower rooms, public pools, gyms) where others have walked with infected feet.

What to Do

- Examine "itchy feet" for white blisters and red spots, especially between the toes.
- Check under the foot for blisters and cracking.
- Try Home Care Tips.

When to Call Your Doctor

Athlete's foot is common and usually does not require any emergency treatment. Call when:

- There is no improvement after two weeks of using the Home Care Tips.
- The toenails are thick and yellow or distorted.
- You suspect another infection.
- The foot is very painful.
- You notice an allergic response to antifungal powder or cream, for example: increased redness, stinging, blistering, skin peeling, or extreme itching after application.

Home Care Tips

Athlete's foot is a common condition requiring simple treatment and good hygiene to cure it. The infection loves sweaty feet because the fungus thrives in warm, moist conditions. Talk to your pharmacist to suggest an over-the-counter antifungal treatment such as Tinactin cream or Caldesene powder.

- Wash and dry both feet thoroughly, especially between the toes.
- Apply the antifungal preparation as directed. Tinactin cream is applied to all affected areas three times per day.
- Continue the treatment for one week after visible lesions have disappeared to prevent recurrence.

- Do not let your child walk barefoot until the fungus has cleared up.
- Have your child wear white socks, preferably made from natural fibers such as cotton or wool. Avoid colored tights or nylons.
- Rotate your child's shoes so that they have a chance to dry out completely. Avoid sneakers and plastic footwear if possible. Sandals are okay.
- Keep your child's towel and washcloth separate to prevent spread of the fungus to other family members.

Additional Information

The fungus that causes Athlete's foot is called *Tinea Pedis*. The condition occurs most frequently in adolescents, but it is found with increasing frequency in younger children, related possibly to the increased popularity of athletic shoes that tend to cause the feet to sweat more compared to other footwear.

Occasionally a prescription ointment will be required, and, in severe cases, an anti-fungal medicine taken by mouth is also necessary.

See Related Areas

Eczema, Rashes, Warts.

BRONCHIOLITIS

Definition

Bronchiolitis is the inflammation of the bronchioles, the smallest airway passages in the lungs. This inflammation causes narrowing of the bronchioles resulting in breathing difficulties and wheezing. Bronchiolitis is an illness that usually affects infants under two years of age. Its onset is usually quick and causes babies to cough, wheeze, and have rapid breathing of over forty breaths a minute. They also have difficulty breathing and sucking at the same time. Bronchiolitis is caused by a number of different viruses; the most common one is the *respiratory syncytial virus (RSV),* which occurs in epidemics almost every winter. This virus is found in nasal secretions of infected individuals and often is the virus responsible for the common cold in adults. It can be much more serious, however, in a baby or young child.

What to Do

- Ease breathing by keeping your baby in an upright position.
- Keep fever down.
- Make sure baby is well hydrated by giving lots of fluids.

- Communicate frequently with your baby's doctor to closely monitor his breathing.

When to Call Your Doctor

Immediately

- Breathing over fifty breaths per minute when not crying.
- Lips become bluish.
- Your child acts extremely sick.
- Your baby is having retractions (a tugging motion between the ribs).
- Fever over 101°F taken rectally lasts more than seventy-two hours.
- You think your baby is getting worse.
- Your baby is extremely drowsy and does not wake to feed.
- Your baby is not interested in feeding and is taking less than her usual amount of fluids.

Home Care Tips

You must carefully watch a young baby who you suspect has bronchiolitis, and be in continuous communication with your doctor to monitor his breathing. There are a few things you can do immediately at the onset of symptoms to prevent them from getting worse. This is particularly useful in a baby who has already had one bout of bronchiolitis.

- Keep your baby in an upright position at all times, even when sleeping. This is best accomplished with an upright infant seat or infant car seat. This position makes it easier for your baby to breathe.
- Keep the air in your baby's room moist by using a cool air humidifier at all times.
- Increase the amount of fluids your baby is taking. For bottle-fed babies, dilute the formula in half using equal parts formula and water. For breast-fed babies, nurse more frequently and ask your doctor about supplemental water bottles. In some cases, your doctor may recommend adding an oral electrolyte solution like Pedialyte for both bottle- and breast-fed babies. For all babies, give frequent feedings with a smaller amount each time so the baby does not tire as easily.
- Control his fever with tepid water baths and fever-reducing medicines. (See section on Fever.)
- Keep your baby in a smoke-free environment. Smoke will irritate his lungs and make breathing more difficult and coughing more frequent.

- A good test to see if your child is breathing okay is to give him something to drink. Drinking is a physical act, and this will challenge his breathing ability. It is a type of "breathing stress test." *If your baby is unable to drink and breathe at the same time, you need immediate medical attention and treatment.* Without treatment, it is possible for a baby or young child with bronchiolitis to stop breathing.

Additional Information

The most critical period for a baby with bronchiolitis occurs two to three days after a cough and breathing difficulties begin. At this point the air becomes trapped in the small airways of the lungs making breathing both difficult and painful.

In most cases, children with breathing difficulties, fever, or trouble eating and sleeping need to be hospitalized. Because bronchiolitis is a virus, antibiotics will not cure it, and often your child will need aggressive respiratory therapies to maintain his airway and keep hydrated.

Children hospitalized for bronchiolitis generally will recover in about a week; however, for several months after recovery, some may have recurring episodes of wheezing with a common cold. While this will require continued monitoring, your child will outgrow this tendency as his airway grows larger, usually around age two.

A new immunization against RSV is available for high-risk individuals including premature babies and babies born with respiratory or cardiac abnormalities. These immunizations are given on a monthly basis during the winter season.

See Related Areas

Allergies, Asthma, Bronchitis, Colds or Upper Respiratory Infections, Cough, Croup, Dehydration, Fever, Pneumonia.

BRONCHITIS

Definition

Bronchitis is the inflammation of the membrane of the larger air passages (bronchi) leading to the lungs. (See Figure 3.1.). Most cases of bronchitis are caused by viral infections that occur usually several times each year as part of a cold. The infection causes the lining of the air passages in the bronchi to swell and the mucus to build up making breathing difficult. Bronchitis usually causes a dry cough that sometimes becomes loose for a few days, thus causing the child to cough up phlegm.

Possible symptoms include

- Fever.
- Dry, hacking cough, changing to a cough that produces green or yellow phlegm.

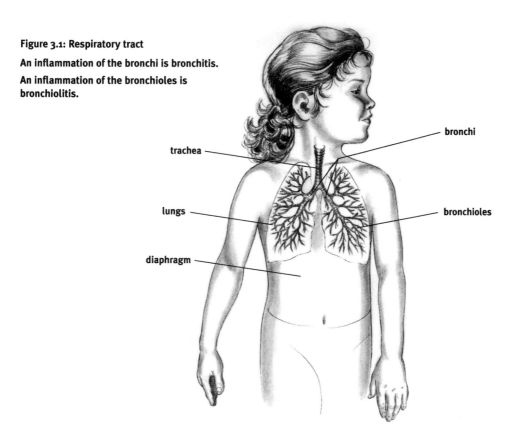

Figure 3.1: Respiratory tract

An inflammation of the bronchi is bronchitis.

An inflammation of the bronchioles is bronchiolitis.

trachea

bronchi

lungs

bronchioles

diaphragm

- Rapid breathing, over forty breaths per minute, with wheezing.
- Loss of appetite.
- Vomiting with the cough.
- Blueness of the lips.

What to Do

- Increase your child's intake of clear fluids.
- Keep fever down.
- Keep your child calm and quiet.
- Use cool air humidifier.
- Avoid exposure to cold air. (This may cause bronchial spasms.)
- Optimize your child's breathing by keeping him in an upright position, even when sleeping.
- Keep your child in a smoke-free environment.

When to Call Your Doctor

- Wheezing or difficulty breathing (drawing in his chest with every breath).
- Retractions (tugging motion between the ribs) during breathing.
- Blueness around his lips.
- Child is unable to speak or is having difficulties making normal sounds.
- Child is unable to swallow.
- Rapid breathing, over forty breaths per minute.
- The fever lasts over a three- to four-day period.
- Persistent cough.
- Your child is acting very sick.
- Your child is unable to sleep.

Home Care Tips

- Don't worry if your child won't eat but encourage him to drink clear liquids. This will keep the mucus loose, prevent dehydration, and help keep fever down.
- Prop your child up when he is sleeping so that he can breathe more easily. Keep babies in an infant seat or an infant car seat while sleeping.
- If your child is coughing persistently, check to see if there is any phlegm. If there is, encourage your child to cough it up. Hold him over your lap if he doesn't understand how to do this, and pat him gently on the back.
- If your child is over two years old and has a dry, hacking cough that interferes with sleep, you may try an over-the-counter cough syrup containing dextromethorphan (without any other ingredients) to help him get some rest. (See Table 1.2 on over-the-counter remedies for brand name recommendations.) If you are unsure about which or how much medicine to give, contact your doctor for the correct dosage. It will be based upon your child's current weight.
- Try to make sure your child has clear nasal passages. For a child under age two, you may have to use saline nose drops and a small bulb syringe to clear his nose. If your child is at least age two, teach her how to clear her nasal passages by pretending to blow out birthday candles with her nose.
- If your doctor prescribes antibiotics, make sure your child receives the full course of treatment even when he starts to feel better.
- Your doctor may also prescribe a bronchodilator (medicine that opens up the airways) to be given by mouth or through a nebulizer.

Additional Information

For children over two years of age, bronchitis is not usually serious. In rare cases, wheezing and vomiting may be troublesome enough to require admission to a hospital.

See Related Areas

Allergies, Asthma, Bronchiolitis, Colds or Upper Respiratory Infections, Cough, Croup, Dehydration, Fever, Pneumonia, Vomiting.

CANKER SORES

Definition

Canker sores are painful, superficial ulcerations that appear in the mouth and lips. They look like small, shallow, gray-white spots surrounded by a bright red circle. They may or may not be associated with a low-grade fever or other symptoms of an illness, but they do tend to recur in cycles.

What to Do

- Examine your child's mouth where she feels pain to look for the characteristic spot surrounded by a red circle.
- Try to prevent your child from touching the canker sore.
- Use Home Care Tips to relieve symptoms.

When to Call Your Doctor

- Canker sores last more than two weeks.
- Fever that lasts more than three days.
- Difficulty feeding or eating.

Home Care Tips

- Encourage hand washing.
- Encourage good oral hygiene to speed up the healing process. Have your child (if able) rinse her mouth with warm salt water two to three times per day.
- Puree foods to minimize chewing when the sores are most painful.
- Avoid acidic foods such as oranges and tomatoes; these tend to cause the sores to sting. Give Popsicles and ice cream; the cold from them may prove soothing.

- If the pain is more severe, try an over-the-counter numbing ointment or solution. Acetaminophen or ibuprofen in the appropriate dose for her weight may also offer pain relief.

Additional Information

Canker sores are very common, occurring in 20 to 50 percent of the population. There is no cure for canker sores; however, most will heal by themselves within one to two weeks. Although the cause of canker sores is unknown and they cannot be prevented, stress does seem to play a role.

See Related Areas

Cold Sores, Rashes, Sore Throat.

CHICKEN POX

Definition

Chicken pox is a common childhood illness, caused by the highly contagious *varicella* virus. The symptoms may include headache, fever, and the chicken pox rash. The chicken pox rash begins as multiple, small, red bumps that progress first into clear blisters, then cloudy blisters that eventually open and drain before becoming dry, brown crusts. The rash usually appears first on the face and trunk and then moves to the extremities. The rash is frequently accompanied by a fever and sometimes headache; it is always very itchy. Sometimes your child has cold-like symptoms for one to two days before she comes down with the rash. The fever is usually highest on the third or fourth day of the illness when the rash is at its peak. Children start to feel better and stop having a fever once they stop getting new spots.

Your child may come down with the disease seven to twenty-one days after being exposed to someone else who has chicken pox. The disease is contagious from a day or two before the rash appears until all the blisters have formed scabs and no new spots have developed for twenty-four hours.

What to Do

- Examine the rash for the chicken pox pattern.
- Relieve the itching with cool baths.
- Keep the fever down.
- Have your child drink cool liquids.
- Keep her fingernails cut short and discourage scratching.

When to Call Your Doctor

- To confirm the diagnosis of chicken pox if you are not sure. (Do not bring your child to the regular office waiting room or clinic because of the risk of infecting other children.)
- Breathing becomes difficult.
- There is bleeding into the chicken pox rash.
- If any spots develop a redness with swelling or red streaks (possible infection).
- You are worried about how the rash looks.
- Your child complains of eye pain, has constant blinking, or you suspect there may be a chicken pox in his eye.
- Fever lasts over four days.
- Your child is feverish, complains of neck ache (unable to touch her chin to her chest), or seems confused or extremely tired when you think she should be feeling better.
- The itching is severe and doesn't respond to Home Care Tips.

Home Care Tips

The goal of home care during chicken pox is to relieve skin discomfort and itching while promoting the final drying and crusting over of lesions. The first three to four days are the most uncomfortable for your child and when she will need the most tender loving care.

- *Give a cool bath every three to four hours for the first few days.* Add four tablespoons of baking soda per tub of water or use one of the commercially available oatmeal baths like Aveeno. These baths are very soothing for skin discomfort and itching, and they may also help to reduce fever.
- Apply *calamine lotion* to itchy spots after the bath. You may give your older child a Q-tip moistened in calamine lotion and let her "paint" the itchy rash with it herself. Do not use Caladryl lotion because that has other medicine in it (diphenhydramine), and too high a dose may be absorbed through the skin. If you need to give special medicine for the itch, give diphenhydramine (Benadryl) by mouth in a dosage appropriate to your child's weight.
- Massaging the "itchy" chicken pox with an ice cube may also provide relief.
- Allow time in between baths for the sores to dry and crust over. If your child is still in diapers, change them frequently and leave them off for periods of time to allow the spots to dry and scab over.

- If you think some of the scabs look infected, put a little antibiotic ointment like Bacitracin on them.

- Keep your child's nails cut short and try to teach her not to scratch, as this can cause infection. Also, have your child wear cotton gardening gloves or cotton socks when she sleeps to decrease scratching.

- Keep fever down with fever-reducing medicines and baths. (See Fever.) DO NOT GIVE ASPIRIN to children and adolescents when they have chicken pox BECAUSE OF THE KNOWN RISK OF REYE'S SYNDROME ASSOCIATED WITH TAKING ASPIRIN DURING A VIRAL INFECTION. Reye's syndrome is a very serious, sometimes fatal, illness that involves brain dysfunction and liver failure. The symptoms (which follow a viral illness like chicken pox in two to seven days) include vomiting, sleepiness, hallucinations, delirium, and aggressive, uncooperative behavior.

- Encourage your child to drink lots of cold fluids. Sometimes there are chicken pox sores in the mouth, and eating may be difficult for a few days. Offer a soft, bland diet and avoid salty foods and citrus fruits. For infants, give fluids by cup rather than by bottle because the nipple can cause pain.

- If mouth sores are an issue, have your child swish and swallow one teaspoon of an antacid solution four times a day after meals or put a few drops of the antacid in front of his mouth after meals. Swishing or rinsing his mouth with water may also provide relief.

- If you notice chicken pox sores in the genital area and urination becomes painful, apply some 2.5 percent Xylocaine or 1 percent Nupercainal ointment to the sores every four hours to relieve pain. This is available without a prescription; ask your pharmacist to help you find it.

- Keep your child away from other children and don't send her to school or day care until she is no longer contagious. Most cases of chicken pox are contagious until all the sores have crusted over, usually for about a week. Your child does not have to stay home until all the scabs fall off; this can take as long as two or three weeks.

Additional Information

Chicken pox rarely leaves any permanent scars unless the sores become deeply infected with skin bacteria or your child repeatedly picks off the scabs. It can, however, leave temporary marks on the skin that can take as long as six to twelve months to fade. One attack usually gives lifelong immunity to chicken pox; however, individuals may later contract shingles that emanate from the same virus.

A chicken pox vaccine is now available. Most physicians recommend it for all children who haven't had chicken pox. It is usually given after twelve months of age, and children under five years old require only a single injection. If you are not sure whether or not your child has had chicken pox, there is a blood test that can be done to confirm either yes or no. Discuss this with your doctor if you are concerned.

Acyclovir is an oral, antiviral medicine that is sometimes used to decrease the intensity of the chicken pox rash. However, this helps only if it is started within twenty-four hours of the first appearance of the sores. Discuss the use of acyclovir with your physician to ascertain if he recommends it.

Siblings usually come down with chicken pox fourteen to sixteen days after the first case. The second case in the family may be more severe with more chicken pox blisters and higher fever than the first.

See Related Areas

Colds or Upper Respiratory Infections, Fever, Impetigo, Pneumonia, Rashes.

COLIC

Definition

Colic refers to prolonged periods of intense crying, usually totaling more than three hours in one day. Colic can begin when a baby is six weeks old and may last until he is approximately three to six months old. An infant with colic usually appears quite healthy and is gaining weight. He is also happy between bouts of crying. The condition erupts suddenly, often occurring in the late afternoon or evening. Usually the baby's face is flushed and his belly hard and tense. His legs may be drawn up and his fists may be clenched.

What to Do

- Stay calm.
- Talk to your doctor to confirm the diagnosis of colic.
- Try Home Care Tips.

When to Call Your Doctor

- If an attack of crying lasts more than two hours. Other causes for crying must be ruled out by your baby's doctor; these might include intestinal obstruction; constipation; food, formula, or milk allergy; or some type of infection.

- Fever over 101°F taken rectally.
- Vomiting with crying.
- Unable to feed.

Home Care Tips

Once a diagnosis of colic is made, parents must find ways to minimize the strain caused by a constantly crying baby.

- Provide a stable, stress-free environment for your baby. Put him on a regular schedule for feedings and naps, thus providing a consistent and predictable day. Write down the schedule and ensure that all caregivers follow it to the letter.
- Evaluate your baby's feeding habits. Look for excess swallowing of air during feeding and gulping. Be sure to burp him effectively after feeding. Have him sit up (at least a 45° angle) in an infant seat or in an adult's lap, for thirty minutes or more after each feeding.
- Try feeding your baby earlier than your previous routine to avoid the gulping that can come with excess hunger. This phenomenon is more likely to occur in bigger babies (weight in the seventy-fifth percentile or greater) because he may be hungry before you expect it.
- Help your baby feel more secure by cuddling, rocking, holding him, and rubbing his back.
- Try placing your baby on his stomach on a warm water bottle or heating pad to ease possible stomach cramps.
- Caregivers should take turns caring for the baby during colicky periods to prevent exhaustion and minimize frustration.
- Take a nap before the usual crying period starts.
- Have a trusted babysitter or other family member watch the child so you can have a break.
- Try low background sounds in your baby's sleeping area like music or a vacuum cleaner. This may prove soothing.
- Provide gentle movement in a baby swing or car ride. There also are crib vibrators available that simulate the sound and movement of an automobile.
- If you are bottle-feeding, discuss with your doctor his thoughts about trying a milk-free diet using a soy formula. Avoid frequent formula changes, however, because one of your main goals is to provide a stable, stress-free environment for your baby.

- Talk to your doctor about using one of the over-the-counter medications for gas. One example is Mylicon drops for infants. (The active ingredient simethicone helps to reduce the surface tension of the gas bubbles in a baby's stomach and small intestine, thus relieving pain.)

- In extreme cases, your doctor may prescribe a medicine to help your baby settle down and rest quietly.

Additional Information

Although the traditional explanation for colic is belly pain, the actual causes are poorly understood. However, some of the following may contribute to the condition:

- *Gas.* One theory suggests that belly discomfort may be caused by air swallowed during feeding that then becomes lodged in the intestines.

- *Abdominal distension.* Prolonged crying may fill your child's belly and intestine with air and lead to crampy pain. Continuous sucking on an empty bottle or pacifier that's not airtight may have the same effect. Either practice can establish a vicious cycle of crying, air swallowing, crampy pain, and more crying. Genuine hunger may also initiate this cycle by making your baby gulp and swallow air as he tries to get his milk faster. (Feed your baby earlier than usual to avoid this extreme hunger.)

- *Air swallowing.* Hungry babies tend to gulp and swallow air with their milk. This causes increased abdominal distension and discomfort. Also, feeding your baby while he is crying may lead to more air swallowing, gas, and pain.

- *Emotional factors.* Family tension and parental anxiety can be aggravating factors. Another theory suggests that colic is caused by a baby's frustration with his inability to cope with some aspect of his environment.

- *Allergy.* Allergy to cow's milk, especially in babies with other family members who have cow's milk allergy, may also be a factor.

See Related Areas
Abdominal Pain, Allergy, Asthma, Constipation, Diarrhea.

COLDS OR UPPER RESPIRATORY INFECTIONS

Definition

The common cold is a viral infection affecting the upper respiratory tract. Entering the body through the nasal passages and throat, the virus can produce any of the following symptoms:

- Sneezing.
- Runny nose or blocked nasal passages.
- Postnasal drip.
- Coughing.
- Sore throat.
- Aching muscles.
- Irritability.

Colds are quite common in children, increasing in frequency as your child comes in contact with more children in a day care or nursery school setting. It's not unusual for some children in these settings to have as many as eight colds a year. It takes the body's defenses ten to fourteen days to overcome the cold virus and return your child to good health.

What to Do

- If your child has any cold symptoms, take his temperature to check for fever.
- Use Home Care Tips for comfort and to relieve symptoms.
- Make sure that your child drinks plenty of fluids.
- Monitor your child's symptoms to make sure they don't develop into something more serious like bronchitis or an ear infection.

When to Call Your Doctor

Immediately

- Wheezing, difficulty breathing, or if he is breathing extremely fast.
- Your child is too sleepy or difficult to wake up.
- Your child is either very irritable or listless.

In the Near Future

- Ear pain as well.
- Fever over 101°F taken rectally.
- Sore throat develops.
- Fever continues after seventy-two hours.
- Infant is under three months old.
- Skin under the nose becomes raw or cracked and may have a golden crust.
- Discharge from nose becomes green or contains pus.

Home Care Tips

Colds often require little care, but they must run their course. The most important thing is to make your child comfortable and prevent the cold from developing complications. Generally the first three days are the worst; then your child should begin to improve and the symptoms will lessen. To help, you can:

- Encourage him to drink lots of fluids. Your child should drink at least a quart of liquid a day. This will help to keep his nasal secretions thin and ease his cough.

- Keep your child's head elevated when sleeping. Elevate the head of the crib for infants or have them sleep in an upright infant seat. Use pillows for older children. You may even try putting the extra pillow under the mattress.

- Take his temperature at least two times a day for the first three days and give fever-reducing medicine as needed.

- Help your child blow his nose properly. For a young child, hold one nostril at a time and ask her to blow her nose. Another tip is to ask your child to blow out pretend birthday candles into the tissue. For a baby, use saline nose drops, such as Ocean, to keep his nasal secretions thinner and runny. You may also use a nasal aspirator to suction the mucus from a baby's runny nose.

- Use Vaseline or petroleum jelly on his nose and upper lip to prevent chafing.

- Use a cool air humidifier at night to ease congestion.

- Consult your doctor about using an over-the-counter decongestant medicine, especially if your child has trouble resting and sleeping.

- Give acetaminophen or ibuprofen in the appropriate dosage for your child's weight for relief of muscle aches, headaches, and fever over 101°F rectally.

Additional Information

The common cold is not a serious illness, but, because it lowers the body's resistance, complications such as bronchitis, ear infection, or even pneumonia can occur. It is most important to give your child lots of extra fluids, including Popsicles and Jell-O, and to watch him carefully to make sure he starts getting better after three days. Consult your doctor if you think he has developed another infection or if a hacking cough is causing sleepless nights. For a baby, call your doctor if he is unable to drink fluids well.

Many children will get as many as five to eight colds a year. It is important for you to stay on top of your child's symptoms and make him as comfortable as possible. Antihistamines are not helpful unless your child has nasal allergies. An oral decongestant containing pseudoephedrine may sometimes help to relieve symptoms. It is not recommended, however, for babies under six months old.

Abdominal Pain, Allergies, Asthma, Cough, Croup, Dehydration, Eye Irritation/Pain, Fever, Headache, Sore Throat.

CONJUNCTIVITIS/PINKEYE

Definition

Conjunctivitis or "pinkeye" is a common infection that causes redness and most often results in discharge from the eye. The word literally means "inflammation of the conjunctiva" (the mucous membrane of the eye). The discharge is sometimes thick and copious and may cause the eye to crust over, especially after sleeping. However, when treated correctly, conjunctivitis is not serious.

The condition may be caused either by a virus or bacteria. It may also be associated with allergies. When it is caused by a virus, the discharge is usually more watery and the eyes may be a little light sensitive. Because it is sometimes also associated with a general viral infection such as a cold or sore throat, it may be accompanied by a fever.

Bacterial conjunctivitis usually has a thick, yellow discharge. In bacterial conjunctivitis, you will often find your child's eyelids "stuck together" after sleeping and lots of crusts caked in her eyelashes. When conjunctivitis is associated with a runny nose, your child may also have an ear infection.

What to Do

- Gently clean your child's eye to remove crusts.
- Check your child's temperature for any fever.
- Apply eye ointment or drops ordered by your doctor.
- Follow Home Care Tips.

When to Call Your Doctor

- To confirm diagnosis of conjunctivitis.
- Fever is also present.
- Your child complains of eye pain.
- Your child's eyelid or surrounding skin becomes red and swollen.
- Eyeball looks cloudy or bloody or you notice sores in her eye.
- Baby is under one month old.
- Eye does not improve after three days on medicine.

Home Care Tips

- Gently clean your child's eye. If the crusts are really thick or stuck, use a warm, moist facecloth as a compress. Then, wet a cotton ball with warm water and gently wash your child's eye from the inner corner to the outer corner until all crusts are gone. Do this every two to four hours during the first day to keep the crusts from building up.

- If your child has a runny nose with thick discharge, make sure to wipe her nose frequently to prevent the spread of infection back to her eye.

- Be sure to wash your hands thoroughly with soap and water before and after you perform your child's eye care. Conjunctivitis is very contagious.

- Make sure to separate your child's washcloth and towel to prevent another family member from getting the infection.

- To apply eyedrops, pull down the lower lid and gently drop the eye medicine in the lower lid. If your doctor has ordered eye ointment, gently pull out the lower lid and squirt a thin line of the ointment into the lower lid. Then dab your child's eye with a tissue. If both eyes are affected, wash your hands between applications and use separate eye medicines that are labeled for the right and left eyes. Sometimes your child will experience blurry vision for a few minutes after you have applied an eye ointment.

- Wash your child's hands frequently to prevent spread of the infection to the other eye. Ask him not to rub his eyes; but as this is typically difficult to enforce, keep him occupied with his hands in motion.

- You may decrease the frequency of eye cleaning as the infection resolves.

Additional Information

Conjunctivitis is very common in young children and spreads quite easily. In order to prevent the spread to other children, keep your child home from day care or preschool until redness and discharge have decreased and she has been on treatment for twenty-four hours.

A *sty* is a localized, non-contagious, red swelling of either the upper or lower eyelid. It is basically a pimple on the eyelid, so it may also be tender or painful. Treat a sty with frequent warm, moist compresses. Antibiotic ointments are usually not needed unless the pimple opens.

See Related Areas

Allergies, Colds or Upper Respiratory Infections, Earache/Infection, Eye Irritation/Pain, Fever, Rashes, Sore Throat.

CROUP

Definition

Croup is an inflammation of the airway around the voice box (larynx) that causes difficulty breathing. Usually caused by a virus, the common symptoms are:

- "Barking seal" or croaking cough.
- Noisy breathing.
- Trouble breathing with the lower chest "caving in" when your child takes a breath.
- Face turning blue or gray.
- Voice or cry is hoarse (laryngitis).

Croup usually affects children between the ages of three months and three years and may last from three to seven days. It is more common in the late fall and early winter and often comes on suddenly and is worse at night.

What to Do

- Keep calm and keep your child calm.
- Try Home Care Tips.

When to Call Your Doctor

Immediately

- Difficulty breathing, shortness of breath, or extremely rapid breathing (more than forty breaths per minute for babies under one year of age and sixty breaths per minute for children over the age of one).
- Child makes a "crowing" sound while resting.
- High fever, greater than 103°F rectally.
- Blueness of lips or nails.
- Child passes out.

In the Near Future

- "Crowing" sound when child is upset or crying.
- Baby is reluctant or resistant to drinking fluids.
- Child is drooling and has trouble swallowing.
- Continued fever for twenty-four hours with other croup symptoms.

Home Care Tips

- Your child's air passages will be soothed by moist air, so steam is the best treatment for urgent care. Take your child into the bathroom, close the door and windows, and turn on the hot water in the shower to create steam. Do not put your child in the shower, but sit with him in a chair or on the toilet. (Do not sit on the floor; there is less steam there.) Open a window for a few minutes to help create more steam. Keep the shower running and stay in the bathroom for fifteen to twenty minutes. If the steam alone doesn't relieve your child's symptoms, carry him outside to the cool night air for fifteen minutes. In the summer, open the freezer door and stand in front of it. If you still don't see relief, call your doctor.

- Remain calm. While the barking, crowing, and noisy breathing sounds are frightening, you need to help your child stay calm. Hold him, rock him, read to him, and help him relax. This may help stop his airway from constricting further and make breathing easier. He will gauge his reaction from you. If you are anxious and fearful, he will be too, and anxiety will increase his breathing rate.

- Encourage clear, cold liquids and try small sips. This will help to keep secretions thin, promote relaxation of his airway, and prevent dehydration. Don't worry if your child does not want to take solids for a few days as drinking is more important. Also, don't worry if your child throws up. This may actually help him clear phlegm and reduce some of the inflammation in his airway.

- Prop up your child in bed with pillows under the mattress or hold him on your lap. It is easier to breathe sitting up.

- After an attack, you may want to sleep in your child's room so that both of you remain calm. You can also make sure his breathing remains good.

- Run a cool air humidifier in your child's room for several nights after an attack to keep the air moist. Clean the humidifier as directed.

- If croup is a recurring problem, consider purchasing a humidifier for your furnace.

- With croup, crying is a good sign. A crying child is able to breathe. His symptoms are improving.

- For a "coughing spasm" (coughing lasting longer than five minutes without pause), give warm fluids to relax the airway. Use warm apple juice or tea if your child is older than six months.

Additional Information

A virus is the most common cause of croup. It makes the cells in the voice box and the airway react by secreting more mucus. The mucus makes the air passages narrower, especially as the mucus dries and thickens. Moist air will help to dissolve this mucus and make it easier for your child to breathe again. Often the combination of warm, moist air (steam) for a brief period of time, followed by cool, moist air (night air) for another brief period of time, is the most effective way to treat an acute episode. This should always be followed by continued cool air with a cool air humidifier. Children usually outgrow croup as their airway gets bigger. The same virus that gives a baby croup will give an older child or an adult laryngitis.

Sometimes croup is confused with another more serious condition called *epiglottitis*. Epiglottitis is an inflammation of the structure at the back of the tongue. It is more serious because it can completely block the airway. Usually, epiglottitis occurs in children between four months and three years of age. Children with epiglottitis tend to tilt their head forward, drool, have a high fever, and lean forward to improve breathing. If you suspect epiglottitis, call for immediate medical help or have someone drive you and your child to your emergency room.

See Related Areas

Allergies, Asthma, Colds or Upper Respiratory Infections, Cough, Dehydration, Fever, Sore Throat.

EARACHE/INFECTION

Definition

Ear pain is quite common in children. Your child may complain about the pain, or he may start pulling on his ear. Some children will also have a runny nose, sore throat, or fever. The condition is often associated with an infection of the ear canal or the middle ear in which fluid accumulates behind the ear drum, causing pressure. See Figure 3.2 for a diagram of the ear.

The eustachian tube is the passage connecting the middle ear to the back of the throat. Nasal congestion can block normal drainage of the middle ear through the eustachian tubes, and this congestion can lead to an infection called *otitis media*. An ear infection can only be diagnosed by a doctor looking into your child's ear.

Ear pain may also result from water accumulation in the outer ear (ear canal). This may cause an infection of the ear canal called Swimmer's Ear, which most often results in a feeling of pain and fullness. Please see specific section on Swimmer's Ear on page 172 for more information.

Figure 3.2 : Diagram of ear

Swimmer's ear is an infection involving the outer ear canal.
Otitis media is an ear infection involving the middle ear.

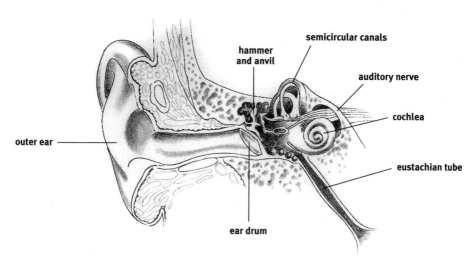

What to Do

- Take your child's temperature and give fever-reducing medicine for temperatures over 101°F taken rectally. These medicines will also help to relieve ear pain.
- Apply a warm cloth over the ear to soothe pain.
- Prop your child up at a 30° angle to promote ear drainage.

When to Call Your Doctor

Immediately

- High temperature over 101°F taken rectally.
- Severe pain, causing constant crying despite receiving pain-relief medication.
- Your child is extremely irritable or very sleepy, has a stiff neck, or looks sicker than ever.
- You suspect your child has put a foreign object in the ear canal.

In the Near Future

- Ear pain with recurrent temperature over 101°F rectally for twelve to twenty-four hours.
- Pus or other drainage from ear.

Home Care Tips

- To help open up the eustachian tubes, prop up your child's bedding so that he can sleep at a 30° angle.

- Tell an older child to yawn, as this helps move the muscles that open the tubes.

- If your child is old enough to drink from a cup, have her swallow water while you pinch her nose. This creates a vacuum in the nose that helps the eustachian tubes to open.

- After you check your child's temperature, give acetaminophen or ibuprofen for the pain as well as the fever.

- Place a drop or two of warm olive oil into his ear. This helps to relax and anesthetize the membrane, reducing the pain.

- Have your child drink plenty of cool liquids.

- Position a baby upright at a 30° angle or higher when giving her a bottle. Do not give a bottle to a baby who is lying down as this position allows fluid to drain directly into the middle ear.

- Use a well-wrapped hot water bottle or warm facecloth placed against the ear to help relieve pain.

- Massage your child's ear to keep the eustachian tube open. Place the fleshy part of your palm, just below your thumb, over your child's ear and rotate the ear in all directions.

- If ear pain occurs after swimming, it is usually caused by irritation of the ear canal by water. (See Swimmer's Ear.)

Additional Information

Ear infections are common in babies and young children because the eustachian tube that connects the throat with the ear is relatively short and somewhat horizontal. Fortunately, children rarely develop permanent hearing problems from recurrent ear infections. The peak age range for earaches is six months to two years of age, but they may continue to occur until your child is nine or ten years old.

Earaches often occur when a child has a cold or an upper respiratory infection. Other things that can cause ear pain include changes in air pressure while in an airplane, foreign objects in the ear, tooth problems, ear injuries, and allergies.

Because babies and young children spend a lot of time lying down, any bacteria or viruses that are in the mouth can pass easily to the middle ear. When this occurs, your doctor may prescribe an antibiotic, which usually starts relieving your child's symptoms after forty-eight hours. Be certain that your child takes the antibiotic for the full length of time prescribed by the doctor even if he is feeling better. If your child's symptoms are not better in five days, consult your doctor. If a child suffers three or more attacks of a middle-ear infection in a short period of time (within six months), your doctor may prescribe a long course of antibiotics at a reduced dose as a preventive measure. Sometimes when a child suffers frequent ear infections, an ear, nose, and throat specialist may be consulted to discuss the possibility of "tubes." These ventilation tubes will aerate the middle ear, clear up infection, and relieve pain.

When your child has an ear infection and air travel is necessary, be sure to provide as much additional comfort as possible. The change of pressure during takeoff and landing can greatly increase the pain. Nasal decongestant drops along with acetaminophen or ibuprofen for pain taken before takeoff and landing may also help. Also be sure that your child is sucking on something during takeoff and landing. You can encourage this by feeding an infant (bottle or breast) or using a pacifier. For an older child, try a lollipop, hard candy, or chewing gum.

See Related Areas

Allergic Rhinitis/Hay Fever, Allergies, Colds or Upper Respiratory Infections, Fever, Headache, Swimmer's Ear.

ECZEMA

Definition

Eczema is a generic term for a sensitive skin condition that produces extremely itchy, red, and dry patches of skin with oozing, scaling, and thickening of the skin. It usually appears on the face, behind the ear lobes, on the neck and hands, and in the creases of the arms and legs. The most common form of eczema is called *atopic dermatitis*. This is an inflammatory skin condition with symptoms of eczema that usually starts when a baby is two to three months old, or at four to six months when she starts taking solid foods. Atopic dermatitis usually improves by the age of three to five years. Common causal factors are certain foods such as dairy products, eggs, and wheat, or skin irritants like wool, detergent, or animal fur. Stress or an emotional upset can also play a role.

Another skin condition similar to eczema involves the sebaceous glands and is called *seborrheic dermatitis*. Lying just under the skin, the sebaceous glands produce *sebum*, the body's own skin moisturizer. Seborrheic dermatitis is commonly found on the scalp of babies (cradle cap), behind the ear lobes, and in the creases around the nostrils, ears, and groin.

What to Do

- If your child is scratching, examine her for any rash, particularly on her face, neck, hands, and skin creases.

- Hydrate the dry skin to ease irritation.
- Report any new food or medicine that your child has had in the last forty-eight hours.
- Use Home Care Tips.

When to Call Your Doctor

- To set up a treatment plan if you suspect eczema.
- Your child is having difficulty sleeping because of the itching.
- Your child has scratched the rash and the skin looks infected (oozing pus-like drainage and/or extremely red skin that is warm to touch).
- Your child has eczema and a fever of 101°F rectally with no other apparent causes.

Home Care Tips

Eczema is not usually serious although it can be very irritating. Careful skin care and avoidance of irritants will go a long way to make your child more comfortable.

- Eczema is very sensitive to soap, so minimize its use and select only mild soap without perfume or scent.
- Decrease the frequency of bathing as this dries the skin. When your child does takes a bath, add a nonperfumed bath oil to the water.
- Always follow washing by hydrating the skin with a greasy emollient cream (such as Vaseline) to keep her skin soft, prevent excess dryness, and reduce itching. Avoid using any product with alcohol in it because this may dry the skin further and worsen the eczema. Alcohol is contained in many of the popular moisturizing lotions, so read labels carefully. When in doubt, ask the pharmacist to interpret the ingredients for you.
- Cut your child's fingernails and toenails short to keep her from breaking the skin when she scratches. She may scratch when she is asleep, so consider using cotton mittens or gardening gloves at night.
- Dress your child with cotton next to her skin whenever possible.
- Avoid overdressing your child. Too much clothing will cause sweating and increase the itch.
- Use a mild, "baby" laundry detergent and make sure that her clothes are rinsed thoroughly to remove all traces of detergent.
- Anti-itch medications such as diphenhydramine are available without a prescription. Follow the directions on the label and give your child the proper dose

for her weight. Because it may make your child sleepy, it's better given at night. Some children react to diphenhydramine by getting a little hyper. If this happens to your child, talk to your doctor about changing to a prescription anti-itch medicine.

- Oatmeal baths such as Aveeno are helpful for some children during a severe eczema attack.

- Consider an elimination diet to determine if there is a certain food that triggers your child's eczema. (See Allergies and Sensitivities to Food.)

- Remove as many irritants from your child's environment as possible, such as pets, feather pillows, wool blankets, etc. (See Allergies.)

Additional Information

It is common for a child with atopic dermatitis to have other allergic conditions like asthma or hay fever. It is thought that a tendency for developing eczema is usually inherited. Most children grow out of atopic dermatitis by age three, but it may continue through adulthood as do other allergic conditions.

If your child has scratched her eczema and the skin becomes infected, your doctor may prescribe antibiotics until the infection is healed. Cortisone creams are the main treatment, and many of these are available over the counter without a prescription. However, cortisone creams should be used very sparingly on a child's skin and only under the direction of your doctor.

See Related Areas

Allergies, Asthma, Eye Irritation/Pain, Head Lice, Rashes, Skin and Rashes (in chapter 6, "Newborn Care and Concerns").

FIFTH DISEASE (ERYTHEMA INFECTIOSUM)

Definition

Fifth disease, also known as *Erythema Infectiosum,* is a mild, contagious disease usually accompanied by fever or cold-like symptoms and a *three-stage rash*. It usually lasts three to seven days but may come and go for three to four weeks. The first stage is a pink rash appearing on the cheeks and ears. Next, the area around the mouth becomes very pale, leading to a "slapped cheek" appearance that is warm to the touch and slightly raised. The distinctive "slapped cheek" rash is harmless and doesn't usually cause itching, though occasionally, older children complain of itching (particularly of the trunk and extremities), along with headache and joint pain. This eruption fades within four days followed one day later by the third stage—a lacy, bumpy, red rash that appears first on the extremities and then on the trunk. The distinctive rash is harmless and causes no itch, pain, or complications; its estimated incubation period is four to fourteen days. Other symptoms may include itchiness, headache, and joint pain.

What to Do

- There is no treatment for uncomplicated cases. The disease will run its course.
- Keep your child comfortable by keeping the fever down.
- Give her extra fluids to increase hydration.
- Give frequent baths to reduce itching.

When to Call Your Doctor

- Your child is irritable or vomiting.
- Your child is getting worse.
- Fever is over 103°F rectally or 102°F orally.

Home Care Tips

This illness almost always takes a simple course and clears up by itself. Your role is usually to provide comfort measures to relieve the symptoms.

- Keep the fever down by using acetaminophen and ibuprofen as recommended in the section on Fever. You may also give these medicines if your child complains of joint pain as one of her symptoms.
- Encourage your child to drink extra fluids including fruit juices, Jell-O, and Popsicles. This will keep her well hydrated and keep her fever down.
- Sometimes the rash is itchy. Frequent tub baths will help to relieve the itch and relax your child.
- If the rash is itchy and interferes with her sleep, talk to your doctor about giving an anti-itch medicine like diphenhydramine at bedtime. Consult your doctor for the appropriate dosage based upon your child's current weight.
- Exposed children will come down with the rash in ten to fourteen days. The disease is contagious during the week *before* the rash begins. Once your child has the "slapped cheeks" or the lacy rash, she is no longer contagious and does not need to stay home from day care or school.

Additional Information

Fifth disease usually occurs in epidemics in a family, school, or day care. The virus that causes erythema infectiosum is called human parvovirus B-19. It is referred to as "fifth disease" because it was the fifth childhood disease with a characteristic rash that has been identified. (The other characteristic-rash diseases include measles, rubella, scarlet fever, and roseola.)

Adults who contract this disease may have pink cheeks and no rash but get joint pain. There is the risk of miscarriage if a pregnant woman is exposed to this virus during her first trimester. Consult your doctor if you are pregnant and think you may have been exposed.

See Related Areas

Allergies, Fever, Headache, Impetigo, Rashes, Roseola, Scarlet Fever.

FOOD POISONING

Definition

Food poisoning is an inflammation of the stomach and/or intestines caused by eating contaminated food. Symptoms usually start within two to twenty-four hours after eating and include abdominal cramps; fever; vomiting; frequent, loose diarrhea; muscle weakness; chills; and loss of appetite. Food poisoning can be very serious in babies and young children as it often causes dehydration.

If the food is contaminated with bacteria, it may release poisons called *toxins*; these will cause an inflammation of the lining of the intestines. Many types of bacteria can cause food poisoning, with the most common being *E. coli* followed by *salmonella, shigella,* and *staphlococci.*

Food poisoning can also occur when your child ingests chemicals and/or insecticides that have been sprayed on fruits and vegetables. In addition, other food-related illness can be caused by contaminated shellfish, botulism, and poisonous mushrooms.

What to Do

- Check your child's bowel movements for mucus or blood.
- If she has diarrhea and vomiting, check for fever.
- Try to figure out if she has eaten some food that might be contaminated.
- Stop all solid foods and give frequent liquids in small amounts to prevent dehydration.
- See Home Care Tips.

When to Call Your Doctor

- Vomiting and diarrhea continue for more than six hours.

- Vomiting is severe and projectile.

- Signs of dehydration, including dry mouth and lips; listlessness; no urine for eight hours; concentrated, dark yellow–colored urine; and in children under age two, a sunken fontanelle (soft spot at the top of the head).

- You suspect that your child has ingested a chemical poison or a poisonous plant.

- Your child's condition has not improved in twenty-four hours with Home Care Tips.

Home Care Tips

In general, there is no special treatment for food poisoning except to replace the fluids and electrolytes that have been lost through diarrhea and vomiting.

- Hold all solid food until vomiting has stopped. Give your child frequent fluids in small amounts. Use a special cup, straw, or teaspoon to encourage intake of fluids.

- Add a special oral electrolyte solution like Pedialyte or Ricelyte for all babies. For children over the age of two, you may give Gatorade or SportAde.

- Have your child rinse her mouth with water after vomiting to get rid of unpleasant tastes in her mouth.

- Offer flat or de-fizzed soda. It may be easier to keep down. Do not give apple juice as this will aggravate the upset.

- Place a pan or bucket next to your child's bed so that she doesn't have to run to the bathroom to vomit.

- Lay a cool facecloth on her forehead. Many kids become sweaty due to vomiting.

- With vomiting and diarrhea it is difficult to give fever-reducing medicine, so use fever-control methods if the fever is making your child uncomfortable. Sponging your child with lukewarm water may be comforting and may help reduce fever. Also keep her cool and refreshed with clean, light clothing.

- If the vomiting is more severe, try giving the fever-reducing medicine by suppository. (This is not helpful with diarrhea, however.)

- Be strict about hand washing. Food poisoning is infectious. Be certain that your child washes her hands after going to the bathroom, and make sure to wash your hands after changing diapers.

- Diarrhea with food poisoning may be explosive. Even if your child is toilet trained, you may want to use "pull-ups" at night because she may not make it to the bathroom.

- Once the vomiting has stopped, slowly reintroduce foods that are easy to digest. Saltines, soups, Jell-O, yogurt, and mashed potatoes make good first foods. You can also try the *BRATT* diet. *B*ananas, *R*ice, *A*pplesauce, *T*ea (clear and diluted), and *T*oast.

- Follow your doctor's instructions for reintroducing formula to a bottle-fed baby. Sometimes you may start with half-strength or quarter-strength formula by diluting it with water.

- Check what your child has eaten over the past twenty-four hours. Separate any foods that you think might have caused the food poisoning, especially meat or dairy products. Ask your doctor if you should save them for analysis by your local health department or throw them out.

Tips for preventing food poisoning

- Refrigerate all food items that tend to spoil, especially in warm weather.
- Cook meats to medium preparation. Use a meat thermometer to check the temperature.
- Refrigerate all leftover cooked foods soon after you are through eating.
- Do not give your child raw eggs.
- Do not let her "lick the bowl" when she is helping to cook sweets (especially cakes and cookies) when raw eggs are used.
- Use an ice pack when sending spoilable foods in a lunchbox to day care or camp.
- Defrost foods completely prior to cooking.
- Carefully reheat leftover foods from the refrigerator.
- Always wash hands thoroughly before and after food preparation. Be sure your child does the same when she is helping.
- Thoroughly clean all countertops and cutting boards before and after food preparation.
- Use separate cutting boards for meats and vegetables in food preparation and periodically replace cutting boards.
- Wash all fruits and vegetables thoroughly before using.

Additional Information

Hospitalization is usually not necessary unless dehydration or fever becomes a problem. However, many forms of food poisoning must be reported by your doctor to the local health department. This agency will often follow up in an attempt to determine the source of food poisoning and to prevent others from getting sick as well.

The gastrointestinal effects of food poisoning can last up to one week, but it may take longer for your child's intestines to return to normal. Some bacteria in the intestine are necessary for normal digestion, and extensive vomiting and diarrhea can wipe out this normal bacterial flora. If your child is over two years of age, there is some evidence that yogurt with live cultures may help to restore the normal flora to her intestines. Read the labels for the words "made with live cultures." These come in both flavored and unflavored preparations and may help your child return to normal after a bout of food poisoning.

Botulism is a rare but powerful type of food poisoning that can be very dangerous in babies and young children. Symptoms of botulism start with a headache and dizziness, then progress to include double vision, muscle paralysis, vomiting, and breathing and swallowing difficulties. Children under the age of one year are susceptible to botulism from spores found in honey. After a child has eaten honey, bacteria from the spores may grow in his intestine, thus producing the toxin that causes the illness. If you suspect botulism, call your child's doctor immediately. Your child will probably need to be hospitalized to receive an antitoxin plus other necessary treatment.

See Related Areas

Abdominal Pain, Allergies and Sensitivities to Food, Dehydration, Diarrhea, Fever, Gastroenteritis, Poisoning, Vomiting.

GASTROENTERITIS

Definition

Gastroenteritis is an inflammation of the lining of the stomach and intestines. The usual symptoms include nausea, vomiting, abdominal pain, diarrhea, loss of appetite, and fever. The most common cause of gastroenteritis in children is the *rotavirus* that runs its course in twenty-four to seventy-two hours. (*Rotavirus* is the name given to a group of viruses that are a major cause of periodic bouts of intestinal and stomach infections in infants and small children. They usually start with fever and vomiting followed by severe watery diarrhea. The vomiting normally lasts less than two days, but the diarrhea can continue for five to seven days. It can be very serious in babies because of the danger of dehydration.) Occasionally, gastroenteritis is caused by a bacterial infection.

What to Do

- Stop all solid food and milk for twenty-four hours.
- Give your child small amounts of clear liquids at frequent time intervals.
- Check for fever.
- Follow Home Care Tips.

When to Call Your Doctor

- Vomiting and diarrhea last for eight hours and you are unable to get your child to keep liquids down.
- Signs of dehydration, including dry lips and mouth; listlessness; no urine for six hours; concentrated, dark yellow–colored urine; and a sunken fontanelle in children under age two.
- Fever over 101°F rectally.
- You suspect food poisoning or botulism.
- Your child's condition does not improve in twenty-four hours using Home Care Tips.

Home Care Tips

- Have your child rest and pursue quiet activities until the vomiting and diarrhea subside. Keep a bowl or bucket near his bed so he doesn't have to run to the bathroom every time he has to throw up.
- Your child will tolerate clear liquids, but give a small amount at a time. The stomach needs to rest and have time to absorb the liquids. If you give a large volume of liquids, your child may vomit. You may want to dilute the liquids with water at first.
- To avoid dehydration, your child should drink at least three ounces of fluid for every pound of body weight in a twenty-four-hour period. Your child may prefer ice chips, Popsicles, and Jell-O in addition to clear liquids.
- When vomiting or diarrhea is severe, add a special oral electrolyte solution such as Pedialyte or Ricelyte for all babies under the age of two. An older child may like Gatorade or SportAde, or you can continue to use the oral electrolyte solution. Chicken soup broth is also another good source of clear liquids.
- Once vomiting has stopped for three hours, you can slowly start to reintroduce solid food. Start with dry toast or saltines. If your child refuses solid foods, follow her lead and continue with liquids.

- The *BRATT* diet is usually well tolerated after vomiting and diarrhea and is a good transition to solid foods. This diet includes *Bananas, Rice, Applesauce, Toast,* and *Tea* (diluted).
- Follow your doctor's instructions for reintroducing formula to a bottle-fed baby.
- Give your child water to rinse out her mouth after she vomits to get rid of any foul taste. Some older children may want to brush their teeth as well.
- Many children get sweaty when they vomit. Lay a soothing cool cloth on her forehead.
- Use fever-control methods if a fever is making your child uncomfortable. With vomiting and diarrhea, it may be difficult to give fever-reducing medicines. Sponging your child with lukewarm or tepid water may help to reduce the fever and make her more comfortable. Be sure that she wears loose, light clothing and changes it frequently when it becomes soiled.
- Do not give nonprescription medicines to stop vomiting. They do not work and may disguise key symptoms.
- Imodium A-D or Kaopectate may prove helpful to slow diarrhea. Check with your doctor if either would be appropriate for your child's illness.
- Make sure your child washes his hands before eating and after using the toilet to prevent spread of infection.

Additional Information

Gastroenteritis can be serious in babies and young children because vomiting and diarrhea can lead quickly to dehydration, the severe loss of essential body fluids, and salt.

Other conditions that appear quite similar to gastroenteritis in many ways include food poisoning, intestinal parasites, lactose intolerance, and celiac disease. Some food allergies also produce symptoms similar to gastroenteritis.

See Related Areas

Abdominal Pain, Allergies and Sensitivities to Food, Dehydration, Diarrhea, Fever, Spitting Up (Reflux), Vomiting.

HAND, FOOT, AND MOUTH DISEASE

Definition

Hand, foot and mouth disease is a *viral infection that causes fever, sores in the mouth, and blisters on the hands and feet.* The virus involved is the *Coxsackie A virus.* Hand, foot, and mouth disease usually begins with a moderate fever (100°F to 103°F), and the appearance of small, round blisters in the mouth. They appear most often on the inside of the cheeks and tongue but may also appear on the lips, gums, and roof of the mouth. Small, round, clear blisters may also appear on the soles of the feet, palms of the hands, and between the fingers and toes. A few children will develop a body rash, particularly on the buttocks.

The disease usually lasts three to seven days but may last up to two weeks. It is most frequent in children under the age of four, and is highly contagious in this age group. The key to the diagnosis is the combination of fever, mouth sores, and blisters on the hands and feet. This illness has no relationship to foot and mouth disease found in cattle.

What to Do

- Examine the rash for the classic pattern.
- Keep the fever down.
- Make your child comfortable using Home Care Tips.

When to Call Your Doctor

Immediately

- If your child starts looking extremely sick or complains of a neck ache and is unable to touch his chin to his chest.
- Your child has a stiff neck and is unable to touch his chin to his chest.
- Your child is vomiting.

In the Near Future

- Fever over 101°F rectally.
- Your child is under six months of age.
- To confirm diagnosis.
- Fever lasts more than four days.

Home Care Tips

Because hand, foot, and mouth disease is caused by a virus, antibiotics will not help. For the most part, the disease must simply run its course, so the goal of home care is to alleviate symptoms and make your child as comfortable as possible.

- Keep fever down with fever-reducing medicines and cool baths. (See Fever.)
- Avoid dehydration by giving your child plenty of cold liquids and soft foods. She may not feel like eating for a few days because of the mouth sores. Ice

cream and Popsicles are good, but avoid citrus drinks as they may irritate the sores. Sucking on ice cubes may help to numb the pain for a short while.

- Apply an antacid solution on mouth sores for pain relief four times a day. For children younger than age four, put a half teaspoon in the front of their mouth after meals and before bed. For children age four and older, apply one teaspoon as a mouthwash after meals and before bed. Have your child swish it around her mouth and then spit it out.

Additional Information

Signs and symptoms of the disease appear two to five days after a child has been exposed to the virus and usually last less than two weeks. The fever tends to last two to three days, mouth sores about seven days, and the rash ten to fourteen days. Your child can return to day care or nursery school when the fever is gone. Hand, foot, and mouth disease is not serious, and most infants and children recover without side effects.

Hand, foot, and mouth disease is occasionally accompanied by viral meningitis. (This inflammation of the central nervous system is the more common, less severe form of the disease. It is said to be self-limiting because children usually recover from it in less than two weeks and don't require antibiotics or admission to a hospital.)

See Related Areas

Canker Sores, Cold Sores/Fever Blisters, Dehydration, Fever, Meningitis, Rashes.

HEAD LICE

Definition

Head lice are *small parasites* that attach themselves to human skin and hair. They are *ectoparasites*, which means that they are completely dependent on the human host's blood for survival. They usually cause intense itching in the scalp but may also cause a rash (from the bites) or swollen glands in the back of the neck. Lice are very hard to see.

The mature louse is a small, wingless, brownish-colored creature. It is easier to see the eggs or nits. Nits are tiny, white, opaque eggs, with a diameter of approximately $\frac{1}{16}$ inch, that are firmly attached to the hair shaft. They are most likely to be seen at the back of the neck or at the temples. Head lice are commonly transmitted by close personal contact as well as by hair devices, clothing, and bedding. They are especially prevalent in nursery schools, day care centers, and elementary schools. If you suspect head lice or if there are any cases in the neighborhood or your child's school or day care, examine your child's hair and scalp for nits in natural sunlight (when possible). A reading light, sewing light, halogen lamp, or flashlight may also be helpful.

What to Do

- DO NOT PANIC!
- Eradicate the lice.
- Remove the nits.
- Treat the environment.

When to Call Your Doctor

- If you are not sure that your child has lice.
- Home care treatment doesn't work.
- Re-infestation of head lice.
- Lice in an infant under twelve months old.

Home Care Tips

Treatment of head lice is a three-step process. All three steps must be followed closely in order to successfully end the infestation and prevent re-infestation.

Examine all other family members and other close contacts for evidence of lice, and treat them as well if you find evidence of lice or nits. Cooperation by all affected persons is critical to end an infestation.

1. *Eradicate the lice.*
   - Apply a medicated anti-lice shampoo or cream rinse designed for lice eradication. Many are available without a prescription from your local pharmacy. Ask your pharmacist where to find them.
   - There are basically two categories of products: (1) permethrin 1 percent (for example NIX) and (2) pyrethrum 0.33 percent (for example, RID, R&C, and most generic products).
   - Follow directions carefully and leave the preparation on for only the recommended time, usually ten minutes.
   - Most initial treatments will kill all live lice, and NIX will also initially kill 70 to 80 percent of the eggs.
   - Depending upon the product you use and the degree of infestation, you might need to apply a second treatment in seven to ten days.
   - If you notice lice on the eyelashes, apply petrolatum twice a day for one week. This will essentially smother the lice.

2. *Remove the nits.*

- "Nit-picking" is an extremely time-consuming and laborious task.

- Separate the hair into sections and use a fine-tooth comb, tweezers, or your fingernails to pick out the tiny, white, opaque eggs. (see Figure 3.3.)

- Nits are hard to see, and the lice move extremely fast. Therefore, it's essential that you search your child's head in a strong light. You can see them best in natural sunlight, weather permitting. Otherwise a halogen light or high-intensity sewing or reading lamp will work best. A flashlight may also be useful, but someone else will have to hold it while you are "nit-picking."

- Don't worry if you don't get all the lice at once; it usually takes a few sessions.

- You may rub heavy olive oil in your child's hair to help with louse hunting and "nit-picking." The olive oil slows them down and makes them easier to pluck.

- Sometimes the nits seem "stuck like glue" to your child's hair shaft. Use a little vinegar on her hair to help loosen them from the hair shaft. There is also a product available commercially called Clear that will help to loosen the eggs from the hair shaft. Follow the manufacturer's directions.

- If you choose to use NIX, it may be better to remove the nits first. Using olive oil, vinegar, or Clear after the shampoo treatment will decrease the efficacy of NIX. See Additional Information.

- NEVER USE KEROSENE TO REMOVE NITS. It is extremely flammable, and using it may cause a serious burn injury to your child. Olive oil will work in a similar fashion and is much safer.

Figure 3.3: Nit removal
The nit is usually found at the base of the hair shaft near the root.

3. *Treat the environment.*

- At the same time you treat your child, you must also treat the environment to end the infestation and to prevent re-infestation.

- Remove loose hair from all combs and hairbrushes. Then soak the combs and brushes in a louse shampoo for one hour, or place in water heated to 150°F for ten minutes.

- Wash hair bows, headbands, curlers, and any other hair accessories in hot water and place in a clothes dryer set on high for a minimum of twenty minutes, or place in a sealed plastic bag for fourteen days.

- Launder all clothing including outerwear, bed linens, and towels in hot, soapy water and place in a clothes dryer on high for at least twenty minutes. Items that can't be laundered must be dry-cleaned.

- You must either launder as above or dry-clean all stuffed animals and "loveys." You must place any of these type of furry creatures that can't be treated in a sealed plastic bag for at least fourteen days. Then examine them for any lice before you return them to your child and your child's bed.

- Vacuum all rugs, upholstered furniture, and mattresses to dispose of any living lice or nits attached to fallen hairs.

- In a severe case of re-infestation, you must seal any items that can't be laundered or dry-cleaned in a plastic bag for thirty-five days to account for the possibility of dormant ova that may hatch later.

- You must continue to clean and monitor the environment throughout the treatment period to prevent re-infestation.

Additional Information

Head lice have no bearing on personal cleanliness and occur without regard to socio-economic status, age, or sex. Many schools and day care centers have a "no nits" policy, so in order to send your child back to school you must painstakingly remove the nits.

Adult female lice have a life span of about one month and lay four to five eggs daily. The incubation period for the ova is variable but averages eight to nine days. However, ova may lie dormant for up to thirty-five days. Ova will then develop into adulthood in ten to fifteen days. Newly hatched nymphs must feed in twenty-four hours in order to survive. Adult lice cannot survive away from their hosts for more than ten days.

If you chose permethrin 1 percent (NIX), you should not use additional products, shampoos, or lotions after the treatment to help remove the nits. If you must shampoo before seven days, use only a mild baby shampoo and no cream rinse or conditioner.

Your initial treatment with NIX should kill all the live lice and 70 to 80 percent of the eggs (nits). Any nits that you missed will hatch into crawling lice within seven to ten days. When NIX is used properly and not diluted with subsequent shampoos and lotions, the new lice should die within twenty minutes of hatching.

There have been reports (*Pediatric News,* April 1997) that some head lice have become resistant to currently manufactured lice medications. Fortunately, most of them seem to respond to a generous application of 100 percent real mayonnaise. Apply a thick layer of mayonnaise to the hair, particularly the scalp, and then cover the entire head with plastic wrap or a tight-fitting shower cap. Leave on overnight when possible or for at least eight hours. Only use this when conventional methods have been tried and there is still a problem. Consult your doctor for further information.

See Related Areas

Bites—Insect and Tick, Rashes.

IMPETIGO

Definition

Impetigo is a *superficial, bacterial skin infection,* usually caused by *streptococcus* or *staphylococcus.* It is contagious by contact and begins with a rash of small red bumps that turn to blisters with a cloudy fluid. The blisters then break and crust over as yellowish brown scabs that look like brown sugar. The scabs are itchy, and impetigo spreads by contact with other parts of the body. Impetigo can occur anywhere on the body, usually where there is a break in the skin from cuts, scrapes, insect bites, poison ivy, or diaper rash.

What to Do

- Wash away all crusts with warm, soapy water and a facecloth twice a day.
- Apply an antibiotic cream two to three times a day.
- Discourage your child from scratching the rash.
- Keep your child home from nursery school or day care while sores are oozing.

When to Call Your Doctor

- Your child is acting very sick.
- Your child has more than one or two sores on her face.
- Your child has a fever over 101°F taken rectally.
- Your child has reddish or cola-colored urine.

- Red streaks run from the rash.
- The rash is spreading or has not healed in ten days with Home Care Tips.
- You suspect impetigo in your newborn baby.

Home Care Tips

- Wash all affected areas with warm, soapy water two to three times a day. Remove the scales by gently rubbing the areas. Use an antibacterial soap such as Dial, Safeguard, or Phisoderm; then pat dry with a paper towel and apply antibiotic cream.
- If the scabs do not rub off easily, apply a little hydrogen peroxide. It will foam and loosen up the scabs. A little bleeding may occur, but it will stop with a little pressure and the application of antibiotic cream.
- Sometimes it is useful to cover the affected area with a gauze bandage after you apply the antibiotic cream.
- Be meticulous about hygiene. Wash your hands and your child's hands before and after treatments. Discourage your child from sucking her thumb, biting her nails, or picking her nose during an outbreak.
- Encourage your child to keep her hands away from the rash. Keep her fingernails short to reduce the risk of spreading the infection to other parts of the body.
- Use an oral anti-itching medicine like diphenhydramine (Benadryl) to help decrease the itch, especially at night.
- Keep your child's washcloth and towel separate from the rest of the family to avoid spreading the infection. Launder them frequently in soap and hot water.
- When the infection has cleared, keep the area moist with lotion or cream. It will remain a little dry even after the infection has cleared up.

Additional Information

Your doctor may choose to prescribe an oral antibiotic in addition to skin care to eradicate the infection. Be sure to finish the medicine—even if the rash seems improved. Impetigo rarely has any serious side effects, but because it is easily spread by contact it should be treated immediately. The infection often occurs in outbreaks in schools, day care centers, and camps. There is no immunity to the infection, and it can recur whenever your child is exposed to the infectious organisms while she has an area of broken skin.

Uncleanliness does not cause impetigo; however, washing with an antibacterial soap will reduce the number and strength of the infectious bacteria on your child's skin.

Instruct your child, at an age you feel is appropriate, about the need to control the spread of infection, the importance of frequent hand washing, and the hazard of sharing washcloths and towels.

See Related Areas

Allergies, Bites—Animal; Bites—Insect and Tick; Cuts, Scrapes, and Wounds; Eczema; Hives; Poison Ivy, Oak, and Sumac; Rashes.

LYME DISEASE

Definition

Lyme disease is a recently identified tick-borne illness that was first discovered in Lyme, Connecticut. *It is transmitted by the bite of a deer tick.* Lyme disease is most often contracted in the late spring and early summer.

Common early symptoms include:

- Non-itchy rash or a red patch at the site of the tick bite, usually a raised red circle with a clear center. (Rash may appear at a different site 30 percent of the time.)
- Fever and chills.
- Headache and backache.
- Severe tiredness and fatigue.
- Malaise or general feeling of sickness.
- Conjunctivitis or red, watery eyes.
- Recurrent attacks of painful, swollen joints, usually the knees, may occur in about half of untreated cases. It becomes chronic in only a very small number of the children affected.

What to Do

- Check your child for ticks. If you see one, remove it immediately with blunt tweezers.
- You can also try to smother the tick by soaking it in oil, as this should cause it to back out.
- Call your doctor if you suspect a deer tick; treatment is most effective if started within ten days of infection.
- Provide plenty of rest for your child.

- Give acetaminophen or ibuprofen as needed for fever control and pain.
- Follow Home Care Tips.

When to Call Your Doctor

Immediately

- If you cannot remove the tick or if the tick's head remains embedded.

As Soon as Possible

- When you suspect Lyme disease so treatment can be started.
- To confirm diagnosis, discuss blood test with your doctor.

Home Care Tips

- Prompt removal of ticks is the best method of prevention. A minimum of twenty-four hours of attachment and feeding is necessary for transmission to occur.
- To remove ticks, use blunt tweezers. (See Figure 3.4.) Grasp tick close to skin and pull with steady, even pressure. Do not squeeze, crush, or puncture tick. (Body fluids may contain infected particles.) Flush tick down toilet or submerse in alcohol. Outdoor camping stores also carry a special tick remover tool that you may want to purchase if you live in an infested area.

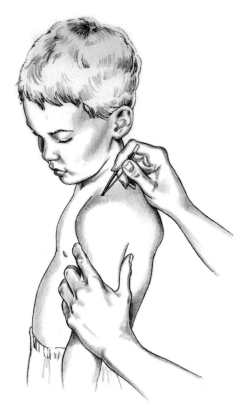

- Disinfect bite site by cleaning with rubbing (isopropyl) alcohol.
- If your child does contract Lyme disease, encourage plenty of rest and treat fever and aches with acetaminophen and/or ibuprofen.

Figure 3.4: Tick removal
Remove the tick with tweezers.

- Report suspicions of Lyme disease to your physician so that antibiotic therapy can be started. Follow your physician's instructions and take all medicines and amounts as directed.

Prevention

- Examine your child's body after playing outside, hiking, etc. Give her a bath after suspected exposure.
- Avoid tick exposure in endemic areas. If you live in an area in which deer ticks are common, mow all weeds and grass around your house frequently to keep it low.
- Teach your child to walk along cleared or paved surfaces rather than walking on grass or in the woods.
- In tick areas, have your child wear long-sleeved shirts that button at the wrists, and long pants. Tuck the pants into her socks, and have her wear closed shoes.
- Have your child use insect repellent when outside in known tick areas. Repellents containing DEET and/or permethrin work best. (DEET concentration should not be higher than 10 percent.) Follow directions. Use the repellent product appropriate for your child's age. Some products may recommend restricting their use for younger children.
- If you live in an area known to have a high density of deer ticks, you might want to use a special anti-tick spray repellent. This works on clothes, not on skin.
- Use flea and tick collars on your pets, and brush them carefully after they have been outdoors.

Additional Information

The deer tick called *ixodes dammini* is a pinhead-sized parasite, and much smaller than the normal or brown tick. It has an oval body covered with a leathery, granulated cuticle and no antennae. Unfed ticks are flat; ticks that have recently fed are blood engorged.

The course of Lyme disease varies from one person to another. Diagnosis is made by evaluating the characteristic rash, history of the flu-like symptoms, potential for exposure to an area of risk (usually wooded areas with overhanging bush where both mice and deer ticks live), and by a special blood test (titer). Unfortunately the titer, or blood test, for Lyme disease is not accurate until three weeks after exposure. A history of a tick bite may only be present in one-third of children who contract Lyme disease. The offending tick is about the size of a sesame seed and can easily be missed upon examination.

Lyme disease has three stages. Recognition of the problem and treatment of the first stage will prevent the other two. Stage 1 occurs seven to ten days after the tick bite. It exhibits the symptoms described in the definition. Stage 2 occurs two weeks to one month after the bite. Untreated Lyme disease may exhibit signs such as heart palpitations, dizziness, shortness of breath, swollen glands, and possibly neurological complications like meningitis or encephalitis. Stage 3 occurs two to six months after the bite but may occur from weeks to years after the tick bite if left untreated. This stage evinces arthritis-like symptoms of joint pain (especially the knees), and less commonly, memory loss, mood swings, or inability to concentrate. With increased awareness of Lyme disease, it is hoped that it will rarely progress to Stage 2 or 3.

See Related Areas

Abdominal Pain, Allergies, Bites—Insect and Tick, Colds, Fever, Headache, Head Lice, Impetigo, Rashes.

MENINGITIS

Definition

Meningitis is an inflammation of the tissues surrounding and protecting the spinal cord and brain. These tissues are called the meninges. Meningitis is more common in infants and young children and seems to occur more frequently in the summer months. There are two kinds of meningitis: bacterial and viral. Bacterial meningitis is a fast-acting, serious infection, but it can be treated successfully with antibiotics when caught early enough. Viral meningitis is more common and less severe. It usually lasts less than two weeks and often can be cared for at home.

Possible symptoms of meningitis include:

- Moderate to high fever (101°F to 106°F, taken rectally).
- Stiff neck or unable to touch her chin to her chest.
- Stiffness or pain in the lower back, interfering with your child's ability to sit properly.
- Extreme lethargy or fatigue.
- Vomiting.
- Headache.
- Bulging fontanelle in children under age two.
- Extreme sensitivity to bright light.
- Drowsiness and confusion.
- Purple-red rash that looks like bleeding under the skin, over most of the body.

Babies and young children often develop a fever at first and then become lethargic, irritable, and often vomit. Some children under age two may become irritable, with a bulging fontanelle and no fever.

What to Do

- If you suspect meningitis, bend your child's head forward and try to touch his chin to his chest. Any stiffness or pain in his neck is cause for worry.
- If your child is under the age of two and has a fever, check his fontanelle (soft spot) for tightness and bulging.
- Shine a bright light at your child to see if it bothers him.
- Get prompt medical attention if you suspect meningitis.

When to Call Your Doctor

Immediately

- *Call your doctor immediately if you suspect meningitis.*
- Fever over 101°F rectally.
- Signs and symptoms of meningitis.

Home Care Tips

Viral meningitis may be treated at home *after diagnosis* by your physician. Bacterial meningitis—which is more life-threatening—is usually treated in the hospital.

For Viral Meningitis

- Monitor your child's fever and use fever-control methods for his comfort.
- Allow your child plenty of rest in bed or on the couch in a family room. Encourage quiet activities.
- Make sure he gets plenty of fluids to drink. If he seems to be urinating less in spite of drinking a lot of fluids, call your doctor. This could be a sign of a hormonal problem with his kidneys.

Additional Information

Diagnosis of meningitis is usually confirmed with a special procedure called a spinal tap or lumbar puncture. This is done by your doctor. Your child will be given a local anesthetic before the procedure. The doctor then places a small, sterile needle into the canal around the spinal column at the base of your child's back. A small amount of spinal fluid is withdrawn and analyzed for any infection as well as the presence of blood cells, proteins, and sugar.

Viral meningitis is caused by a large number of viruses. They may be transferred through contact with infected respiratory secretions as well as stool. The incidence of viral meningitis associated with poliomyelitis and mumps has been reduced because most children receive their vaccinations against these organisms.

Bacterial meningitis is also caused by a variety of bacteria. Some of the more common ones include: *streptococcal, pneumococcal, meningococcal, staphylococcal haemophilus,* and influenza bacteria. Analysis of bacteria from the spinal fluid will help the doctor choose the best antibiotic to treat your child. These antibiotics are usually given intravenously for at least ten days and until the fever is gone. There is a vaccination to prevent bacterial meningitis caused by *haemophilus influenza-B*. Make sure your child has received this vaccination as part of his regular immunization program. It is given at two months, four months, six months, and twelve to eighteen months. The incidence of bacterial meningitis in children under the age of five has been markedly reduced by the haemophilus influenza-type B (Hib) vaccination.

Encephalitis is inflammation of the outer tissue of the brain. The symptoms are very similar to meningitis, and the illnesses can sometimes be confused. Encephalitis symptoms include a sudden fever (101°F to 106°F rectally), headache, stiff neck and upper back, seizures, nausea, and vomiting. Meningitis can also progress to encephalitis. The most common causes are viral infections. A lumbar or spinal tap is needed to confirm the diagnosis, and hospitalization is necessary for encephalitis. Once a child has been discharged from the hospital, keep him comfortable and well fed. You may also need to help with exercises if he has any lasting muscle weakness or stiffness.

See Related Areas

Dehydration, Fever, Headache, Neck Pain.

PINWORM

Definition

Pinworm is an infestation of the intestinal tract by small, *parasitic roundworms*. Pinworms are the most common worms infesting children in the United States, and are very easily spread. Pinworm infestation produces few symptoms, but the most common is severe itching around the anus, buttocks, or vagina, especially at night. Your child may also show restlessness during sleep. Some girls may also experience vaginal irritation.

What to Do

- Contact your doctor if you suspect pinworms.
- To see the worms, wait one to two hours after your child has gone to sleep.

Then examine the anal area with a flashlight. Pinworms are white and resemble a piece of sewing thread, about a quarter-inch long. They move extremely quickly.

When to Call Your Doctor

- To verify diagnosis and prescribe treatment.
- If the skin around the anal area is red and/or tender.
- Itchiness around the anal area has not resolved after one week of treatment.

Home Care Tips

- Strict family hygiene is a critical part of the treatment. *Wash hands frequently*—especially after toileting and before eating.
- Keep all fingernails trimmed short and clean.
- Have your child wear tight cotton underpants. Change underpants twice daily, in the early morning and at bedtime.
- All towels, bed linens, and underclothes should be laundered in hot water and dried in a clothes dryer for at least twenty minutes. Avoid shaking bedding and clothing prior to washing.
- All family members should be treated at the same time. Your doctor will prescribe an anti-worm medicine and a program for its use.
- Warm baths may ease itching and anal irritation.
- Apply a zinc oxide ointment such as Desitin or Balmex to the anal area if it is irritated from itching.

Additional Information

The course of a pinworm infestation is benign and easily treated. Pinworms are extremely hardy and can survive for long periods of time in dirt, dust, furniture, sheets, clothing, stuffed animals, and even in the fur of house pets. They are spread through close contact or by sharing food or clothing. Recurrences are common, particularly in large families and day care.

Pinworms are almost never observed in the doctor's office. They are most active at night when they come out to lay their eggs. Your doctor may ask you to help with a "scotch tape" test to confirm the diagnosis. Basically, you will receive instructions to press a sticky piece of scotch tape against your child's anus at night or before toileting in the morning to "catch" the worms, and then, lay the tape sticky side down on a clear glass slide and bring it to the doctor's office the next day.

If your child has had contact with another child who has pinworms, do not treat her unless you see evidence of pinworms. Be alert for anal tenderness and especially anal itching. If your child has a pinworm infection, your doctor will treat your child as well as other members of your family with the medication. Consult your doctor if you are at all concerned.

See Related Areas

Constipation, Rashes.

PNEUMONIA

Definition

Pneumonia is *an inflammation of one or more areas of the lungs*. It may be caused by a viral or bacterial infection; a mycoplasma infection; or by a foreign object (such as a peanut) that has been inhaled into the lungs. In young children, pneumonia often starts with an upper respiratory infection, ear infection, or bronchitis. Its onset can be sudden.

Possible symptoms for pneumonia include:

- Difficulty breathing—including rapid breathing, possibly the nostrils flaring, grunting sounds, or pain associated with breathing.
- Dry, repetitive cough.
- Fever over 100°F rectally.
- Vomiting usually induced by a severe cough.
- Headache or abdominal pain.

Pneumonia is diagnosed by your child's doctor after a careful examination in which she listens to your child's breathing with a stethoscope. She then can confirm the diagnosis by sending your child for a lung X ray. A blood test and sputum culture may also be done to help with the diagnosis. Early treatment of pneumonia is essential to prevent complications.

What to Do

- If your child has a cold or infectious illness and her condition worsens, check for a dry cough and difficulty breathing.
- Monitor her temperature for signs of fever.
- Give your child plenty of fluids to prevent dehydration.
- Use a cool mist humidifier.
- Avoid smoke around your child.

When to Call Your Doctor

Immediately

- Your child's condition becomes worse, and she has difficulty breathing.
- Fever is greater than 101°F rectally, and your child is uncomfortable.
- Lips and/or nails are bluish in color.
- Your child's sputum is tinged with blood.

In the Near Future

- Your child coughs up thick, yellow sputum.
- Your child is reluctant to feed regularly.
- Your child seems to have a prolonged cold and feels very tired or is unable to participate in her usual activities.
- Coughing is interfering with sleep.
- Cough lasts over two weeks.

Home Care Tips

- Prop up your child in bed to at least a 30° angle; this may help her breathing. Babies may be most comfortable resting in an upright infant seat or car seat.
- If your child has bacterial pneumonia, the doctor will prescribe antibiotics. Be sure to give the medicine at the prescribed times and finish the medication as directed, even if your child starts to feel better. The antibiotics will help reduce the severity of the disease and speed recovery. They are also given to prevent the spread of infection both inside and outside the lungs.
- Antibiotics may be used to treat pneumonia caused by a mycoplasma; they are not useful for pneumonia caused by a virus, however.
- Give your child plenty of fluids to drink. When she feels like eating, give her foods that are easy to digest such as soup, fruit, and yogurt.
- Relieve fever symptoms as necessary to keep your child comfortable.
- Encourage rest and sleep.
- Check with your doctor about using a cough suppressant medicine if coughing is interfering with sleep at night. Use a cough expectorant medicine during the day if the sputum is thick and hard to cough up.
- Keep your child's room well ventilated but not hot and stuffy.
- Keep your child away from smoke.

Additional Information

All pneumonia is serious, especially in a very young child; however, the disease is very treatable today. There are rarely any complications associated with viral pneumonia, and complications associated with bacterial pneumonia are unusual in an otherwise healthy child. Infants and young children who have never been exposed to a particular strain of a virus or bacteria are more susceptible to pneumonia. The disease is most dangerous for infants under one year of age and the elderly because those both groups have less effective defenses against illness.

Both bacterial and viral pneumonia can occur at any time during the year, but they occur more frequently during the winter months when people spend more time indoors and bacteria and viruses spread more easily.

Bacterial pneumonia is more serious than viral pneumonia. It begins when bacteria settle in the air sacs of the lungs. These sacs subsequently become inflamed, causing cough, fever, and rapid breathing. When bacterial pneumonia is treated with antibiotics your child will show improvement in two to four days. Recovery is gradual; however, it is very important to continue to give the antibiotic for the length of time your doctor prescribed, even when your child starts to feel better.

Viral pneumonia may be severe, but it's usually mild and thus may go undetected. A child with viral pneumonia may seem to have a prolonged cold with a persistent cough (sometimes lasting for several weeks). He may feel very tired, but not sick enough to go to bed; for this reason, viral pneumonia is often called "walking pneumonia." Sometimes when viral pneumonia is diagnosed, your child will need to rest for a few days to help speed recovery.

See Related Areas

Abdominal Pain, Allergies, Asthma, Bronchiolitis, Bronchitis, Colds or Upper Respiratory Infections, Cough, Croup, Dehydration, Diarrhea, Earache/Infection, Fever, Headache, Swollen Lymph Nodes, Vomiting.

POISON IVY, OAK, AND SUMAC

Definition

Poison ivy rash is *an allergic skin reaction to oils in the poison ivy plant.* Oils from similar plants such as poison oak and poison sumac can cause the same skin irritation. Poison ivy rash occurs most frequently in the spring when the plant oils are plentiful and exposure is greatest.

Once contact is made, the first sign of the rash usually appears within eighteen to seventy-two hours. It may, in rare cases, appear as long as twenty-one days after contact. The rash is intensely red, sore, and extremely itchy. Pinhead-sized blisters may appear on the sores as the rash progresses and can merge to form blisters as large as one-half inch in diameter. Second and third exposures to poison ivy result in a rash in twelve to seventy-two hours. The blisters usually dry up in ten to fourteen days.

What to Do

- Use cool compresses to relieve itching.
- Discourage scratching.
- Keep your child's fingernails short.
- Use Home Care Tips.

When to Call Your Doctor

- The rash is severe.
- To confirm the diagnosis.
- Your child develops a fever of 101°F rectally.
- You think the rash may be getting infected.
- Your child has swelling and pain around the eyes, nose, lips, and genitals.
- You have difficulty controlling the itch.

Home Care Tips

- If contact with poison ivy is seen or suspected, wash the affected skin immediately with soap and water to remove the poison ivy plant oils. Scrub under fingernails with a nail brush to make sure all plant oil is removed. (The oils penetrate the skin within ten minutes and can't be washed off after that time.)
- Wash any clothing and shoes that have come in contact with the poison plant with soapy water to prevent it from spreading further.

Once the Rash Has Developed

- Keep your child cool and comfortable because sweating and heat will make the itching worse.
- To soothe the rash, use cold compresses or cool baths with an oatmeal solution like Aveeno.
- Have your child wear loose, comfortable cotton clothing if the rash is in an area normally covered by clothing. Poison ivy on the arms, legs, and face can be left open to the air.

- If scratching is extensive and/or interfering with sleep, use anti-itch medicine, given by mouth. *Do not apply anti-itch creams that contain diphenhydramine* because the amount of medicine absorbed through the skin cannot be measured and you can easily end up giving your child too much. (This includes Caladryl and Benadryl creams and lotions.)

- You may apply an over-the-counter cortisone cream like Cortaid to relieve the itch.

- Apply calamine lotion to help soothe the rash. It will also help dry the blisters.

- Keep your child's fingernails cut short. Constant scratching of poison ivy rash may result in infection.

- Secondary infection is common with poison ivy, so check previously affected patches of skin for oozing blisters or crusting.

- As your child becomes older, teach him to recognize the poison ivy, oak, and sumac plants so that he can avoid future contact.

Additional Information

Poison ivy usually does not spread when a child touches or scratches the rash. It only spreads when the plant oil is spread from the source to other parts of the body. The kind of contact made with the plant determines the pattern of the rash. If your child has touched the straight edge of the poison ivy leaf, her rash will be in a linear pattern. If the plant oil gets on her hands and under her fingernails, a more scattered pattern may occur.

Dogs and cats may also get coated with poison ivy oils and spread it to the family. Give your pets a warm, soapy bath to remove the plant oil from a pet's fur if you suspect that contact has occurred.

Infected poison ivy rashes need to be treated by a physician. When medication is ordered, be sure to complete all the medicine as instructed—even when the rash appears to be improving.

See Related Areas

Allergies, Boils, Impetigo, Rashes.

POISONING

Definition

Poisoning occurs when your child swallows a drug, chemical, plant, or other nonedible item that may include acids, alkalis, and petroleum products. Examples are toilet bowl cleaners, drain cleaners, lye, automatic dishwasher detergent, clinitest tablets, ammonia, bleach, kerosene, gasoline, benzene, furniture polish, and lighter fluid. Other poisonous substances include most drugs, chemicals, and some plants. The most dangerous prescription drugs for overdose include barbiturates, clonidine, digitalis products, narcotics, lomotil, darvon, tofranil, and other tricyclic antidepressants. The most dangerous over-the-counter drugs are iron and aspirin.

What to Do

- Call your emergency response service (911) when life-threatening symptoms are present (coma, confusion, trouble breathing, or seizures).
- Call your local POISON CONTROL CENTER for all other questions.
- Use your fingers to sweep any swallowed pills or solid poisons out of your child's mouth.

When to Call Your Doctor

- If referred by the POISON CONTROL CENTER.

Home Care Tips

- PREVENTION is key! Keep all harmful substances out of reach of children and in a locked cabinet whenever possible.
- Never change the original container for a toxic substance. Your child may mistake it for something harmless and drink or eat it.
- Keep the phone number of your local POISON CONTROL CENTER in a visible location near your telephone.
- Have *syrup of ipecac* available in your medicine cabinet. The POISON CONTROL CENTER may advise you to use it to induce vomiting—*give only upon the recommendation of the poison con-*

Syrup of Ipecac Dosage

Nine to twelve months: two teaspoons (10 ml)

One to six years: three teaspoons (15 ml)

Older than six years: six teaspoons (30 ml)

trol center. (Vomiting may sometimes cause additional damage and delay proper treatment.) Give the proper dose of ipecac with eight ounces of water or clear fluids to help speed delivery, and have your child walk around. Once vomiting begins, repeat clear fluids until vomiting comes back clear.

- Sometimes the POISON CONTROL CENTER advises you to give your child a glass of milk or activated charcoal if you have it. Always check first. If you don't have the proper substance, take your child to the nearest emergency room for treatment.

Additional Information

Sometimes your child will ingest harmless (nontoxic) substances as well. It's always a good idea to call the POISON CONTROL CENTER to verify what course of action you should take.

Lead poisoning is another area of concern for children under age five. Children often eat, chew, or suck on lead-painted surfaces. Lead can be found in dust and paint chips in older homes as well as painted toys, furniture, and playground equipment made before 1978. Headache is the first sign of lead poisoning. Talk to your child's doctor about having a blood test for lead if you live in an older home or apartment. This is also important if you are doing home renovations. Lead dust stirred up during renovations is a major cause of lead poisoning in young children.

See Related Areas

Allergies and Sensitivities to Food, Choking, Gastroenteritis, Headache.

RINGWORM

Definition

Ringworm is a common fungus infection of the skin that appears as small, round, red or pink patches that grow to about the size of a dime. When it appears on the body, it is called *tinea corporis*; on the head, *tinea captitis*; in the groin *tinea cruris*; and on the foot, *tinea pedis*. There usually is a small area of clearing at the center and a raised, rough, scaly border. It may be transmitted from a fungus infection, infected puppies or kittens, or through soil.

What to Do

- Check your child's body for any other areas of rash.
- Check your child's temperature to make sure she doesn't have a fever.
- Use Home Care Tips.

When to Call Your Doctor

- If more than three spots are present.
- Pus is draining from the affected area.
- Scalp is involved (may need special medicine).
- If the infection does not seem to go away after home care treatment.

Home Care Tips

- Use an over-the-counter antifungal cream like Micatin, Tinactin, or Lotrimin for skin infections and apply it two times a day to the rash and one inch beyond its border.
- For scalp infections, use an antifungal shampoo like Selsun Blue twice a week.
- The infection should begin to go away in about a week but continue to use the antifungal cream for at least seven days after the rash has cleared to ensure that the fungus is gone.
- Keep your child's skin cool and dry because fungal infections tend to spread in a warm, moist environment.
- Have your child wear cotton clothing over the infected area and change it frequently if the area becomes moist. If the infection is on your child's foot, you should have him change his socks two to three times a day.
- Ringworm of the skin is mildly contagious as it requires direct skin-to-skin contact to spread. After forty-eight hours of treatment, it is no longer contagious so you do not need to keep your child home from day care or nursery school.

Additional Information

The ringworm fungus can affect different parts of the body. *Jock itch,* a common fungal infection in the groin area of boys, and *Athlete's foot,* an infection of the skin between the toes and on the soles of the feet, are also caused by the ringworm fungus. Hair and scalp ringworm are often treated with an oral antifungal medicine. Another form of fungal infection of the skin is called *tinea veriscolor.* See under Rashes and Table 2.2, Common Rashes and Treatment on pages 84–85.

If your child has ringworm and you have a puppy or kitten, take the animal to the vet to determine if it has become infected and treatment is required.

See Related Areas

Allergies, Athlete's Foot, Eczema, Rashes, Warts.

ROSEOLA

Definition

Roseola is a short-term viral illness affecting infants and children under the age of two. It is marked by a high fever of 103°F to 106°F rectally that lasts for three to four days. Sudden onset of a high fever may also bring febrile convulsions. As the child's temperature returns to normal, a total body rash breaks out, and this rash lasts from one to three days.

What to Do

- Monitor your child's temperature for signs of fever.
- Give acetaminophen or ibuprofen in an appropriate dosage for fever control.
- Cool your child with frequent tepid baths or sponging.
- Increase fluid intake to ensure good hydration.

When to Call Your Doctor

- If your child has a febrile convulsion or seizure.
- Fever is greater than 101°F rectally.
- Your child appears very sick.
- Your child is vomiting.

Home Care Tips

Roseola is difficult to diagnose since the rash doesn't appear until after fever subsides and is usually gone after the third day. The disease usually runs its course with only treatment for fever, and there are rarely any complications. Home care is aimed at making your child comfortable since you often won't know the diagnosis until the fever breaks.

Additional Information

Roseola is contagious from the onset of fever until the rash is gone. Be aware of your child's fever if you have heard that Roseola is going around his day care or nursery school.

See Related Areas

Allergies, Chicken Pox, Convulsions or Seizures, Fever, Rashes.

SCARLET FEVER

Definition

Scarlet fever is an illness caused by *streptococcal* (group A) bacteria. It causes fever, sore throat, strawberry red patches on a "furry-looking" tongue, and a rash of small red spots that eventually merge. (Often the sore throat will appear twenty-four hours before the rash.)

The rash is bright red with a sandpapery feel and lasts about a week. Resembling a bad sunburn, it usually starts on the chest and neck and then merges within twenty-four hours to include the entire body. There is also increased redness in the skin folds of the elbows, armpits, and groin. The only area excluded from the rash is the area around the mouth. Sometimes the skin where the rash was prominent flakes or peels off for up to two weeks or more.

Your child might also complain of belly pain and have swollen lymph glands in the neck.

What to Do

- Check for fever and sore throat.
- Check his tongue to see if it looks furry with bright red strawberry patches.
- Give your child plenty of cool liquids to drink.
- Give antibiotics as prescribed by your doctor.

When to Call Your Doctor

- Fever over 101°F rectally and complaint of sore throat, tummy ache, swollen glands, or a rash.
- To obtain a throat culture.
- If no improvement after forty-eight hours on antibiotic or if child seems worse.
- If child improves and then seven to fourteen days later develops fever; headache; abdominal pain; loss of appetite; swelling; joint pain; or dark, cola-colored urine.

Home Care Tips

- Administer antibiotics as prescribed. If you have trouble getting your child to take the medicine, call your doctor for advice. Also see tips on giving medicines to children in chapter 1.
- Use fever-reducing measures to keep your child comfortable.
- Give your child plenty of cold fluids. This will help keep him hydrated with his

fever. He may also have trouble swallowing because of the sore throat, and so cool liquids and foods may be soothing. Avoid orange juice and carbonated beverages as they may be difficult to swallow. If you do want to give cola or ginger ale to your child, let it go flat first.

- Puree his foods if painful swallowing is interfering with eating.

- Encourage rest for the first twenty-four hours when the symptoms are usually their worst.

- Give cool baths to soothe the rash and keep down the fever.

- For a child over age three, sucking on a lollipop may help relieve the sore throat. Throat lozenges are not recommended for children under age five because of the danger of choking.

- Give acetaminophen or ibuprofen in the appropriate dosage for your child's weight for pain and for fever over 101°F.

Additional Information

Scarlet fever and its complications (including rheumatic heart disease and nephritis, a serious kidney infection) caused very serious health problems for children during the first half of the twentieth century. However, since the use of penicillin to treat "strep" infections, it's no longer a dreaded disease. Today, children are treated very effectively with antibiotics and rarely suffer complications from this disease. The disease is sometimes now referred to as *Scarletina* or scarletina rash.

Scarlet fever and "strep" throat can spread through the family. You might want to take other family members to the doctor for a throat culture if they have any of the symptoms. Your child is contagious until she has been taking antibiotics for forty-eight hours. After that time, she may return to day care or preschool even though the rash may still be present. The rash itself is not contagious, and it can persist or even wax and wane for a period of time after the clearance of the strep infection.

Make sure that your child takes the full course of antibiotics for the recommended number of days and doses. Even if your child is feeling better and the symptoms are gone, the streptococcal infection may not be totally eradicated, and stopping the medicine too soon could lead to recurrence. It is also important to never use any leftover antibiotic from a friend or other child because it will make any subsequent throat culture inaccurate. Replace her toothbrush after she has been on the antibiotic for forty-eight hours, and again after she has finished the course of antibiotics prescribed by the doctor, as this may prevent reinfection.

See Related Areas

Abdominal Pain, Allergies, Earache/Infection, Fever, Headache, Rashes, Sore Throat, Swollen Lymph Nodes.

SWIMMER'S EAR

Definition

Swimmer's ear, also known as *otitis externa,* is an *inflammation of the ear canal* that leads to the eardrum. It is usually red, painful, and itchy. It may be caused by bacteria, fungus, trauma, excess wax production, or a foreign object in the ear. It is called swimmer's ear because, when swimming, water can get trapped in the canal causing the lining to become wet and swollen. This wet environment leaves the ear canal prone to infection. Wax buildup also traps water and increases the risk of swimmer's ear.

What to Do

- Have your child shake her head or hop on one foot on the affected side to remove water after swimming or shampooing.
- Dry her ear canal after water exposure.
- Give acetaminophen or ibuprofen in the appropriate dosage for your child's weight to relieve pain.
- Follow Home Care Tips.

When to Call Your Doctor

- Ear pain and fever over 101°F rectally.
- Dark-colored or foul-smelling discharge from her ear.
- If the earache is associated with trauma or injury to her ear.
- You think there is a foreign object or insect in your child's ear.

Home Care Tips

- With an external ear problem, it is imperative to *keep the outer ear and ear canal as dry as possible* because a wet, moist environment is the perfect medium for bacteria and fungus to grow. The goal is to clean and dry the outer canal of the ear without doing further damage to the irritated top layer of skin. Some guidelines are:
  - No swimming for three to five days.
  - Avoid shampoos (without protection).
  - Do not use cotton in ears; it will retain moisture.
  - Do not use earplugs or cotton swabs.
  - Wipe water from the ear with a towel. Be gentle; the ear canal is very tender.
  - Dry ear with a hair dryer on low setting, twenty inches away from skin.

- Apply prescription eardrops as directed. Continue to use for the amount of time prescribed even if your child feels better. The acute pain should subside within forty-eight hours.

- To use eardrops, lay your child on her side with the affected ear up. Pull her earlobe up and back and then administer the eardrops without letting the dropper touch the ear. Have your child remain in this position for at least five minutes to allow absorption of the medicine.

- Make sure that you remove all ear wax when your child has swimmer's ear. To do this, place two drops of half-strength hydrogen peroxide into the affected ear each night for two to three weeks. You can make half-strength hydrogen peroxide by mixing equal amounts of hydrogen peroxide and water. It's best to dilute only a small amount each time. For example, mix one-eighth cup water and one-eighth cup hydrogen peroxide. Be sure to label the diluted mix and keep out of reach of small children.

- If you think your child has excess ear wax, use wax-softening eardrops to remove the wax. Do not use Q-tips to remove ear wax because you may just push excess wax further into the ear, or you may injure your child's eardrum.

- If your child seems susceptible to swimmer's ear, use an over-the-counter product such as Swim-Ear on an ongoing basis to combat bacteria after swimming or shampooing. Another technique for preventing swimmer's ear in the susceptible child is to place one drop of rubbing alcohol in the ear canal both before swimming and when she gets out of the water. This will tend to dry any water that gets into the canal.

Additional Information

Recurrences of swimmer's ear are common, especially in adolescents who swim, shower, or shampoo daily. In addition to eardrops, your doctor may also prescribe antibiotics to clear up a more serious case of swimmer's ear. Children who are more susceptible to swimmer's ear may benefit from having their ears cleaned by a physician before swimming season. Then parents can give over-the-counter eardrops containing boric acid (such as Swim-Ear) at the end of each day.

The swelling of the ear canal that can accompany swimmer's ear may lead to temporary hearing loss. Hearing will come back once the ear is treated and swelling decreases.

See Related Areas

Earache/Infection, Eczema.

THRUSH

Definition

Thrush is a *yeast infection in the mouth or on the tongue* caused by the fungus *Candida albicans*. It causes no symptoms other than characteristic white spots or patches inside the oral cavity. Thrush usually occurs in babies under six months of age, and it can cause irritation of the mouth that may interfere with feeding. Generally, older children who develop mouth thrush are either in poor health or have been taking certain antibiotics for a long period of time.

What to Do

- Check the inside of your child's mouth for white patches that look like dried milk but will not wipe away.
- Check for fever.
- Apply antifungal solution when prescribed by your doctor.

When to Call Your Doctor

- To confirm diagnosis and receive prescription for antifungal solution.
- If the sores are extremely painful.
- Bleeding is present.
- If your baby develops fever, cough, or digestive symptoms.
- Your baby refuses to drink liquids.
- The white patches last after two weeks of treatment.
- Signs of dehydration such as very dry mouth, no tears, or no urine for eight hours are apparent.

Home Care Tips

- If antifungal solution is prescribed, give your child a small amount of water before taking the medication to rinse the inside of her mouth. Use a small syringe or medicine dispenser to place the antifungal medicine inside your baby's mouth.
- It also may be helpful to swab a 1 percent gentian violet solution (available without a prescription) with Q-tips on the white patches four times a day after meals. Please note that gentian violet may be a bit messy.
- Give extra fluids.

- Monitor your baby's intake of fluids to make sure she is drinking enough. Try a soft infant nipple with a large opening if she refuses the bottle or breast. You can also try using a cup.
- Use fever-reducing and pain medicines as directed by your child's doctor.
- Wash your hands frequently. If breast-feeding, wash nipples well both before and after feeding. Allow to air-dry.
- Double-check your cleaning procedures for nipples on the bottles. If you are breast-feeding, you may need to use a medicated cream on your breasts. Ask your doctor for recommendations.
- Wash toys well to prevent reinfection.
- Prolonged sucking can irritate the mouth; if your child is using a pacifier, allow it only at bedtime or seriously consider eliminating it all together. In addition, the pacifier is often the source of reinfection. If your child still needs it, you should replace it with a new pacifier when the infection is gone.
- If you are nursing, you may apply the antifungal solution to any irritated or open areas on your nipples to minimize reinfection.

Additional Information

If treated properly, oral thrush is not serious, though it may last for two to three weeks. Occasionally, poorly sterilized nipples on bottles, contaminated hands, or infected breast nipples may spread the fungus. Children who have been taking antibiotics may develop mouth thrush because antibiotics eliminate the normal bacteria present in the mouth and allow the fungus to grow.

The same fungus that causes mouth thrush can also appear as a rash in the diaper area of babies (or in the vagina of adolescent girls and women). Rarely, the fungus may also appear as a rash in the skin folds of the neck, especially when the child is drooling and keeping the area wet. This rash may also appear when your child is taking antibiotics for another problem.

See Related Areas

Canker Sores, Cold Sores, Fever, Rashes.

URINARY TRACT INFECTIONS

Definition

A urinary tract infection (UTI) is *an infection in any part of the urinary tract system including kidneys, bladder, and urethra.* In some cases, the part infected is the lining of the bladder, and this is called *cystitis*. The most common symptoms are pain when passing urine and the need to urinate more frequently (urgency). The range of symptoms include:

- Pain or burning sensation when passing urine.
- Increased frequency of the need to urinate but passing only small amounts of urine or a feeling of urgency to urinate.
- Fever.
- Foul-smelling urine.
- Cloudy urine.
- Lower abdominal or back pain.
- Children previously toilet trained may have "accidents."
- If your child is too young to talk, suspect a problem if she begins to cry regularly while passing urine.

What to Do

- If your child complains of pain or frequency of urination, check her temperature.
- Check her urine to see if it is cloudy or unpleasant smelling.
- Give her extra fluids to drink.
- Check for fever.
- Make sure your child is having normal bowel movements and is not constipated.

When to Call Your Doctor

- Your child complains of pain or burning when she urinates.
- Fever and any change in urinating (or symptoms as above).
- Frequent urination, more often than once every two hours.
- Only able to pass small amounts of urine at a time.
- Urine appears to contain blood.
- Abdominal, side, or back pain with fever greater than 101°F rectally.

Home Care Tips

- Make sure your child is getting plenty of fluids to drink to increase urination. Cranberry juice is a good liquid if you suspect a urinary tract infection.
- Place a hot-water bottle against her back if she is complaining of low back pain.

- Teach your daughter to wipe from front to back after urinating so that her urethra is not contaminated by material from her bowels.
- Make sure that your child takes all medication as prescribed. Sometimes the doctor may ask you to administer the medicine at specific time intervals; be certain your child finishes the medicine as prescribed even if the symptoms have gone away and she feels better.
- Do not use bubble baths. Many of these solutions change the pH around your child's urethra, making her more susceptible to urinary tract infections. This is especially true for girls because of the possible contamination of the vaginal-urethral area by anal bacteria.
- Give acetaminophen or ibuprofen for pain and fever.

Additional Information

A urinary tract infection is always serious and requires immediate medical attention and follow-up. Girls suffer from more urinary tract infections than boys because the female urethra is much shorter than the male urethra, making it easier for bacteria to enter the bladder.

See Related Areas

Abdominal Pain, Constipation, Dehydration, Fever, Vaginal Pain/Itching.

WARTS

Definition

A wart is a *virus* that causes a raised, round, rough-surfaced lump on the skin. There are brown dots within the wart and a clear boundary with the normal skin. Sometimes you will see small black dots in the lumps. These are blood vessels, not dirt. Warts can appear singly or in large numbers over all parts of the body including the face and genitals.

What to Do

- Try Home Care Tips.

When to Call Your Doctor

- If you are not sure the lump is a wart.
- The warts continue to multiply.
- Home Care Tips don't work.
- Your child is uncomfortable and wants the warts removed.

Home Care Tips

Most warts will go away on their own in two to three years without any treatment. With home treatment, warts usually disappear in two to three months. If the wart is in an area that particularly bothers your child, talk to your doctor about possible solutions.

- Home care treatment of warts can be done with one of the over-the-counter wart-removing acids (high concentration of salicylic acid) that will destroy the wart tissue.
- Ask your pharmacist to recommend the latest home kits available. Most are applied once a day, but follow all directions on the product. Be sure to protect the surrounding (normal) skin so that the acid does not destroy it as well.
- The topical treatment usually works faster if it is applied after soaking the affected area with very warm water. It is also helpful to cover the wart with an adhesive bandage after you have applied the treatment.

Additional Information

There are several different kinds of warts, all of them caused by a member of the same virus family called the *human papilloma* virus. Types of warts include:

- *Common hand warts.* These are usually found around the nails, on the fingers, and on the back of the hand.
- *Flat warts.* These are smaller and less rough than hand or foot warts, and usually grow in large numbers—twenty to one hundred at a time. They can appear anywhere.
- *Foot warts.* These are called plantar warts and are usually found on the sole of the foot. Plantar warts often grow in a group the size of a quarter or larger and are usually flatter because of the pressure of walking. They may also cause pain.

Because warts are caused by a virus, they are probably passed from person to person. It takes several months from the time of first contact to the time when the warts grow large enough to be seen. The risk of catching hand, foot, and flat warts is small; however, genital warts do seem to be very contagious. Wart viruses seem to occur more easily if the skin has been damaged in some way. This may explain the high frequency of warts in children who bite their nails. Warts eventually are rejected spontaneously by the body's immune system and disappear permanently.

See Related Areas
Athlete's Foot, Rashes.

CHAPTER FOUR

Common Injuries

BASICS OF FIRST AID

Definition

First aid is the immediate care given to an injured or suddenly ill person. It does not take the place of medical care but is the temporary assistance given until the need for proper medical treatment can be determined. Children are prone to accidents because they are naturally curious and often unaware of danger. Although most accidents are relatively minor, it is important that you know what to do in case of a serious accident. (Also see chapter 5, "Emergency Situations.")

When your child is injured *it is always important that you stay calm*—taking the time to think and use your common sense. For children, most first aid is given for cuts, scrapes, and bruises. Every house should have a first aid kit that is fully stocked and checked regularly. It needs to be kept in a safe, accessible place and out of reach of young children.

What to Do

- Stay calm.
- Take time to think and use common sense.
- Keep important phone numbers by the telephone including your child's doctor, 911 or your emergency medical service, the poison control center, your local pharmacy, and a trusted neighbor.
- Have a first aid kit stocked, up to date, and in a secure place.

When to Call Your Doctor

- For all emergencies.

- When your first aid and Home Care Tips don't seem to work.
- You are worried you are not doing the right thing.
- Your child seems to be sicker than you originally thought.

Home Care Tips

- Assemble a first aid kit and make sure everyone in your household and all care-takers for your children know where it is. Make sure it is kept in a safe, secure, and accessible location.
- Discuss principles of first aid and common accidents for each age group with your child's doctor at regular well-child visits.

Checklist of First Aid Supplies

- Ace or elastic bandages, three or four inches wide.
- Adhesive tape.
- Antihistamines.
- Band-Aids in assorted sizes.
- Calamine lotion for itching.
- Cotton balls.
- Cotton swabs.
- Fever- and pain-reducing medicine.
- First Aid handbook
- Gauze bandages in two- and four-inch squares, and some gauze rolls.
- Hot-water bottle or heating pad.
- Hydrogen peroxide.
- Ice pack (a disposable chemical one or ice bag).
- Ipecac syrup.
- Petroleum jelly.
- Rubbing alcohol.
- Safety pins.
- Scissors.
- Sling.
- Steri-strips.
- Thermometer.
- Tweezers.

Additional Information

All caretakers and babysitters for your child should be prepared for an accident or injury, or the possibility of sudden illness. Make certain to give each of them a tour of your home, including the location of your first aid kit, your telephone, emergency telephone numbers, medicines for your child, flashlights, fire extinguisher, and fire escape route. Also review any regular medicines your child takes, any over-the-counter medicines your child might need, and what to do in case of an emergency.

BITES—ANIMAL

Definition

This includes a bite or claw wound from any pet, farm animal, or wild animal. Most bites are from dogs or cats. In most cases, a pet dog or cat will not have rabies; however, if a pet has been sick and/or the attack was unprovoked, rabies should be considered. Cat bites become infected more often than dog bites, and claw wounds are treated the same as bite wounds as they, too, are contaminated with saliva.

The main risk from bites by domestic farm animals is serious wound infection, while small indoor pets like hamsters, white mice, guinea pigs, and domesticated rabbits pose no risk for rabies. Even bites that penetrate the skin are usually not serious because these animals don't eat dead animals. However, bites from rabies-prone wild animals is a most serious concern. Rabies is a fatal disease. Bites or scratches from a bat, skunk, raccoon, fox, coyote, wild dogs and cats, or any large wild animal are especially dangerous. These animals can transmit rabies even if they have no symptoms. Bats have transmitted rabies even without a detectable bite mark. Squirrels do carry rabies but have not been found to transmit it to humans. If there is any question, your local public health department can provide information about the local animal population.

What to Do

- Stop any bleeding with direct pressure.
- Cleanse the wound thoroughly.
- Observe the bite closely for three to five days for any signs of infection, particularly fever or local swelling, redness, pus, or tenderness around the wound.

When to Call Your Doctor

- You suspect the animal may carry rabies.
- The bite is on the hands, face, or feet.
- You have trouble stopping the bleeding even with direct pressure for twenty minutes, or the wound is gaping (open) and may need stitches.

- To check your child's tetanus immunization status.
- If the wound looks tender, red, swollen, or drains pus.
- Your child has a fever over 101°F.

Home Care Tips

- Thorough cleaning of the wound is the most important part of care. Wash all wounds immediately with soap and water for ten minutes, scrubbing vigorously enough to make it re-bleed a little. Then, remove any remaining saliva by flushing the wound thoroughly with running tap water. Apply an over-the-counter antibiotic ointment and cover with a gauze bandage.
- Wash the wound daily with soap and water and apply an over-the-counter antibiotic ointment twice a day for three days. Keep the wound covered between treatments with a gauze bandage.
- Give ibuprofen or acetaminophen at the dosage appropriate to your child's weight for pain.
- Carefully watch the wound for three to five days for any sign of infection.
- If the rabies status of the animal is unknown and rabies is a consideration, contact your local public health department and animal control department. If necessary, the rabies vaccination should be given to your child within seventy-two hours.

Additional Information

Sudden, quick, and loud behavior toward an animal can provoke even a beloved pet to bite. Wild animals are most likely to attack when they feel cornered or frightened. In addition, more and more individuals are keeping attack animals for pets, and the "pet" may feel that an approaching small child is a predator and go into his attack mode.

Teach your children to play calmly in order to avoid frightening animals with loud sounds or sudden movements. Also teach your child not to approach or touch strange animals. Always ask the owner's permission first and state, "Is your dog friendly to children? May I pet him?" Then teach your child to let the animal smell his hand first before he gently strokes the animal under the chin. If possible, demonstrate the technique to your child.

Instruct your child that if he is attacked by a dog, he should stand tall and still like a tree, or lie flat like a rock. Tell him not to make eye contact with the animal because many species consider this to be sign of predatory aggression.

See Related Areas

Bites—Human, Bleeding, Basics of First Aid, Puncture Wounds.

BITES—HUMAN

Definition

Human bites occur when the skin is punctured, usually by teeth. Human bites are more likely to become infected than are animal bites. Most toddler bites do not pierce the skin, though they may result in bruising. Bites on the hands cause an increased risk of complications.

What to Do

- Stop any bleeding with direct pressure.
- Wash the wound with soap and water.
- Watch the bite closely for three to five days for signs of infection, including fever, local swelling, redness, pus, or tenderness around the wound.

When to Call Your Doctor

- Trouble stopping the bleeding even with direct pressure for twenty minutes.
- You think that stitches will be needed to close a gaping wound.
- Wound looks tender, red, swollen, or drains pus.
- Your child has a fever over 101°F.
- To check your child's tetanus immunization status.

Home Care Tips

- Immediately wash the bite wound with soap and warm water. Then rinse the wound vigorously by holding it under running tap water. If it's in an area that can't be held under the faucet, rinse with warm water from a pitcher. Then apply an over-the-counter antibiotic ointment and cover with a gauze bandage.
- Twice daily for the next three days, continue wound care by washing with soap and water, applying the over-the-counter antibiotic ointment and covering with a gauze bandage.
- Carefully watch the wound for three to five days for any signs of infection.
- Give ibuprofen or acetaminophen in the dose appropriate to your child's weight for pain. Discontinue the medicine if you suspect a wound infection. Both of these medications also reduce fever; if you suspect infection, discontinue usage until you can determine if infection is present.

Additional Information

It's natural for teething babies to take a bite out of just about anything, including themselves and a sibling. Usually this has no harmful intent, but two- and three-year-old toddlers are prone to bite when they are angry. It is best to work with them to channel their anger in more appropriate ways. It's also a good time to start repeating the phrase, "You need to use your words."

See Related Areas

Bites—Animal, Bleeding, Puncture Wounds.

BITES—INSECT AND TICK

Definition

Many insect bites are difficult to distinguish unless you actually see the bite as it is occurring. Bites from mosquitos, harvest mites, fleas, and bedbugs cause itchy red bumps. Horsefly, deer fly, gnat, fire ant, blister beetle, and centipede bites usually cause a painful, red bump. Within a few hours, fire ant bites can change to blisters or pimples. Spider bites cause redness, pain, and swelling. Ticks attach themselves to the skin and must be removed, as tick saliva may cause tissue destruction. Most insect bites will hurt or itch for one to two days, and occasionally an insect bite may cause an allergic reaction.

What to Do

- Relieve symptoms with Home Care Tips.
- Remove any ticks promptly.
- Keep bite area clean.

When to Call Your Doctor

If your child experiences any of the following

- Wheezing or difficulty breathing.
- Pale or sweaty appearance following a bite.
- Continued discomfort or swelling.
- Development of flu-like symptoms following a tick bite.
- An allergic reaction.
- A rash or skin spot.

Home Care Tips

For Itchy Insect Bites

- Rub an ice cube over the bite for fifteen minutes or apply a cool compress.
- Apply calamine lotion over the bite area. Aluminum salts (found in roll-on deodorant), astringents like witch hazel, or a paste made by mixing one

tablespoon of vinegar with three tablespoons of cornstarch will also decrease the itch.

- If the itch seems severe, apply 1 percent hydrocortisone cream two times a day.
- If the bite gets a scab on it from itching, apply an over-the-counter antibiotic ointment two times a day and cover it with a Band-Aid to protect it from further scratching.
- If the itch is interfering with your child's sleep, give him some diphenhydramine medicine by mouth at bedtime in the appropriate dose for your child's weight.

For Painful Insect Bites

- Rub an ice cube over the bite for fifteen minutes.
- Give ibuprofen in the appropriate dose for your child's weight for its pain relief and anti-inflammatory effects.
- There is folklore (though medically unsubstantiated) that a paste made with meat tenderizer or baking soda and water will relieve the pain and discomfort. Apply the paste to the skin and keep it in place with a moist cloth for twenty minutes.

For Tick Bites

- Promptly remove the tick by pulling the visible part directly back with a tweezer.
- Grab the tick firmly with tweezers as close to the skin as possible. Pull the tic straight out with steady, gentle pressure.
- Do not apply heat, cold, or any chemical substance to the tick prior to removal.
- Do not squeeze the tick or crush it. This may inject more venom into your child.
- Check with your doctor if you are in an area known for Lyme disease or Rocky Mountain Spotted Fever. Prompt medical treatment is needed.

Additional Information

Despite the large number of individuals who receive insect bites, relatively few have a bad allergic reaction. Babies and younger children usually experience severe swelling following an insect bite compared to an older child or adult. A simple mosquito bite, for example, can cause a small child's eye to be swollen closed. Only a few species of spiders, such as black widows, tarantulas, and brown recluse spiders, cause severe allergic reactions that require emergency medical attention.

See Related Areas

Allergies; Hives; Impetigo; Poison Ivy, Oak, and Sumac; Rashes; Stings.

Injuries

BROKEN BONES

Definition

A broken bone or fracture is a break, crack, or buckling of a bone. Most children break a bone at least once in their lives. The most common bones that are fractured during childhood include those of the arm, leg, ankle, foot, toes, nose, hand, and fingers. Older children may easily break the collarbone from falls or blows to the shoulder.

Fractures may be open or closed. An open fracture occurs when the bone sticks through the skin, and may damage muscles and blood vessels. A closed fracture is a complete or incomplete break that does not puncture the skin. A common closed fracture in children is a greenstick fracture in which the young bone of the child bends and breaks incompletely, sometimes resembling a crack. A buckle or *torus fracture* occurs horizontally along the side of a long bone (such as the shin bone or an arm bone), causing it to buckle rather than break. A compression fracture occurs when force compresses a bone, causing it to shatter. See Figures 4.1a–4.1h for examples of types of fractures.

Figures 4.1a–4.1h: Types of Broken Bones

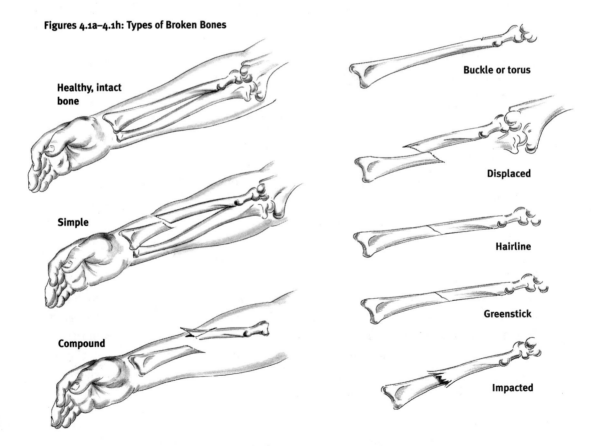

Healthy, intact bone

Simple

Compound

Buckle or torus

Displaced

Hairline

Greenstick

Impacted

What to Do

- Call 911 if the bone is sticking through the skin, and take your child to a hospital by ambulance. If you have a sterile gauze pad nearby, cover the open wound with it but don't attempt any wound cleaning.
- Compare the injured area with the same region on the other limb.
- If a limb appears to be bent or curved, don't try to straighten it.
- If there is no bone sticking through the skin but your child cannot move the affected area without pain, stabilize the joints above and below the affected area and take him to the emergency room.
- If there is bleeding, apply direct pressure.
- Apply ice to the affected area, and keep the area elevated after you have immobilized it.
- Keep your child warm and calm while waiting for help.
- Don't give your child anything to eat or drink in case he needs anesthesia to set the broken bone.

When to Call Your Doctor

Immediately

- The bone is sticking through the skin—call 911.
- You suspect a broken bone.
- Trouble breathing.
- Unconsciousness.
- Extreme pain.
- Limb is cold, blue, or numbed.
- Limb looks deformed.
- Child is pale, sweaty, or dizzy.

In the Near Future

- Unable to bear weight on affected limb.
- Moderate pain.
- Decreased use or movement of limb.
- Noticeable swelling.
- Injury to elbow with a lot of swelling.

Home Care Tips

In most cases, take your child to the emergency room or doctor's office if you suspect a broken bone. An X ray may be needed, and a brief discussion about this with your child will be helpful. If your child has broken a bone and needs a cast, ask for specific instructions. Some casts (those made from fiberglass) can get wet, while plaster casts need to be kept dry.

Some general cast care tips include:

- Keep the affected area elevated for twenty-four to forty-eight hours after the injury to reduce swelling.
- Give ibuprofen or acetaminophen for minor pain.
- Itching is a common problem with casts. Ask your doctor about using Q-tips to relieve itching under the cast. Give diphenhydramine by mouth in the dose appropriate to your child's weight to help relieve itching at night so that your child can get a good rest.
- Call your doctor for severe pain or pressure within the cast or increasing coolness or blueness of the fingers or toes. In these cases, your doctor may need to apply a new cast.
- Once the cast is removed, your child may feel weak but should gradually increase his activity. If this is a problem, call your doctor.

Additional Information

Nursemaid's elbow is a slipped ligament in the elbow joint that connects one of the forearm bones. It is a common occurrence in some babies and small children and is caused by pulling on the child's arm. The child will not use the arm because of pain at the elbow. Your doctor can reposition the arm with a special twist. There is usually a click, and the child almost instantaneously regains full use of the limb.

See Related Areas

Sprains.

BURNS

Definition

A burn is an injury to the skin caused by contact with hot liquids, a hot object (such as a stove or iron, fire, flames, or electrical outlet), or exposure to chemicals or the sun. There are four important considerations for determining the seriousness of a burn injury:

- *Size of the area of skin burned.* The larger the area of skin that is burned, the more serious the injury.
- *Depth of the skin injury.* This is the "degree" of burn. Third-degree burns are the deepest and most serious. They affect the full thickness of the skin and require immediate medical attention. Skin grafts are needed for complete healing. Second-degree burns are also serious and require medical attention. First-degree burns, such as a sunburn, will usually heal on their own in two to three days.
- *Location of the burn.* Any burn is serious, but burns involving the face, hands, or perineal area (groin) require professional medical attention.
- *How the burn occurred.* The mechanism of the burn injury and the surrounding environmental factors are important to know in order to treat the injury properly.

What to Do

- *Stop the burning process.* Immediately remove all of the child's clothing including diapers. This prevents entrapment of any heat, liquids, or chemicals that can deepen the burn.
- *Cool the burned area.* If the area is not too large (no bigger than the size of one arm), cool the affected areas with cool water. This prevents the burn from deepening. Keep cooling the area as long as it feels hot or until you get professional medical attention.
- *Never use butter* or any type of ointment on a burn as it may lock in heat and cause a deeper and more serious injury.
- Get medical attention. Second- and third-degree burns require professional medical attention.

When to Call Your Doctor

Immediately

- Any burn that is deeper than a sunburn and bigger than the palm of the child.
- Blisters bigger than two inches across.
- Child does not feel pain in the area that was burned.
- Any fire that occurred with your child in an enclosed space—even if you don't see any skin burns.
- Burns on the face, hands, or groin area.
- Your child has shortness of breath or trouble breathing.
- All burns related to electrical contact, including lightening.

- Loss of consciousness, even briefly.
- All burns caused by chemicals.
- Story of how the burn occurred doesn't make sense.

In the Near Future

- Sunburn in an infant.
- Large sunburn in an older child that doesn't heal in two days.
- Burn seems to be getting worse or you notice pus.
- Fever with a temperature greater than 101°F taken rectally.
- Tetanus immunization is not up to date or you are unsure of your child's immunization status.

Home Care Tips

Only first-degree burns can be treated at home without professional medical supervision.

- Give ibuprofen for pain and to decrease inflammation.
- Make sure your child drinks plenty of liquids.
- After the burned area has been cooled with cool water or cool facecloths, you may apply a soothing lotion or ointment. Aloe vera gels are very soothing for a first-degree burn. Make sure that whatever ointment or lotion you apply does not contain alcohol as this will be drying and cause stinging.
- Do not break any blisters. Leave them intact. They will heal on their own.
- If the blisters break on their own, gently wash the area with soap and water. After the area dries, apply an antibiotic ointment.
- For second-degree burns your doctor will prescribe a special cream, instruct you how to apply it, and show you how to care further for your child's injury.

Additional Information

Burns are very serious—even those that appear deceptively minor. If you have any questions, call your doctor. Medical professionals estimate the size of a burn in terms of the percentage of body area affected. You can think of your child's palm as 1 percent of his body and make a rough estimate of size from that.

The depth of injury is very hard to determine, and often this depth is uneven. There may be areas of first-, second-, and third-degree burns all in the same wound. In most cases, if you are unsure you should bring your child to a doctor.

Third-degree burns are the most serious and require prompt medical attention. They affect the full thickness of skin, including the dermis and epidermis. Often there is no pain or feeling with a third-degree burn because the nerve endings have been injured. The color may be white or brown, charred, or cherry red, depending upon what caused the burn, and there is usually no bleeding. Skin grafting is often needed for healing. Second-degree burns involve the entire top layer of skin (epidermis) and some of the second layer (dermis). Second-degree burns are very painful and require a doctor's care. Most will heal when treated with a special prescription cream in two to three weeks. First-degree burns cause a reddening of the top layer of the skin, making it feel painful and warm to the touch. Some first-degree burns produce teeny water blisters that usually heal in two or three days.

Prevention is the best treatment for burns. Most burns suffered by small children involve hot liquids. So, never drink hot liquids (such as tea, coffee, or hot soup) with a squirmy child on your lap or when breast-feeding. Use care when cooking. Keep handles pointed in and avoid dangling electrical cords around crock pots, etc. Set the water temperature for your house lower than 125°F. Hot water running from the tap can burn the sensitive skin of infants and young children. When running a bath, run cold water first in case the child falls in accidentally.

Teach your child what to do in case of a fire. Have fire drills and instruct children to get out of the house safely and meet at a special spot. Emphasize that they should not go back for a special toy and not hide in a closet. Make sure that an ambulatory child knows how to exit from her bedroom. Change the batteries in your smoke detector at least once a year (the switch to daylight saving time is a good yearly habit) and protect the areas around fireplaces, wood stoves, and other heating units. Teach children appropriate behavior around fire and grills. Be as careful when you finish a fire as when you start it. Keep matches in a safe place, and when your child is old enough, talk to her about the safe use of matches. Teach your children what to do if their clothes catch on fire and make sure they know how to "stop, drop, and roll." Practice safety at all times. Your children will learn from the example that you set.

See Related Areas

Emergency Situations, Poisoning, Sunburn.

CUTS, SCRAPES, AND WOUNDS

Definition

Unfortunately, children fall frequently—and most cuts, scrapes, and wounds are usually the result of these accidents. A cut is an injury that breaks the skin and causes bleeding. A scrape or *abrasion* occurs when the skin's surface is not actually broken but rubbed so that the capillary blood vessels under the skin ooze a little. A wound is usually a deeper cut that also injures some of the underlying tissue. Small cuts and scrapes can be treated at home while some wounds may need medical attention for suturing, deep cleaning, or to stop excessive bleeding. Cuts that need sutures or stitches are deep and leave the skin edges separate.

What to Do

- Apply direct pressure to stop the bleeding.
- Keep the injured area elevated above the heart.
- After the bleeding has stopped, wash the area with soap and warm water.
- Apply a bandage to keep it clean.
- See Home Care Tips.

When to Call Your Doctor

- Large cuts that gape open.
- Trouble stopping the bleeding with direct pressure for twenty minutes or more.
- Deep or large cut on face or hand.
- Redness, tenderness, warmth, or pus around wound.
- Cut or abrasion on head with any change in behavior.
- Fever develops.
- Any question about need for tetanus immunization.

Home Care Tips

- The best treatment for small cuts is to wash them well with soap and warm water. After you're sure that no dirt, glass, or other foreign body is present, you can rinse with hydrogen peroxide or hold under running tap water to rinse thoroughly.
- Pat the skin dry or let air-dry for five minutes.
- Cover the area with an over-the-counter antibiotic ointment and apply a Band-Aid or appropriately-sized gauze bandage and bandage tape.
- Change the bandage when it becomes soiled and follow the same routine of washing the area with soap and water, flushing the wound, drying the area, and then applying a fresh Band-Aid or bandage.
- Bandages will protect the injured area from additional injury and promote healing by keeping out dirt. If a scrape is on an area that rubs, an additional gauze bandage may be needed for padding.
- When you change the bandage look for signs of infection like pus draining from the wound or a large, red, warm area surrounding the wound.
- Don't apply adhesive tape directly on the wound because removal will be painful and restart bleeding.
- Let your child bathe normally and change the bandage as needed.

If your child has received sutures (stitches)

- Do not wash the area for twenty-four hours.
- Then gently begin "suture care." The exact nature of suture care will be determined by your doctor. Usually it involves a gentle cleaning of the stitches and then application of an over-the-counter antibiotic ointment. It is often easier to clean the stitches on a child using a Q-tip.
- Ask your doctor when swimming and bathing will be allowed. Usually it is forty-eight hours after your child has received stitches.
- Be certain to have your child's stitches removed on the correct day, as stitches removed too late may leave marks on the skin.

Additional Information

Most cuts, scrapes, and wounds that are going to become infected do so in the first three days following the injury. A small area of redness or pinkness, approximately an eighth of an inch, around the wound is normal but shouldn't spread. This small reddened area is very common around stitches and is not a sign of infection. Pain and tenderness are also common but should decrease, not increase, with each passing day.

Some wounds are referred to as *lacerations*. Lacerations generally slice through the skin and underlying tissues including fat, blood vessels, nerves, tendons, and ligaments. When blood vessels are involved the bleeding can be considerable, and prompt medical attention is always required.

All wounds heal by scarring, but how visible the scar remains depends on how deep the wound is, how long it takes to heal, and where it is located on the body. The healing process can continue for as long as six to twelve months for deeper wounds, and you can expect any scar to keep fading throughout that time.

See Related Areas

Bites—Animal, Bites—Human, Fever, Puncture Wounds, Rashes, Tooth Trauma.

FACIAL INJURIES

Definition

There are a number of injuries that may occur to the face, and the most common affect the eyes, mouth, teeth, and nose.

Eye injuries. Normal vision is a good sign that an injury to the eye is not severe. However, eye pain may occur from scratches on the eye surface, and a small object in the eye rim may cause blood in the front of the eye and loss of vision.

Mouth injuries. Although they are usually not serious, mouth injuries can cause problems if not taken care of. Small cuts on the inside of the mouth or tongue will often bleed a lot and may need stitches to heal properly. Children who fall with an object such as a pencil or lollipop stick in their mouth may injure internal structures and require stitches.

Dental injuries. Dental injuries occur from blows to the teeth or from falls. Injuries can cause teeth to become tender, sensitive to cold or touch, loose, cracked, knocked out, or displaced. Bleeding often occurs at the margin of the teeth and gums.

Often a facial injury may also involve a *nosebleed*, and, in these cases, direct pressure is the best treatment. (See the section on Nosebleeds for more information.)

What to Do

- Make sure that your child has no trouble breathing.
- Check your child's vision.
- Assess bleeding if present to see extent of cut or wound.
- Determine if a tooth problem is affecting permanent or primary ("baby") teeth.

When to Call Your Doctor

- Your child has loss or blurring of vision.
- You see blood in the front part of the eye.
- There is injury to a tooth. (Call a pediatric dentist.)
- Your child fell with an object in her mouth, and there is a puncture wound.
- She is having a lot of eye pain.
- There is a lot of bleeding that doesn't stop after twenty to thirty minutes.

Home Care Tips

- You can apply ice packs over a cool cloth to ease the swelling of facial injuries. Ice packs can usually be applied for fifteen to twenty minutes every two to three hours.
- Pressure will help to stop bleeding. Take a gauze bandage or clean cloth and hold it over the site for twenty minutes. (If you are unable to stop the bleeding after twenty minutes, call your doctor.)
- If a tooth is loose, try to put it back in place with gentle pressure and take your child to a dentist. If a permanent tooth cannot be held in place, place it in room temperature milk and take it to the dentist with your child. For a tooth to be successfully reimplanted, it should be done within two hours of injury.
- See Nosebleed if applicable.

Additional Information

It is important to see a pediatric dentist even for a knocked-out baby tooth. There is always the possibility that the root of a permanent tooth may be injured. There might be valid concerns regarding spacing when a baby tooth is knocked out traumatically. These questions need to be evaluated.

See Related Areas

Cuts, Scrapes, and Wounds; Eye Irritation/Pain; Nosebleed; Toothache; Tooth Trauma.

FROSTBITE

Definition

Frostbite is skin damage—similar to a burn—caused by exposure to severe cold. The hands, feet, and face (particularly the cheeks, tip of the nose, and ears) are most susceptible to this type of injury. Mild frostbite causes a lot of pain; a more severe case causes loss of sensation. The affected area will turn white and may or may not have blisters. The severity of frostbite is influenced by the duration of exposure, the intensity of cold as determined by the combination of temperature and wind-chill factors, and the rate and method of rewarming.

What to Do

- Remove any wet clothing in contact with the skin.
- Loosen all constricting garments.
- Check body temperature to rule out hypothermia (body temperature less than 96°F).
- Cover area immediately with dry clothing.
- Rewarm the area gradually using a heating pad set on a medium setting, or a hot-water bottle wrapped in a towel.
- As rewarming can be painful, give pain medicine as necessary.
- Encourage your child to drink warm liquids.

When to Call Your Doctor

- If the area exhibits blistering and/or numbness.
- You notice swelling of a suspected frostbite area.
- Your child's body temperature registers below 96°F on a household thermometer.
- You aren't sure if there is frostbite, but you are very suspicious.

Home Care Tips

- PREVENTION is the best remedy.
- In cold conditions, wear several layers of loose, warm clothing. This protects better than one heavy, well-fitting garment.
- Generally, mittens work better than gloves at keeping hands warm and preventing frostbite. For extreme weather conditions when your child must be outside, or when winter sports will keep him outside for long periods of time in very cold weather, consider purchasing mitten or glove liners to wear under mittens.
- Always wear a face mask, earmuffs, mittens, and heavy boots when dressing for extremely cold temperatures or if wind-chill factors increase the danger from cold temperatures.
- Always remove/change wet clothing when possible. Wet skin increases the cooling and freezing rate, and wet clothing will cause conductive heat loss from the part covered. Send extra clothes (especially extra socks and mittens) with your child when she is engaged in winter sports.
- Teach your child to use a "buddy system" when he will be outdoors in severe cold. Teach both children to check each other's noses, faces, and ears for evidence of frostbite.
- If you are suspicious of frostbite on the hands, help your child warm up via natural body heat by placing her cold hands under her armpits or in her groin area.

In the event that you suspect your child may have frostbite:

- Do not rub any frostbitten area. This may cause further tissue damage. Protect the area from trauma—especially if it is swollen.
- Keep the affected part elevated.
- *Never use ice or snow* on any suspected area of frostbite.
- Watch for any blisters or signs of tissue damage. Do not puncture blisters as they will heal best if protected and left alone.
- Encourage your child to drink warm liquids like hot chocolate.
- Do not expose the affected areas to any further extremes of temperature, including heat.
- Expect future hypersensitivity to cold and increased susceptibility to repeated frostbite of the affected areas.

Additional Information

Hypothermia occurs when the *core body temperature is less than 93°F or 35°C*. When your child needs aggressive warming of his entire body, transport him to the nearest hospital.

If you are doing a lot of driving in areas where cold temperatures and snow are common, keep a blanket, flashlight, radio, extra batteries, and a candle in your car trunk. The candle is particularly useful if you become stranded because it can provide heat as well as light in desperate situations.

See Related Areas

Burns, Rashes.

PENIS INJURY

Definition

Penis injury includes an object falling on a child's penis, or events in which the penis gets stuck in a zipper or under a toilet seat. It usually happens when a young boy is in a hurry.

What to Do

- Use a cold pack to reduce swelling if a heavy object has fallen on your son's penis.
- Offer ibuprofen in an appropriate dose for pain and swelling.
- If your child's penis is caught in a zipper, don't attempt removal unless it appears easy to do so.

When to Call Your Doctor

- To get help removing a penis from a zipper.
- You are not sure what to do.
- Your son has pain when he urinates.
- There is excessive swelling. (There may be bruising and swelling for four or five days.)

Home Care Tips

- Apply antiseptic cream to a damaged penis three times a day to soothe the area and prevent infection. Let your son apply the cream himself if he wants to.

- Give your child a bowl of warm water to pour over his penis when he urinates to ease the stinging. He will probably complain of discomfort for forty-eight hours.
- Leave the skin open to the air as much as possible to promote healing and prevent rubbing.
- Have your child rest and do quiet activities to lessen the chance of accidentally bumping himself.

See Related Areas

Cuts, Scrapes, and Wounds; Scrotum or Groin Swelling.

PUNCTURE WOUNDS

Definition

A puncture wound occurs when a foreign object cuts through the skin and causes an injury deeper than it is wide. They can be distinguished from cuts, scrapes, and other wounds by their narrow surface opening and the fact that they tend to bleed less than other wounds. Most puncture wounds in children are caused by nails, pins, knives, needles, splinters, animal or human bites, sharp pieces of glass, or fish hooks. Puncture wounds usually seal over quickly so there is a greater chance of wound infection with this type of injury.

What to Do

- Call 911 or an emergency medical service for life-threatening puncture wounds caused by a gunshot or a knife.
- Clean minor puncture wounds thoroughly.
- Follow Home Care Tips.
- Give acetaminophen or ibuprofen for minor pain.

When to Call the Doctor

Immediately

- Puncture is deep and has occurred on head, chest, abdomen, or a joint.
- Tip of the object is broken off or missing.
- Foreign object is embedded too deeply to be easily removed.
- Foreign object is embedded in face, eye, or hand.
- Your child won't stand or bear weight on a punctured foot.

- The puncturing object or setting was extremely dirty (barnyard, construction site, or landfill).
- To verify tetanus immunization status.
- Severe pain.
- Dirt or debris is seen in the wound but can't be removed using Home Care Tips.
- Fever over 101°F rectally.
- Wound looks infected (redness, red streaks, swollen, extreme tenderness).

Home Care Tips

- Soak in warm, soapy water for fifteen minutes. Then carefully inspect the wound for any signs of dirt or foreign debris. It's okay if the wound bleeds a little.
- Flush the area with running tap water if it's in an area where you can apply it. Otherwise, pour water over the wound from a cup or pitcher to flush out any foreign material.
- When it looks clean, apply an over-the-counter antibacterial ointment and then cover with a Band-Aid.
- Soak the area and reapply the antibiotic ointment two times a day for two days.
- If possible, keep the injured area elevated for the first day.
- Give acetaminophen or ibuprofen for pain in the dose appropriate to your child's weight. The pain should be greatly lessened the second day.
- Puncture wounds are at higher risk for infection, including tetanus, than other wounds because they are often difficult to clean. If you have any doubts, please call your doctor or take your child to an emergency room to have the wound thoroughly inspected, cleaned, and treated.

Additional Information

Folklore tells us that tetanus occurs only from a puncture wound by a dirty object such as a rusty nail. Tetanus bacteria, however, are just as likely to occur in a puncture wound caused by a clean object and are found in soil contaminated with animal feces. They thrive in dark, deep places such as a puncture wound, and a current tetanus immunization is critical to prevent infection in your child. When in doubt, check with your doctor.

Splinters often cause a superficial puncture wound and most can be removed at home. Wash your hands with soap and water and sterilize a needle or tweezers by soaking it for five minutes in boiling water. Cool the needle or tweezers thoroughly for ten minutes before using it on your child. If the splinter is poking out, use the tweezers to pull it out at the same angle. If it is slightly embedded under the skin, you can use the tip of the needle to loosen it and then remove it with tweezers. After the splinter is removed, follow Home Care Tips for a puncture wound. If you are unable to remove the splinter, call your doctor. Some splinters may be left to work themselves out (with frequent daily soaking in warm water) or your doctor may want to remove it.

See Related Areas

Bites—Animal; Bites—Human; Bites—Insect and Tick; Cuts, Scrapes, and Wounds.

SPRAINS

Definition

A sprain is a stretched or torn ligament (the ropelike tissue connecting the bones of the body and giving strength and stability to the joints). Sprains in children most often involve the ankle ligaments, but they can occur any time a child lands forcefully on a joint, usually after falling. A sprain most often results in swelling of the affected joint, tenderness of the surrounding area, pain, and decreased joint movement.

When a child's joint hurts after a forceful twisting, it is usually a sprain. If the pain is severe and the child cannot move the joint, he should be examined by a doctor to make sure that he does not have a fracture.

What to Do

- Most moderate and mild sprains heal with prompt home treatment.
- Make sure your child rests the affected joint. The more an injured ligament is used, the more slowly it will heal.

When to Call Your Doctor

- If you think there may be a fracture or if you are not sure.
- Your child is unable to move the affected joint.
- If swelling and pain do not decrease within forty-eight hours.
- Your child is limping.

Home Care Tips

- *RICE*, an acronym for *Rest*, *Ice*, *Compression* and *Elevation*, is the first aid guideline for sprains.

- Any injury heals better with *rest*. Make sure your child rests the affected area as much as possible for at least the first forty-eight hours.

- Supports such as slings or crutches should be used to minimize motion of the affected joint.

- An ice pack should be applied to the injured area for approximately twenty to thirty minutes every two to three hours for the first twenty-four to forty-eight hours after injury. When you first apply the ice pack your child will complain of cold, then burning, aching, and numbness. This cycle usually takes twenty to thirty minutes. Remove the ice pack when he complains of numbness.

- There are different ways to apply cold to an injury. You can make an ice bag by putting crushed ice, ice cubes, or snow into a double plastic bag, hot water bottle, ice bag, or wet towel. Apply a dual layer of a wet cloth over the injury, and then the ice bag. Often you can use an elastic or Ace Bandage to hold the ice bag in place. You can also use a *chemical snap pack*. These sealed pouches contain two chemical envelopes that, when squeezed, mix the chemicals and produce a cooling effect. They can only be used once but are convenient when ice is not readily available.

- You can achieve *compression* of the injured area and help prevent swelling with an elastic or Ace Bandage. Your child should wear the elastic bandage continuously for the first eighteen to twenty-four hours after injury. Loosen at night but do not remove.

- Elastic bandages come in different sizes for different body parts. Depending upon the age and size of your child, try to use a bandage that is appropriate for his affected joint. For children under the age of five, a one- or two-inch Ace Bandage will probably suffice.

- To apply an elastic bandage, start several inches below the injury and wrap in an upward, overlapping spiral. You usually stretch the bandage to about 70 percent of its maximum length to achieve adequate compression. Leave fingers and toes exposed for observation. Pain, pale skin, numbness, and tingling are signals that the bandage is too tight.

- To minimize swelling, use a pillow or cushion to elevate the injured area in conjunction with ice and compression. When possible, try to raise the injured area above the level of the heart for the first twenty-four to forty-eight hours after injury. *Do not elevate if you suspect a fracture. Call your child's doctor.*

Additional Information

Repeated sprains of the same ligament can result in permanent loss of elasticity. Following an examination of the affected joint, an orthopedist (a bone and joint specialist) may recommend surgery to regain normal functioning.

See Related Areas

Broken Bones; Cuts, Scrapes, and Wounds; Limb Pain.

STINGS—INSECT

Definition

Stings are most commonly inflicted by bees and wasps. Both leave a small puncture wound in the skin—with bees generally leaving the stinger in the wound and wasps doing so occasionally. Reactions from an insect sting range from mild to severe, but most stings cause only local irritation, pain, and swelling. Pain or burning at the site usually lasts one to two hours, while swelling can continue to increase for twenty-four hours and last from three to five days. Some people are allergic to bees and have a severe reaction after a sting, including breathing difficulty, hives, and shock. These reactions require emergency medical treatment.

What to Do

- Keep calm and keep your child calm.
- Remove the stinger.
- Other stinging insects should be brushed off your child's skin to prevent them from stinging again.
- Follow Home Care Tips.

When to Call Your Doctor

- Wheezing or difficulty breathing.
- Tightness in the chest or throat.
- Loss of consciousness, or your child has fainted or passed out.
- Previous allergic reaction to a sting.
- Your child is stung by more than five bees/wasps at once.
- Sting was inside the mouth.
- Swelling is huge.
- Sting looks infected.

Home Care Tips

- If there is a stinger present, remove it by scraping it out of the skin with a credit card, or fingernail.
- Do not squeeze the area because this will inject more venom into your child from the sac at the top of the stinger.
- After the stinger has been removed, rub an ice cube over the site for fifteen minutes.
- Apply cool compresses to the sting area to provide relief.
- Give acetaminophen or ibuprofen for pain relief.
- If the itching is severe, give diphenhydramine by mouth in the proper dose for your child's weight.

Folk remedies for relief from insect stings

- Apply a paste made of meat tenderizer and water over the sting site.
- Squeeze a fresh lime over the sting area.
- Make a paste of baking soda and water and apply it for twenty minutes, held in place with a moist washcloth.
- Make a thick paste of three tablespoons of cornstarch and one tablespoon of white vinegar. Paint it over the sting and leave it on until it dries.

Additional Information

A child who has had an allergic reaction to a stinging insect should wear a medical alert bracelet or some kind of identification indicating the allergy. Never let him play alone outdoors, and keep a *"bee sting kit"* handy. The bee sting kit usually has the medicine *epinephrine* (in the correct dose for your child's weight) in a special syringe ready for injection. You should make this emergency kit available to your child's day care provider and preschool, and make sure that the adults in those settings as well as all babysitters are instructed how to use it.

Bacteria under the fingernails can easily contaminate a scratched open area; if your child scratches a sting too much, she can develop a bacterial infection such as impetigo.

See Related Areas

Allergies, Bites—Insect and Tick, Hives, Impetigo, Puncture Wounds, Rashes.

STINGS—JELLYFISH

Definition

Most jellyfish stings occur when the ocean water gets warmer and jellyfish come in closer to shore. You can't avoid them in the water because they are extremely difficult to see. Heed lifeguard warnings on days when jellyfish are plentiful and avoid the water completely if there are warnings of Portuguese man-of-war jellyfish, as their stings are extremely painful and sometimes toxic.

What to Do

- Remove any remains of jellyfish (tentacles or clear Jell-O–like crystals).
- Follow Home Care Tips.

When to Call Your Doctor

Immediately

- Wheezing or difficulty breathing.
- Tightness in the chest or throat.
- Loss of consciousness or your child has fainted or passed out.
- Previous allergic reaction to a sting.
- Your child has been stung multiple times or by a Portuguese man-of-war jellyfish.
- Extreme swelling.

Home Care Tips

- Use a towel or a stick to remove any jellyfish remains. Do not use your bare hands because you may receive remains of the venom.
- After you are sure that all remains have been removed from the skin, wash the area with soap and water if available.
- Apply ice or cold compresses to relieve the pain.

Folk Remedies for jellyfish stings

- Make a paste of meat tenderizer and water and apply directly to the sting area.
- Apply a compress soaked in vinegar on the sting area. (There are vinegar stations on the beaches in Australia, near the lifeguard chairs, to treat jellyfish stings on the beach.)
- Make a paste of baking soda and water and apply to the sting area. After it dries, scrape it away removing any remaining remnants of jellyfish.

Additional Information

Jellyfish stings are very painful and can keep discharging venom into the skin until they are totally removed. Some children will have an allergic reaction to a jellyfish sting, and if your child has one, always keep identification on him or near him with this information.

See Related Areas

Allergies, Rashes.

SUNBURN

Definition

Sunburn is a common, painful skin condition that results from overexposure to sunlight or a sunlamp. The skin is tender, red, warm to the touch, and may be quite painful. Most sunburns are first-degree burns; however, prolonged sun exposure can cause blisters or a second-degree burn.

What to Do

- Check for fever and treat if present.
- Give your child extra fluids to drink.
- Follow Home Care Tips.
- Prevention is best. Routinely apply sunscreen on your child when he is playing outdoors; use sunblock (usually containing zinc oxide) if he is sensitive to sun exposure.

When to Call Your Doctor

- Your child has fainted or is too weak to stand.
- There are a lot of blisters.
- Your child is unable to look at lights because of eye pain.
- Your child is under one year old, and the sunburn covers an area more than five times the size of your baby's palm.
- The sunburn looks infected, for example draining pus, red streaks, or extreme tenderness and swelling.
- Your child shows symptoms of *sun poisoning* including rash, chills, fever, and nausea, and sunburn is extensive including blisters.

- Your child shows signs of dehydration such as dry mouth, no tears, or no urine for eight hours.

Home Care Tips

- Give acetaminophen or ibuprofen (in the proper dose) for pain relief. Ibuprofen is also helpful in reducing swelling because of its anti-inflammatory effects.
- Give lots of cool liquids and Popsicles to replace fluids absorbed by the sunburn and to prevent dehydration and dizziness.
- Have your child take a cool bath or use cool compresses several times a day to reduce pain and swelling. Add two ounces of baking soda to the tub for a soothing effect, and always avoid soap on a sunburn as it can irritate.
- Leave blisters intact. If any break, you may trim the extra skin and apply an over-the-counter antibiotic cream to decrease infection.
- Apply a 1 percent hydrocortisone cream to the sunburn. If used early and three times a day for two days, it may reduce swelling and pain.

Additional Information

The pain and swelling from sunburn start at approximately four hours after exposure, peak at twenty-four hours, and will begin to improve after forty-eight hours. Use comfort measures after prolonged sun exposure to ease your child's pain. As healing begins, the upper layer of skin starts to peel. This layer—which was injured by the sun's ultraviolet rays—falls off to make room for new, healthy skin. Peeling begins three to ten days after a sunburn and ends when the skin is fully healed, usually within a week.

Anyone can be sunburned, and getting too much sun can be dangerous—especially for children. Infants, young children, and light-skinned, fair-haired people are particularly susceptible, but even children with dark skin need protection. Practice prevention by avoiding overexposure and using sunscreens and sunblock. When taking your baby or young child outside, be sure that his skin is covered and that he is wearing a wide-brimmed hat. Remember to reapply sunscreen lotions throughout your child's sun exposure, particularly after swimming. It's also a good idea to avoid the bright sunlight of the day between 11 A.M. and 2 P.M. Use sun protection on cloudy days, too, as the sun can be every bit as strong.

Some medications can also increase your child's sensitivity to sunlight. Check with your doctor if your child is taking any medicines and carefully read all non-prescription medicine labels.

See Related Areas

Dehydration, Fever, Rashes.

TOOTH TRAUMA

Definition

An injury to the jaw can damage teeth by fracture, displacement, or loss of a tooth. Injuries also can cause the teeth to become tender and sensitive to touch, heat, or cold. A dentist should attend any injuries to permanent teeth immediately—and as soon as possible for any injuries to primary or "baby" teeth. Injuries to baby teeth may influence the permanent teeth if they interfere with the root.

What to Do

- Call a pediatric dentist or your local emergency room for more severe problems.
- If a tooth is loose, try to reposition it with gentle pressure.
- Displaced or knocked-out teeth should be attended to immediately. Put a knocked-out tooth back into the tooth socket and hold it there until you can get to a dentist. If this is not possible, place the tooth in milk and take it with you to the dentist or emergency room for reimplantation.
- Use pressure to stop bleeding. (A facecloth in the mouth works well.)
- Check for a fever if you suspect an abscess.

When to Call Your Doctor

- A permanent tooth has been knocked out or injured.
- For referral to a dentist.
- Your child has fever or facial swelling.
- You are unsure what to do.

Home Care Tips

- Use acetaminophen or ibuprofen in the dose appropriate to your child's weight to relieve pain.
- Apply an ice pack to the area of the jaw that seems to·be painful, for twenty minutes at a time to increase comfort.
- Have your child wear appropriate protective gear for sports and athletic activities to prevent tooth injury.

Additional Information

Injury to a tooth or surrounding bone may cause loosening, dislocation, or fracture. For a tooth to be successfully reimplanted, it should be done within two hours of injury.

See Related Areas

Facial Injuries, Toothache.

CHAPTER FIVE

Emergency Situations

True emergencies are best handled by experts: however, there are situations in which your quick actions could save your child's life. Every parent should be able to do the following:

- Recognize an emergency situation.
- Distinguish between a medical problem that you can treat at home and one that needs emergency attention.
- Initiate treatment for life-threatening problems while help is on the way.

Children are naturally curious and also often unaware of danger. This makes them prone to accidents. When you approach your child in a potential emergency situation, *stay calm so that you do not create panic in your child.* You need to act quickly and effectively.

RECOGNIZING AN EMERGENCY

There are situations when *emergency medical help* is required. These are usually readily apparent. We have put together a short list of examples concerning when *you should call 911 or an emergency rescue service* or take your child to the nearest hospital emergency room. These include:

- Your child has *stopped breathing* or is *breathing with tremendous difficulty* and his lips are turning blue. He may be working hard to breathe but doesn't seem to be able to catch his breath.
- Your child is *behaving in a very unusual way,* and his level of awareness or activity is markedly decreased. He may have an *altered state of alertness* or be difficult to arouse and seem *close to unconsciousness.*

- Your child's heart has stopped beating.
- Your child has *a burn* that is bigger than a quarter, or your child was trapped for even a few seconds in a room or building that caught on fire.
- Your child has *a deep cut that will not stop bleeding* after applying direct pressure for thirty minutes, or seems to be bleeding excessively.
- Your child has fallen from a significant height and appears to have deformed limbs.

There are many other circumstances when the degree of seriousness isn't as clear-cut. If your child has any of the following symptoms, *call your doctor immediately* and whenever in doubt, trust your instincts and call your doctor.

- *Sick newborn* (any baby less than one month old who appears sick).
- *Severe pain* and child doesn't want to be touched or held.
- Drooling and *difficulty swallowing*.
- *Stiff neck;* a child over the age of three cannot touch his chin to his chest.
- *Suspected serious neck injury.*
- Child *can't walk* (after he has learned to walk).
- Extreme fatigue, too *weak* to cry, *floppy*, or *hard to wake up*.
- *Purple or blood-red spots* on the skin.
- The symptoms are persistent and don't seem to be getting better.
- The symptoms are changing and there are new symptoms, or they are getting worse.
- Your child looks or behaves sicker than he ever has before.

If these signs and symptoms appear during your doctor's office hours, she may arrange for your child to be seen in an "urgent care" office. In this case, your child will be examined by a physician or pediatric nurse practitioner who will evaluate your child. After your doctor's office hours, utilize your emergency medical services or the closest hospital emergency room.

ABC'S

The first course of action when you see an emergency is to perform a quick scene survey. Check the area for immediate danger to the child and yourself. If you can safely approach the victim, check the *ABC's*. This stands for *Airway, Breathing, Circulation* (pulse). Trouble within these areas usually indicates an emergency.

First look for a *clear airway* and *normal breathing*. Look at your child's chest to see movement of rise and fall with each breath. Listen for normal or abnormal breathing noises. Feel for air movement by placing your hand near your child's mouth.

Then check circulation by feeling for your child's *pulse* or *heartbeat*. You can put your ear to your child's chest to listen for a heartbeat or feel the child's neck for a carotid pulse or wrist for a radial pulse. (See Figures 5.1a and 5.1b.) Even if you feel a pulse, check whether it is a very fast or very slow pulse. Feel your child's hands and feet for warmth. Look at her skin color. You don't want to see a blue or gray color that might indicate decreased oxygen circulating in your child's body. Also under circulation, check for any *bleeding*. If your child is unconscious, check for breathing and a pulse. Again, check for any bleeding.

If your child can't move, don't attempt to move him yourself; call for help. Compare one side of his body to the other. Problems with any of the ABC's generally indicate an emergency.

Know how to contact the *emergency medical service* in your area. In many areas, it's *911*.

In a true emergency, you will not have time to consult a book. We recommend that all parents and caregivers take a course in *Cardiopulmonary resuscitation* (CPR). CPR training courses are offered by the Red Cross, American Heart Association, and many local hospital and community groups. CPR combines rescue or mouth-to-mouth breathing (See Figure 5.2a) with chest compression (See Figure 5.2b) to get the heart pumping again. Use CPR when someone's breathing and heart have stopped. You need only use rescue breathing if he has a pulse (heartbeat) but is not breathing. If you have

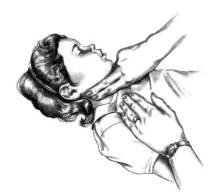

Figure 5.1a: Carotid pulse
Find the Adam's apple and move two fingers to the side, to the groove between the Adam's apple and the neck muscle. Press in.

Figure 5.1b: Radial pulse
Find the bone on the thumb side of your child's wrist. Press in with your fingers.

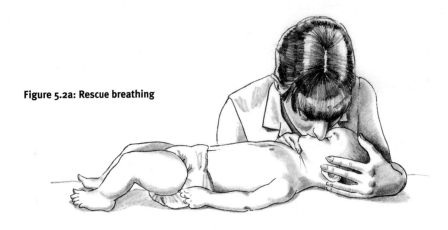

Figure 5.2a: Rescue breathing

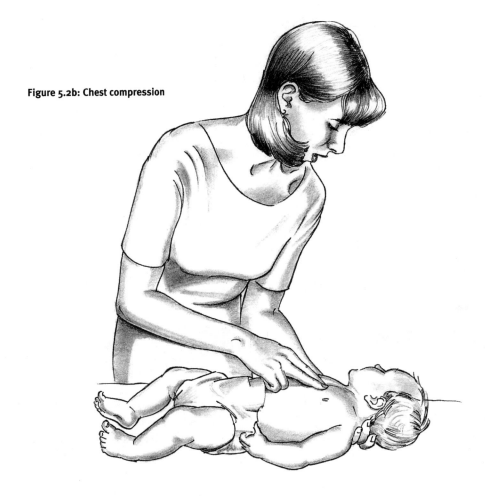

Figure 5.2b: Chest compression

been trained in CPR, you may start it when appropriate; otherwise it's best to activate your emergency medical system and get help as soon as possible.

When you call 911 or your emergency medical service, be sure to have as much information ready as possible, including the following:

- Victim's location. Give street address, landmarks, etc.
- Your phone number and name.
- Tell what happened to the best of your knowledge including the victim's condition—consciousness, breathing, pulse, bleeding, bone protruding, unable to move, etc.
- Number of people needing help.

Do not hang up the phone until the dispatcher has all the information she needs.

AIRWAY

The airway consists of the passages between your child's nose, mouth, and lungs. If your child is unconscious, her tongue may have slipped back and blocked her airway.

To open up your child's airway, lay your child on a firm surface. Place one hand on her forehead and the other under her neck. Press gently on the forehead and tilt the head back. (see Figure 5.3.) Babies have very short necks and soft windpipes. Be careful not to tilt a baby's forehead back too far. You know it is in the right position when you can see directly down her nostrils. Take your hand from behind her neck and lift the bony part of her jaw up so her chin pushes forward. This will also bring the tongue

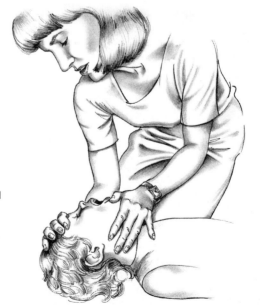

Figure 5.3: How to open your child's airway
Open your child's airway by pushing back the forehead slightly and lifting up the bony part of the jaw.

up and open her airway. Check again for breathing. If your child is still not breathing after you have tilted her head back and opened up her airway, take a look inside her mouth to see if there is something blocking it. Turn your child's head to the side. Carefully, put your index finger in her mouth and run it along the inside. Quickly remove anything you feel. Be careful not to push anything further down her throat. With a very young baby, don't put your finger inside her mouth unless you can see something there and you are sure there is no risk of pushing it further down the throat. If you expect that your child has choked on something, see Choking.

ANAPHYLAXIS

Anaphylaxis, or *shock*, is a severe, life-threatening reaction characterized by a variety of symptoms. The most common ones include:

- Generalized hives.
- Severe swelling of the eyes, skin, tongue, or throat.
- Difficulty breathing.
- Wheezing.
- Nausea and/or vomiting.
- Diarrhea.
- Low blood pressure.
- Fainting.
- Heart rhythm disturbances.

These reactions occur within minutes of eating or exposure to an offending substance. Substances that commonly cause this kind of very serious and life-threatening allergic reaction include:

- Foods such as peanuts, shellfish, milk, eggs, and fish.
- Medicines such as penicillin, aspirin, and drugs containing sulfa.
- Venom from the stings or bites of insects such as honeybees, yellow jackets, hornets, wasps, or fire ants.

If you think that your child is having an anaphylactic reaction, call 911 or your emergency medical response system immediately.

BLEEDING

If blood is spurting out or pooling around your child, act at once. Put direct pressure over the bleeding area with a clean cloth. If none is available, use your fingers or the palm of your hand. *Raise the injured area* above her heart level if possible and *press hard* directly on the wound. Also, try to press the injured area against the underlying bone. *Do not use a tourniquet.* Direct pressure for at least fifteen minutes is often needed. If it doesn't stop within thirty minutes, or if blood seems to be spurting out, get professional medical help. Keep putting pressure directly over the bleeding area while you call or send someone else to call your emergency medical services for further assistance.

CARBON MONOXIDE POISONING

Produced by burning fuels such as gas, wood, kerosene, or oil, carbon monoxide is a very dangerous gas that has no color, taste, or smell. Babies and young children are poisoned more quickly than adults, and symptoms are similar to the flu. They include:

- Headache.
- Fatigue.
- Shortness of breath.
- Weakness.
- Dizziness.
- Nausea.
- Confusion.
- Loss of muscle control.
- Vision problems.

If you or your child have any of these symptoms and you think there is a chance of carbon monoxide poisoning, *get out of your house (or automobile) immediately and call 911 or your emergency medical service.* You should also consider installing a carbon monoxide detector in your home.

CHOKING

Choking occurs when the airway is blocked by a foreign object. Babies and young children tend to put everything in their mouths, so it's imperative that you keep small objects out of reach. Choking (especially in children under the age of five) is caused most often by either a bit of round, hard food, or a small toy. Hot dogs are the most common food that children choke on, so always cut them in small pieces, not round slices. Thickly spread chunky peanut butter is also known to be a common choking hazard in young children. The most common toy that causes choking in a child is a broken or deflated balloon. These are a particular hazard because they are so difficult to dislodge.

You can recognize partial airway obstruction in your child from coughing, a high-pitched noise, or skin that is ashen in color. (On dark-skinned children, an ashen color is best seen on the lips and inside the mouth.) More complete obstruction is present when your child is unable to speak or cry, breathe or cough. Usually a person choking clutches his throat with one or both hands.

If your child is under the age of one, place her face

Figure 5.4: Removing a foreign object for children under twelve months of age

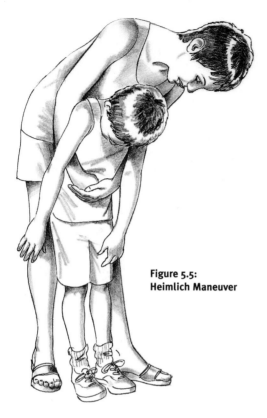

Figure 5.5:
Heimlich Maneuver

down across your arm or your knee and give five sharp thrusts between the shoulders until the object is coughed out. (See Figure 5.4.)

You also should know how to give abdominal thrusts—the *Heimlich Maneuver*. Stand behind your child using your own body to help support him in a standing position. Place one finger on the belly button and with the other hand find the edge of your child's rib cage. This is the spot for your fist. Wrap your arms around him. Place one closed fist (thumb toward the body) in the spot you just found. Grab and cover this fist with your other hand. Keep your elbows pointed out away from his body. Give three thrusts inward and upward toward the head. (See Figure 5.5.)

CLOTHES ON FIRE

The tendency is for a child to run when her clothes catch on fire; however, this only fans the flames and causes them to spread. Instead, throw her down on the ground and roll her over and over to smother the flames. You can also try smothering the flames with a blanket, coat, or any large, heavy fabric. If you cover her quickly and completely, the flames will extinguish without burning you. Remove the child's clothing as soon as possible, cover your child with a sheet or blanket, and call your emergency medical services. With an older child, teach her to *stop, drop, and roll* in case her clothes ever catch on fire. Practice doing this at least once a year during fire prevention week, or after a family fire drill.

DROWNING

Quickly pull the child from the water. Hold her tilted head over your arm to help water drain out. For a bigger child, lay her on her side. If the child is not breathing, start rescue breathing at once. Open the airway by lifting up the jaw and pushing back the forehead. (See Figure 5.3.)

For babies, cover the nose and mouth with your own mouth and administer two slow breaths into the child's airway. Look to see the child's chest rise and fall. If it doesn't, check the position and make sure that you have a tight seal over the baby's nose and mouth so that air can get in. Then give short gentle puffs of air every three seconds. For an older child, position the head the same way, then pinch the nose and tightly seal the child's mouth with your own. Again, give two slow breaths and look to see if the child's chest rises and falls. Continue giving short, gentle puffs of air every three to four seconds until the child starts breathing on her own or until emergency medical help arrives.

ELECTRIC SHOCK

If your child comes in contact with a live electrical wire, he becomes part of the circuit. Don't touch him. Switch off the power at the source. If that is not possible, use a dry, nonmetallic object such as a broom or cushion to move the wire away from the child. In the meantime, call for help. Your child needs emergency medical help and transportation to the closest emergency room where he may receive a thorough examination for internal injuries.

FALLS FROM HEIGHT

Falls are a part of life for children—and one of the biggest causes of injuries. Of concern are falls from a height greater than the height of your child. Babies and small children are particularly at risk of falling out of windows. A screen will not protect your baby from falls, so install window guards on all windows above the first floor.

An emergency situation will arise when the fall is from a substantial height and you suspect head trauma, spinal cord injury, internal bleeding, or broken bones. Warning signs include:

- Altered state of consciousness or confusion and disorientation.
- Slurred speech.
- Persistent vomiting and weakness.
- Abnormal gait if he can get up and walk.
- Severe headache.
- Bleeding from the ear or bruising behind the ear.
- Inability to move extremities symmetrically.
- Tender, localized swelling of a body part.
- Severe pain.

If any of these symptoms are present, do not move your child unless she is in a hazardous location. Call 911 or your emergency medical service and get professional help as soon as possible.

Follow the ABC's discussed on page 210 and check your child's airway, breathing, and circulation. Cover her with a blanket, try to keep calm, and stay with her until help arrives. In hot weather, be aware of the possibility of heat exhaustion. In cold weather be aware of hypothermia. If you suspect a spinal cord injury, do not move your child. Do not attempt to take off any helmet she may be wearing.

HEAD INJURY

Children frequently fall and hit their heads. Most of the time the result is only a bump and/or a mild headache. If you suspect anything more, treat it as an emergency. A serious head injury or *concussion* may result in unconsciousness, dizziness, or vomiting. If your child has any bleeding or drainage from his ears or nose after a blow to his head this may indicate a *skull fracture.* Possible symptoms of a serious head injury include:

- Unconsciousness.
- Headache.
- Confused or dazed state.
- Extreme sleepiness or drowsiness.
- Vomiting.
- Discharge of blood or clear yellow fluid from the nose or ears.

If your child complains of a headache but seems alert, have her lie down and rest. But watch her closely to make sure that she does not lose consciousness. If there is an open wound, there will probably be a lot of bleeding, so apply direct pressure over the wound. If you have trouble stopping the bleeding, you should take her to the nearest emergency room for evaluation.

HOUSE FIRE

In a house fire, the most important thing is to *get out of the house—fast.* Check a closed door for heat. If it is hot, do not open it; use your alternate exit from the room instead. *Never go back for anything.* Have a designated meeting place for your family when everyone gets out. Report the fire from a neighbor's house. If you or your child have been in a house fire and in a closed room, have the paramedics take you to the nearest emergency room to be certain that there is no airway damage and no carbon monoxide poisoning.

To ensure you are alerted to a possible house fire, especially when you are asleep, make sure your smoke detector is working, and change the batteries every time you change the clocks for daylight saving time. Have fire drills in your house and practice leaving the house and meeting at a special place. Emphasize to your children the importance of getting out of the house and not going back for pets or special toys. In the event of a house fire, your best chance for the survival of your family is to have a plan of escape ready—and practice it.

SWALLOWING A POISONOUS SUBSTANCE

If you think your child has eaten something poisonous, find the original container and check the label for its ingredients. *Call your poison control center immediately* and tell them what you think your child has swallowed. Always keep the telephone number of your poison control center with your emergency telephone numbers near your main telephone. If it was something that he ate outside, take a sample of a few of the leaves or berries. If he has swallowed a medicine, save the container and label even if it is empty.

Some possible symptoms that your child has swallowed a poison include:

- Empty or open container known to have poison in it near your child.
- Burns around his mouth if he has ingested a corrosive poison.
- Convulsions for no apparent reason.
- Poisonous leaves or berries near your child.
- Vomiting and diarrhea.

If your child has swallowed a possible corrosive substance such as bleach, lye, plant food, or weedkiller, do not try to make him vomit. Anything that burns going down will burn going up. Get him to the emergency room immediately.

Quickly ask your child to tell you what he has eaten in case he later becomes unconscious. If you are certain it was not a corrosive poison that he swallowed, ask the poison control center about giving him syrup of ipecac. If your child is unconscious, put him in the "recovery position" (see Figure 5.6, page 221) to keep his airway open. Then call 911 or your local emergency medical service.

UNCONSCIOUSNESS

Call your emergency medical services immediately. You can tell she is unconscious if she fails to respond when called by name in a loud voice, tapped on the chest, or shaken gently as you would to wake someone up. Do not move the child unless she is in an unsafe location. Loosen her clothing (especially around the neck and waist) and raise her legs.

Unless you suspect a serious head injury or spinal cord injury, place your child in the recovery position. Position her on the side or stomach with her head turned to the side, in order to prevent her from choking on saliva.

Figure 5.6: Recovery position

CHAPTER SIX

Newborn Care and Concerns

Not many years ago, new mothers and their babies were routinely kept in the hospital for a full week after birth. Now many babies and moms go home in less than twenty-four hours, and so it's more important than ever that both parents understand the principles of caring for their newborn. If this is your first baby, always try to choose his doctor, pediatrician, or family physician before delivery. It's also good idea to meet with the doctor during the last trimester of your pregnancy for what is called a prenatal visit, and often this visit is without charge.

While you are still in the hospital, take time to closely examine your baby and ask the staff any questions you may have. If possible, be present with your doctor for the newborn's physical exam. When you leave the hospital, make a list of telephone numbers of people you can call for help, and a list of questions as you begin to care for your baby. Be certain to get the phone number of the nurses at the newborn nursery; they are particularly helpful at helping to determine what is going on with your baby during that often scary first week at home. (See Table 6.1.)

This chapter has been prepared as an aid and immediate source of information to help you care for your new baby during the first four weeks of life. It will not replace your baby's doctor but will help you answer common questions and organize your thoughts when you do need to call your doctor. In general:

- Trust your instincts.
- Look at your baby as an individual and figure out his patterns.
- Use written instructions as a guideline and adapt them to your baby.
- Recognize that at times you may be unsure of what to do and realize that this is normal.
- Call your baby's doctor and/or the hospital nursery with your questions.
- Relax and enjoy your baby!

The rest of this chapter is arranged in alphabetical order listing common terms and potential problems associated with new babies. If you cannot find the term you are looking for, please consult the index. For more detailed information about specific symptoms associated with illness, please refer back to chapters 2 and 3. Remember though: *If you think your newborn is sick, call your doctor immediately!*

Table 6.1

Important Phone Numbers
The Baby's Doctor: _____
The Baby's Doctor: _____
The Hospital's Newborn Nursery: _____
The Hospital's Newborn Nursery: _____
A 24-Hour Pharmacy: _____
A 24-Hour Pharmacy: _____
Emergency Transportation: _____
Emergency Transportation: _____
Closest Hospital Emergency Room: _____
Closest Hospital Emergency Room: _____

APGAR SCORE

The Apgar score is a quick early reference of your baby's condition immediately after birth. It was developed by Dr. Virginia Apgar as a practical guide for assessing how a newborn is adjusting to life outside the womb. The test is conducted at three specific times: *one minute after birth, five minutes after birth, and again at ten minutes after birth.* There are five areas the doctor looks at to determine the Apgar Score:

- **Appearance** or the baby's color.
- **Pulse** or the heart rate.
- **Grimace** or reflex irritability in response to stimulation of the sole of the foot or **Grasp** reflex of the hand.

- Activity level or muscle tone.
- Respiration or breathing effort.

A score of zero to two is given for each of these areas. Zero indicates some lack in a criteria, and two indicates a high score. The doctor is mostly assessing transition—he wants the score to improve from the first measurement to the last. A low score doesn't necessarily mean something is wrong, but it will alert the medical staff that they need to conduct a particularly close observation. The baby's doctor will also be made aware of the Apgar score for future follow-up.

APPEARANCE OF NEWBORNS

Newborn babies often look a bit odd at first, but many of these newborn characteristics are temporary. For example, your newborn's face may be puffy. Her nose may be flattened and her ears pressed tight to her head. Her head may look unusually large and even be cone-shaped at first. She may have soft bumps (swelling) under the scalp. This elongation and swelling of the skull occur as a result of "molding" during passage through the birth canal. The important thing is not to worry—your baby will look more like the babies in books after a week or two.

Examine your baby very carefully soon after birth. Ask questions about anything that looks unusual to you. You need to have a baseline reference regarding how your baby looks so that you can note any changes in appearance as they occur. For example:

Color

Your baby's skin should be soft and smooth with pink or peach hues after the initial adjustment period is over. Sometimes in light-skinned babies the hands and feet may be slightly paler for a few days due to sluggish circulation. In babies with darker skin tones, the hands and feet may remain slightly paler. This is unrelated to the baby's circulation and solely concerns normal pigmentation. (See also Skin and Rashes.)

Skin

Some babies are born with a cheesy white covering on their bodies. This is called *vernix caseosa* and it protects their skin while they are in utero. It will disappear within a few hours of birth. Some babies are also born with fine hair called *lanugo* covering their shoulders and back. This hair usually disappears once they reach three months of age.

Head

Your baby's head accounts for approximately one-quarter of his body length at birth. The baby's skull bones are joined by soft connective tissue that allows them to overlap slightly so that the head can fit through the birth canal. Some babies may have a slightly cone-shaped head shortly after birth because of this. Don't be alarmed. Within a few days, your baby's head will be the usual rounded shape. There are two "soft spots" or *fontanelles* where the bones of your baby's head have not yet come together. The front or *anterior fontanelle* is diamond-shaped and located right at the top of the head. It usually closes by age one, although in a few cases it may remain open until age fifteen to eighteen months. The back or *posterior fontanelle* is shaped more like a triangle and is much smaller. It is located just above the bulge in the back of the head. It usually closes by two months of age. You may occasionally notice these soft spots throbbing. Don't worry. They are covered by a strong membrane, and there is no danger associated with normal handling.

Eyes

All babies are born with a shade of blue or blue-gray eyes. It will be three to six months or longer before their true color is apparent. Babies can see right away and see best at a distance of approximately twelve inches. Studies have shown that newborns prefer to look at human faces, particularly their parents'. Sometimes you may see a little bleeding in the whites of your baby's eyes right after birth. This is from the birth process and isn't anything to worry about. (Refer to the section on Jaundice if you see any yellow color in the white part of your baby's eyes.)

BATHING YOUR BABY

In the hospital, your baby will be cleaned as soon as he warms up after birth, and then bathed as he needs it. Once you are home, you will need to set up a routine that works for your household. Some parents choose to bathe their baby every day; generally, a complete bath two to three times a week is fine. Keep the water level below the belly button or give sponge baths until a few days after the umbilical cord has fallen off. Getting it a little wet will not cause any problems, but submerging the cord may interfere with its drying and could cause infection. The diaper area should be washed with each diaper change, and his face should be washed as needed throughout the day to prevent irritation from feeding.

For a complete bath, pick a warm area in your home. Many parents use the wash basin from the hospital or a baby bath. Be sure to check the water temperature with the inside of your wrist before you put your baby in to make sure it is not too hot. The rule of thumb is to bathe the baby "from clean to dirty." Start with the eyes and face and finish with the rectum. Some parents like to spread the bath over a few days. Wash the head and hair one day, the body the next, and the arms and legs the next. The first few times you bathe your baby you may want to have another person help until you gain your confidence. Remember, just be organized and gentle—and you will do fine. During cold weather, you may want to give your baby a sponge bath rather than total immersion.

Don't answer the phone and try not to be interrupted while you are bathing your baby. You want to be as efficient as possible. *Never leave a newborn or young child alone in a bath.* If you must leave the room for any reason (i.e., to answer the telephone or the doorbell), wrap up your baby in a warm towel and take him with you. As your baby gets bigger and is able to sit up, bath times will be correspondingly longer with more time for play. Be sure to cover the faucet with a protective padded cover, available at toy and baby stores.

Table 6.2

For a Complete Baby Bath

- Select a warm room or area.
- Gather all your supplies:
  - mild soap
  - baby shampoo
  - soft facecloth and towel
  - basin or baby bath
  - small cup of water for hair washes
  - soft hairbrush
- Fill the baby's bathtub or hospital basin half-full with warm, not hot water. Feel the water temperature before you put your baby in to be sure it is not too hot or too cold.
- Sit your baby in the water, holding him with your hand at his back and under his arms.
- Wash eyes and face first and then proceed down the body. Wash diaper area last.
- Use a cup to wet hair. Scrub gently with mild baby shampoo. Use a soft brush on your baby's scalp if you notice any cradle cap. Rinse with water in cup.
- Take baby out of bath and wrap in a towel. Towel-dry quickly so that baby does not become cold. Dress as appropriate to weather.
- **NEVER LEAVE YOUR BABY ALONE IN OR NEAR WATER.**

BEHAVIOR OF NEWBORNS

Some newborn behaviors may look a little odd to you, but they are normal for new babies and usually are not signs of any problems or areas of concern. A newborn has an immature nervous system and exhibits many jerky movements and reflexes that in most cases are completely normal.

Breathing

Babies normally *breathe much faster than adults*, sometimes taking forty to sixty breaths per minute. They also may have an irregular breathing pattern and *make a lot of noise when they breathe*, especially when they are asleep. Babies pant and can stop breathing for three or four seconds at a time.

An irregular breathing pattern is normal if:

- your baby is content.
- the rate is less than sixty breaths per minute.
- a pause is less than six seconds.
- your baby does not turn blue or have a bluish color to her lips and nails.

Occasionally, babies will take rapid, progressively deeper breaths to fully expand the lungs. This range of breathing is normal.

Noises

In addition to breathing noises, you may also hear gurgling noises due to secretions in the throat.

Hiccoughs (or Hiccups)

Occasionally babies have hiccoughs. Your baby might even have had them while he was still in your uterus. Hiccoughs are common when the baby swallows a lot of air, and they often occur after feedings. They may last as long as ten minutes but will go away on their own. Burping the baby, giving a pacifier or bottle or breast may help, but sometimes hiccoughs just have to run their course.

Trembling

Chin trembling, lower lip quivering, and jitteriness of arms and legs during crying are all normal newborn behaviors. These type of movements will decrease as the nervous system matures.

Yawning

Yawning is normal and doesn't necessarily mean that your baby is tired; he may just be taking a big breath.

Also see Reflexes.

BIRTHMARKS

A birthmark is a discoloration or raised area on the skin. Birthmarks are very common and most go away on their own. Some of the common birthmarks are "stork bites," "strawberry hemangiomas," and "mongolian spots."

Stork Bites

You may notice reddish-purple spots on the eyelids, nose, or the back of the neck that almost look like a rash. These skin discolorations are birthmarks called stork bites. They usually fade during the first year.

Strawberry Hemangioma

This is a raised, red birthmark that resembles a strawberry. It usually grows darker for a period of months and then disappears.

Port Wine Stain

A port wine stain is a purple-reddish patch that may be slightly raised. It frequently appears on the face and limbs and is more common in children with blond hair. It may fade, but it does not go away.

Mongolian Spots

This bluish-gray flat birthmark resembles a bruise and usually appears on the lower back or buttocks. It is more common on children with darker skin and usually fades after two years.

Congenital Nevus

A nevus is similar to an ordinary brown mole but is present at birth. It may be accompanied by hair. It will not go away and should be surgically removed before adolescence. Some nevi can, in fact, develop into melanoma.

BOWEL MOVEMENTS

For the first day or so, your baby will have very dark, tar-colored, sticky bowel movements called *meconium*. This substance filled the intestines in utero and is quickly excreted. Afterward, if you are bottle-feeding your baby, the bowel movements become green and then yellow. After your baby has begun taking one to two ounces of formula at each feeding, she may also have a bowel movement after each feeding, and have as many as six movements a day. Often with bottle-fed babies, this settles down after a short while and may decrease to as little as one bowel movement a day. Do not worry as long as they remain soft each time.

Breast-fed babies start out the same as bottle-fed babies with dark, tar-colored meconium stool. Stools then will turn mustard color and be loose and seedy looking. For the first six weeks, your baby's bowel movements will be fairly frequent, often six times a day or after each feeding as with bottle-fed babies. After about six weeks of age, they may begin to decrease. Occasionally, there are breast-fed babies who will have a normal bowel movement only once every three days or so. Do not worry as long as the movement is not very hard. If a baby is receiving only breast milk, she is unlikely to become constipated.

Many babies will cry or appear to strain when they are having a bowel movement. If the movement is relatively soft, do not worry. For the first one to two weeks, your newborn's bowel movements will be soft and sometimes runny. Sometime after this, infants begin to develop firmer bowel movements. *It is very unusual for a baby to become constipated.* Iron in the formula may harden the bowel movement, but that shouldn't cause you to stop the iron. There are easy ways to soften a bowel movement such as adding a little table sugar to the formula. Discuss this with your doctor if it is a concern. Some babies cry with every bowel movement even when the consistency is soft and normal. However, if you feel your baby is constipated, discuss the possibility with your baby's physician.

BURPING

Burping gets rid of air swallowed from sucking or crying. Bottle-fed babies take more air in when feeding than do breast-fed babies. If your baby swallows a lot of air while feeding, he may think his stomach is full and stop taking formula. If the air is released by burping, there may be room for more milk. Generally, newborn babies should be burped after they take one to two ounces or when switched from one breast to the other. Occasionally, a baby should be burped before feeding if he has been crying and swallowing air.

In general, there are three positions for burping your baby:

- Hold your baby against your chest and gently rub his back. (See Figure 6.1a.)
- Sit your baby on your lap with your dominant hand supporting his chin and gently rub his back. (See Figure 6.1b.)
- Lay your baby across your lap and gently rub his back.

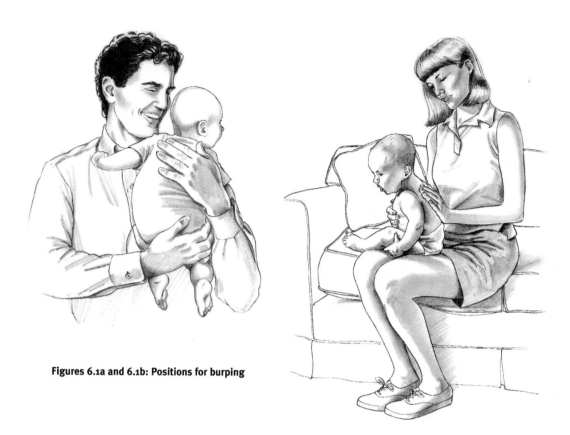

Figures 6.1a and 6.1b: Positions for burping

If he won't burp, lay him on his stomach for a few minutes and then pick him up and try again. Sometimes this causes air bubbles to shift and come up. Occasionally, babies don't need to burp, especially if they are breast-fed; don't struggle for more than ten minutes. And don't worry if your baby doesn't burp easily; after a few weeks, you'll get to know your baby's pattern and be quite proficient.

CAR SAFETY

All babies and children under forty pounds must be buckled into appropriate car seats when riding in an automobile. For the first year or until your baby weighs twenty pounds, an infant, rear-facing car seat should be used. (See Figure 6.2.) Most often they should be placed in the back seat of the car. Infant car seats should never be used where there is an air bag because there is a real danger of the baby suffocating should the bag inflate. A special clip must be used when car seats are restrained using the lap shoulder

harness-type seat belt. Read all the directions on your baby's car seat and from your automobile owners' manual to make sure that the car seats are installed correctly. Always complete and return the product's registration card to ensure that you are contacted in the event of a recall.

· If you need to pick up your child to feed or comfort him, pull over to a rest stop or a safe area off the road. Babies and young children should not ride in cars unless they are buckled into the proper safety restraint.

Figure 6.2: Rear-facing car seat

CIRCUMCISION

Circumcision is the surgical removal of the skin at the tip of the penis (foreskin). This procedure is done for religious or social reasons, or personal preference. If you choose a nonritual circumcision for your newborn son, it can usually be done before you leave the hospital. The doctor may advise you to apply Vaseline or an antibiotic ointment to the circumcised area with each diaper change for the first twenty-four hours after the procedure. No other treatment is usually needed as the area heals. If you notice redness beyond the circumcised area, yellow discharge, pus, or a bad odor, call your doctor. (See Figure 6.3.)

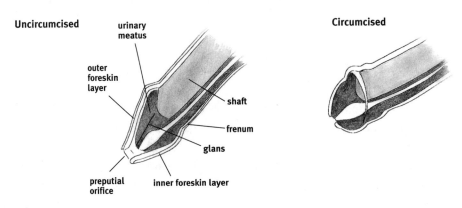

Uncircumcised — urinary meatus — outer foreskin layer — shaft — frenum — glans — inner foreskin layer — preputial orifice

Circumcised

Figures 6.3

COLDS AND RUNNY NOSES

Babies are nose breathers and do not know how to breathe out of their mouths. They usually don't get colds but often sound stuffy because of mucus in their nasal passages. This is normal and will usually clear up on its own. Occasionally, you may want to help clear his nose by using the small rubber bulb syringe from the hospital to gently suck mucus out of the nose. This is called a nasal aspirator, and usually the hospital gives you the one used in the delivery room. If you did not receive one, it can be bought in a regular drugstore. Ask your pharmacist for assistance to buy the correct one. A cool air humidifier is also quite useful in your baby's room if he has a runny nose. It will help clear his nasal passages so that he can suck easier.

What to Do

Occasionally, babies do get real colds in their first month or so of life. If you think your baby is developing a cold, you should:

- Make sure he is drinking plenty of liquids. (If you are breast-feeding, have your baby nurse more frequently. If you are bottle-feeding, add extra water to each bottle and feed more frequently, e.g., every two to three hours.)
- Use a constant cool air humidifier.
- Clear his nose with a nasal aspirator as needed. (It may also help to put two or three drops of a saline solution such as Ocean Nasal Mist into the baby's nose and then use the aspirator to remove the mucus.)
- Take his temperature in the morning and afternoon and when he feels warm.
- Watch his breathing to make sure he isn't struggling.
- Elevate the head of his bed when he's sleeping and keep him sitting up in an infant seat at other times.
- Watch your baby for the development of a cough and a constant runny nose.
- Look for loss of appetite.

Call Your Doctor Immediately About

- Any fever with a temperature greater than 99°F (37.2°C), taken rectally.
- Rapid breathing, more than sixty breaths per minute.
- Difficulty breathing (baby sucks in chest when he takes a breath).
- Baby is unable to drink and breathe at the same time.
- Marked change of behavior, either extreme fussiness or disinterested and unresponsive.
- Dusky color, extreme paleness, or a blueness around the lips or fingernail beds.

During cold season, you should try to minimize your baby's contact with anyone who has a cold. In many cases this is not possible. However, anyone with a cold who has contact with newborn babies should carefully and frequently wash their hands before handling the baby and wear a hospital mask, if possible. It is particularly helpful to wear a hospital mask when feeding your baby if you have more than a mild cold to avoid breathing directly on your baby's face. This will decrease the baby's chances of catching your cold. You should also avoid big crowds in small places when possible.

COLIC

Colic refers to prolonged periods of intense crying. It begins suddenly, and often the baby's face is flushed and his stomach is hard and tense. His legs may be drawn up and his fists clenched. Colic usually starts when a baby is six weeks old and may last until he is approximately three months old. See the section about Colic in chapter 3 for more information.

CORD CARE

The cord clamp placed around your baby's umbilical cord during delivery is usually removed twenty-four to forty-eight hours after birth. Initially, you may be given an antibiotic ointment to apply around the base of the cord. To do this:

- Wash your hands.
- Squirt a little ointment directly on the area or on a Q-tip or your fingertip, and carefully dab it around the connection of the cord and your baby's skin.

After twenty-four hours, you usually switch to 70 percent rubbing alcohol applied at least three to four times daily. This will help the cord dry out.

- Wash your hands.
- Dip a Q-tip or cotton ball in a rubbing alcohol solution.
- Gently dab around the base of the cord three to four times per day. (See Figure 6.4.) (Some parents use the alcohol with every diaper change until the cord falls off.)
- You may also use alcohol prep pads if you have been given some by the hospital staff.

Your goal now is to dry out the cord so that it will fall off. It usually falls off anywhere from five to ten days after birth, but it may stay attached for up to three weeks. Many people recommend that you don't get the cord wet in the bath and that you fold down the diaper to help it dry out. (Newborn disposable diapers often come with a

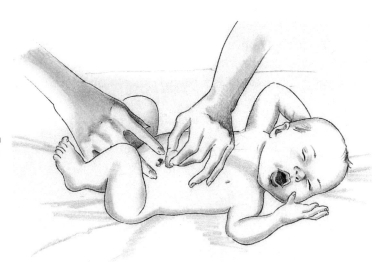

Figure 6.4: Umbilical cord care
Dip a Q-tip or cotton ball in alcohol and carefully wipe from the base in a circular motion to more distal points.

wedge cut out for the cord.) Occasionally when the cord falls off, the stump will bleed a little or have a slight discharge. This is normal as long as it stops in a day or two. You can put a little of the antibiotic ointment on it like you did the first day. If the area has an unusual discharge or is very red, you should call your baby's doctor to have it checked to be sure that it isn't infected. Sometimes there is a little extra tissue in the area that tends to bleed. It is called a *granuloma*. This also needs to be treated by your baby's doctor.

CRYING

In the first few days of life, babies don't usually cry very much because they aren't very hungry and are still a little sleepy. This will gradually change as your baby wakes up and feels hungry. Also, it commonly takes several weeks for a newborn's tear ducts to function; don't expect to see tears immediately. Crying is a baby's way of letting you know that he needs something; often he is hungry and needs to be fed, or he is wet and needs to changed. However, there are many different reasons babies cry. These include:

- Hunger.
- Wet or uncomfortable.
- Being undressed.
- Overstimulated.
- Cold or hot.
- Frustrated.
- Wants human contact; wants to be held.
- No apparent reason.

Crying does not hurt a baby, though it is often worrisome for parents. Often, crying babies just need to be held. *You can't spoil your baby during the early months of life.* A few generations ago it was thought that crying was good for a baby because it exercised his lungs. There is no real proof of this, and sometimes we just don't know why a baby cries. There are some logical steps you can take when your baby does cry:

- Correct obvious problems such as hunger or a wet diaper.
- Pick him up and cuddle him.
- Wrap the baby snugly in a receiving blanket (swaddling).
- Rock him in bed, swing, or cradle.
- Gently pat or rub his back.
- Sing, play music, or talk to your baby.
- Walk around with him in a front pouch or baby sling.
- Take him for a walk in the stroller.
- Some parents feel that laying a baby in a baby basket or strapped into an infant seat on a washing machine or dishwasher while it is running is helpful. (The vibration and steam may help lull him to quiet sleep.)
- Take him for a ride in the car in his car seat.
- Lay him swaddled in bed with a warm, not hot, water bottle wrapped in a towel so that it won't burn his tender skin.
- Use a pacifier (if you are not opposed to this). The crying energy may go into sucking, and the rhythm may be soothing.

Sometimes the baby will continue to cry, and the crying itself is his ultimate relief. Colic doesn't usually start until the baby is six weeks old. See the section on Colic in chapter 3 for more information.

DIAPERS

Diapers today are available both in cloth and disposable varieties. Parents typically make a choice based on their lifestyle and environmental concerns. The rate of diaper rashes is about the same regardless of which type is used. Whichever one you choose, it is important to:

- Change wet and soiled diapers frequently to prevent rashes and irritation.
- After the diaper is removed, rinse your baby's bottom with a wet washcloth.
- *Clean the genital area carefully in girls by wiping from front to back.* Also, carefully clean the creases of the vaginal lips (the labia). This prevents infection

from entering the urethra or the vagina. *In boys, carefully clean the scrotum.* Disposable baby wipes are also available and are quite convenient, particularly when you are away from home. Be aware, however, that they usually contain alcohol and may dry skin. Some contain a perfume scent that some babies may exhibit an acute sensitivity to. See section on Skin and Rashes for information about diaper rash.

DRESSING AN INFANT

Newborns are very susceptible to heat loss at birth so they must be covered with a dry, warm blanket immediately. In some cases, a heating lamp may be needed to help the baby stay warm right after birth. You should be alert to your baby's temperature during the first four or five days and make sure to keep him warm. After that, dress your baby to *accommodate the room temperature and the season.* He should wear as many layers of clothing as an adult would wear. A common mistake is overdressing a baby in summer. A baby should be dressed for comfort in his environment. Once your baby weighs about seven pounds, he will do a good job of regulating his body temperature. Usually an infant will wear an undershirt, diaper, a one-piece outfit or shirt, and pants with socks. In winter, a baby needs a hat because there is often not much hair to protect him from heat loss through his bare head. In the summer, be sure to protect him from too much sun exposure and sunburn. If you are uneasy about putting clothes over his head while he is small, buy clothes that have side snaps. As long as you support your baby's head while changing him, you will not hurt him. If this is your first baby, have a nurse or experienced parent show you how to hold your baby while you change him until you become more confident.

EYE CARE

Soon after your baby is born he will be given special eyedrops in each eye to prevent serious infection. In some cases, these drops will cause mild irritation that should resolve itself in three days. Sometimes a newborn's eyelids are a little puffy for a few days because of the pressure on the face during delivery.

Once you are at home, you only need to keep his eyes clean with the regular bath. Use a clean facecloth and *wipe his eyes from the inner corner (near the nose) to the outer.* If your baby's eye is continuously watery, he may have a blocked tear duct. This means that the channel that carries tears from the eye to the nose is blocked. This is very common and usually corrects itself by twelve months of age. Sometimes newborns have a lot of yellow discharge from their eyes. You need not worry as long as the whites

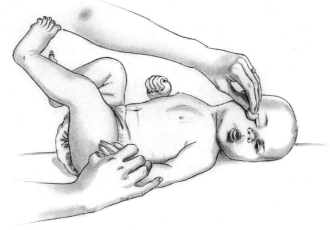

Figure 6.5: Baby eye care
Use a clean facecloth or damp cotton ball to wipe discharge from your baby's eyes.

of his eyes remain white. If you are noticing this discharge, you might want to wipe his eyes, always from the inner corner near the nose to the outer, with a clean facecloth or cotton ball dipped in warm water, three times a day. (See Figure 6.5.) Be sure to wash your hands before and after you wash your baby's eyes. Call your doctor if the whites of the eyes become red or if there is a lot of discharge and you suspect the presence of an infection.

FEEDING

Whether you choose to breast-feed or bottle-feed, feeding time is special for your baby. He is getting his hunger satisfied as well as receiving love and attention.

- Try to make your baby's feeding time relaxed and pleasant.
- Sit comfortably in a favorite chair.
- Try to avoid any distractions, especially during the first few months.

There is a very strong argument for breast-feeding whenever possible. However, you must do what is most comfortable and practical for you, your baby, and your household. At first your baby will need to be fed every two to three hours. This is because most newborn babies will drink only three to four ounces or less at each feeding. As your baby begins to take a larger volume during the day, he will begin to skip a night feeding. This eventually will happen but generally not before the end of the first month. Also, if your baby was born with a low birth weight, you will need to feed him through the night for a longer period of time in order to give him a chance to gain weight and catch up on his growth.

All newborn babies lose weight during the first three or four days of life. You should not be worried by an eight- to twelve-ounce weight loss because this is normal.

Your newborn baby is getting enough to eat if he has a wet diaper at least six times a day. This is true for both bottle- and breast-fed babies. After this you should see a steady weight gain which your doctor will follow with you. In general, your baby requires fifty calories per pound of ideal body weight each day. Standard formulas and breast milk contain approximately twenty calories per ounce. (See Table 6.3, "Sample Food Requirement for a Baby.")

Occasionally a newborn baby may develop a *sucking callus* or blister in the center of the upper lip. This is caused by constant friction at this point during bottle- or breast-feeding. It will disappear as the time between feedings increases and in some babies may last until they use a cup. A sucking callus may also develop on the thumb or wrist.

Table 6.3

Sample Food Requirement for a Baby	
Formula	Baby needs 50 calories per pound, per day. Formula and breast milk each have approximately 20 calories per ounce.
Example	A 10-pound baby
Requirement	50 calories x 10 pounds = 500 calories/day. 500 calories: 20 calories per ounce = 25 ounces of formula or breast milk each day.

This formula is a guide. A baby's appetite may also vary from day to day and this fluctuation is normal. A baby may also have an increased appetite during growth spurts. For newborns this will usually occur at around seven to ten days, three to six weeks, and approximately three months.

Guidelines for Breast-Feeding:

- Breast-feeding is both an art and a learned skill that will take four to six weeks to master.
- When you decide to breast-feed, massage your nipples with a softening cream during your last trimester and continue this practice between feedings to toughen the nipples and minimize cracking from the baby's strong suck.
- Find a comfortable position and hold the baby in your arms with his body entirely on his side, his lower arm around your waist, and his head in the bend of your elbow. (See Figure 6.6.)

- Support your breast with your free hand, placing your thumb above the nipple and your other fingers below. Gently tickle your baby's lips with your nipple until he opens his mouth. Pull him in close to you with the nipple centered close toward his mouth. You may need to reposition the baby a few times before he latches on properly.

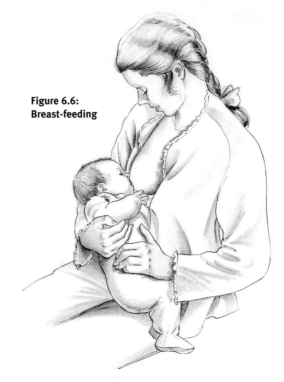

Figure 6.6:
Breast-feeding

- Frequent feedings during the first few days encourage milk production with minimal engorgement. Most breast-fed babies nurse eight to twelve times a day during the first two weeks of life.

- You can tell that your baby is sucking well and getting enough breast milk when:

  1. The feedings are not painful. (With proper latch you feel tugging but not pain.)
  2. You can hear your baby swallowing.
  3. The baby's nose and chin touch your breast.
  4. You get a letdown of milk.
  5. Your baby is having many wet diapers and gaining weight.

- A breast-fed baby doesn't always eat on schedule. Some days he will want more than others. Don't give formula, water, or sugar water unless told to by your baby's doctor. These days of increased appetite often correspond with growth spurts.

- Take care of your breasts. Washing them once a day in the shower is sufficient. Breast milk is a natural lubricant and can be lightly applied to the nipples after each feeding. Be sure to let the nipples dry for about five minutes after each feeding. (Note: Soap and alcohol will dry the skin around your nipple and will remove the natural coating that keeps your nipples clean and soft.)

- If your breasts become engorged, use moist heat (warm compresses or a shower) on your breasts and massage them gently before nursing. Hand

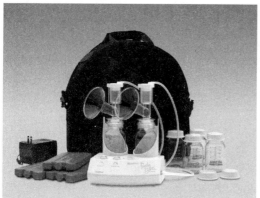

Figure 6.7a: Purely Yours portable electric breast pump with tote bag from Ameda Breastfeeding Products.

Figure 6.7b: Elite electric breast pump from Ameda Breastfeeding Products.

express or pump milk until the areola softens, then encourage your baby to nurse. Breast-feed frequently when your breasts are engorged and, after nursing, apply cold packs briefly to the breasts to relieve swelling.

- Continue to eat a good variety of the same basic foods that were important during pregnancy. Be sure to drink at least two quarts of liquid per day.

- Nap when your baby naps. You need the rest to keep up with the night feedings.

- If you intend to return to work while you are still breast-feeding, begin to evaluate breast pumps. There are many different ones available. Check with your doctor or lactation staff about recommendations. See Figures 6.7a and 6.7b for examples of breast pumps on the market.

- "Relief" bottles may be given after a minimum of three weeks of full-time nursing. You may use breast milk or formula for relief bottles. Recommended storage times for breast milk are:

> Refrigerator: twenty-four to forty-eight hours
> Freezer inside of refrigerator: two weeks
> Separate door freezer: three to four months

- Most pediatricians recommend breast milk for babies until age nine to twelve months. If you decide to wean before nine months, talk to your baby's doctor about how to introduce formula.

- Before you take any medicines, check with your baby's doctor about their effect on breast-feeding and on your baby. Any medicine, food, or alcohol that you take is also given to your baby through breast milk.

Guidelines for Bottle-Feeding

- Find a comfortable position and hold your baby with his head in the bend of your elbow. His head should always be higher than his stomach. (See Figure 6.8.)

- Commercially prepared formulas come in many forms including powdered, liquid concentrate, and ready to feed. You need to find the right one for your budget and lifestyle. Often a combination will work best. Whatever you choose, be sure to read the directions carefully and mix them in accurate amounts. It is a good idea to mix the formula in an amount that will last for twenty-four hours at a time. Always keep prepared formula refrigerated until it is time to use it.

- *Use a commercial formula that is fortified with iron* during your baby's first year. Whole cow's milk should not be given to babies before twelve months of age because of the increased risk of iron-deficient anemia (the milk hinders iron absorption) and the possibility of cow's-milk intolerance.

- Be sure that the formula fills the nipple at all times so your baby doesn't swallow excess air.

- At first offer your baby a bottle every two to three hours during the day. By the fourth or fifth day, he should be taking two to three ounces per feeding. It is usually not necessary to wake a sleeping baby at night to feed him unless specifically instructed to do so by your doctor.

Figure 6.8: Bottle-feeding

- It should take your baby twenty to thirty minutes to finish a bottle. If it takes longer, or if he takes only one to two ounces and then is hungry an hour later, you may need a larger nipple. You can buy a nipple with a larger hole or you can make the hole larger yourself. It is safer and more sanitary to just buy a nipple with a larger hole and a faster flow. In general, we recommend orthodontically-designed nipples for your baby.

- Your baby will typically need six to eight feedings per day during the first month of life. Table 6.3, "Sample Food Requirement for a Baby," on page 239 is one guide for how much formula a newborn may take. Another way to calculate ounces per feeding is to add three to your baby's age in months (with a maximum of eight ounces at five or six months). These formulas are only guides, and it is normal for your baby's appetite to fluctuate. Pour an extra ounce into your baby's bottle for those occasions when he is increasingly hungry.

- Start using eight-ounce bottles as soon as your baby finishes the four-ounce bottles quickly. You want to avoid your baby swallowing a lot of air by sucking on an empty bottle.

- Babies can drink formula at any temperature, except when it is too hot. Do not heat formula in a microwave because the temperature will be uneven and may have some extremely hot spots that could burn a baby.

- Many doctors now believe that sterilization is not necessary or may recommend sterilization only during the first three months. Talk this over with your baby's doctor. If you have a dishwasher, you may be able to use it to care for all the bottle-feeding equipment.

- Babies do not routinely need extra water. If you think your baby needs water for hydration, consult with your baby's doctor.

- Most pediatricians recommend continuing formula or breast milk until a baby is nine to twelve months old.

FEVER

It is not normal for a newborn baby to have a fever. Any fever of 99°F or 37.2°C (rectally) *should be reported immediately to your doctor.* Babies should have their temperature taken rectally. See chapter 1 for information on how to take a temperature. Never take an oral temperature on a baby or young child. It will not be accurate and it is not safe. Keep infant acetaminophen drops (Tylenol, Tempra, etc.) in the house in case you need it. It comes with a small medicine dropper to measure out the proper dose of medicine for a baby. Check with your doctor to determine the appropriate dose for your baby's age and weight. See the section on Fever in chapter 2 for further information.

HAIR LOSS

Most babies lose at least some of their hair. *This is normal*. There is nothing that you can do about it, and there is no reason to worry. Some babies lose it gradually while the permanent hair is coming in; others lose it rapidly and may become bald for awhile. Permanent hair usually begins to appear by the age of six months. Sometimes it is the same color as before and sometimes it changes.

JAUNDICE

Jaundice is a *yellow coloring of the skin and eyes*. It is usually caused by the normal process of breaking down red blood cells into a substance called *bilirubin*. Since your baby's liver is not ready to handle this increase of bilirubin just yet, he will become jaundiced for a day or two. Then his liver will start maturing and the jaundice will go away.

Physiological, or common jaundice, usually appears during your baby's first week of life. If your baby is very yellow or if it occurs during the first day or two after birth, special tests will be performed to evaluate his condition. Newborns often leave the hospital within forty-eight hours of birth. This leaves parents with the responsibility of observing the degree of jaundice in their baby. The amount of yellowness is best observed by viewing your baby unclothed in natural light by a window. Most babies with jaundice cease becoming more yellow by four to five days of age. The yellow then starts to fade. Breast-fed babies take longer to clear their jaundice.

Jaundice can worsen due to:

- ABO disease—when mothers with type O blood may have babies with type A or B blood and thus have mild incompatibility.
- Rh disease—incompatibility of the Rh factor in the blood between the mother and baby.
- The reabsorption of bruise marks after a difficult delivery.

Jaundice usually will dissipate faster when your baby is taking larger quantities of breast milk or formula. This keeps her well hydrated and helps to move her bowels faster.

If your baby is very yellow, the doctor may put him under special lights called "bili-lights," which help to get rid of bilirubin faster. You should talk to your baby's doctor about the specific cause and treatment of your baby's jaundice. If you are at home and your baby becomes yellow and lacks energy, call your baby's doctor immediately.

MUCUS

During the first few days of life, your baby may have a lot of mucus in the nose and the back of his throat. This is normal and occurs frequently in newborn infants. The sticky, colorless secretion may cause him to gag or vomit. Don't force him to drink. Let him take what he wants. *It usually decreases after a day or two.* You may want to use the nasal aspirator to clear his nose before feeding: be sure to hold him with his head upright. If excess mucus continues after three or four days, be sure to discuss it with your baby's doctor.

REFLEXES

By the time your baby is born, his nervous system has developed defenses to help him cope with life outside the uterus. Some of these defenses are called reflexes and are protective mechanisms for your baby. At times, you may notice your baby has the "jitters," which is especially evident in his arms, legs, and mouth. It is common for a baby to have a trembling chin and quivering lower lip. This is because his nervous system is trying to adjust to life outside the uterus. These occasional jitters are normal.

Newborn babies also have frequent hiccoughs and sneezing. It often is very comforting for babies to be wrapped snugly in a receiving blanket (swaddled) with their arms and legs tucked in close to their body.

Rooting Reflex

This is your baby's natural tendency to turn toward a touch on his upper lip or cheek. This is helpful when you feed your baby. Touch your baby's cheek near his mouth with a nipple, and he will turn toward the nipple and open his mouth at the same time.

Suck-Swallow-Gag Reflex

This allows your baby to take in liquids, swallow them into his stomach, and prevent liquids from going into his lungs. As he continues to mature, this reflex develops a more even rhythm so that feeding becomes much smoother.

Moro or Startle Reflex

When a loud noise is made, you will see your baby throw his arms and legs out from his body and then quickly move them into an "embrace" position. It is not known why this reflex is present, and it usually disappears in about six months.

Grasp Reflex

When you place your finger into your baby's hand he will grasp it. To get him to release your finger, stroke the back of his hand.

SIGHT AND HEARING

Newborns have amazingly well-developed sight and hearing. Initially, your baby can see to a distance of about twelve inches. She can see forms and will soon surprise you by following you with her eyes, especially if you are wearing black and white or some brightly colored clothing. Because a newborn's eye muscles do not always work well, you may see your baby cross her eyes occasionally. This should improve as she matures. If it doesn't, point it out to your baby's doctor at one of her well-child visits. You may need to see a specialist.

Your baby's hearing is extremely well developed at birth, and she often will recognize her parents' voices right away. Many newborn nurseries are now doing hearing tests on babies before they go home from the hospital. Talk to your baby often. Play soft music. Your voice will become increasingly comforting to her as you call out "I'm coming!" when she starts to cry.

SKIN AND RASHES

Newborns have delicate, sensitive skin that is prone to a myriad of different rashes as they get used to their new environment.

Acne

Newborn acne develops in approximately 30 percent of babies. It usually occurs on the face as small red bumps. It begins at three to four weeks of age and lasts until four to six months of age. The cause seems to be related to the transfer of the mother's hormones to the baby just before birth. It is temporary, and no treatment is required. There is no relationship between newborn acne and teenage acne.

Milia

Some babies have small white dots on their faces that look like whiteheads. They usually occur on the nose and cheeks but may also be seen on the forehead and chin. These are called *milia* and are caused by blocked pores. They will disappear with time and without any treatment.

Lanugo

Fine hair on the baby's back and shoulders is called *lanugo*. It will eventually fall off, especially as you bathe him.

Newborn Rash

Often newborns will develop a red, raised rash that looks like numerous insect bites. It often becomes evident around two days after birth up to two weeks. This is called newborn rash or *erythema toxicum*. It is harmless and will eventually fade. It does not need any treatment.

Diaper Rash

Diaper rashes may develop in the genital area from prolonged contact with moisture and waste products. It is important to keep the diaper area as clean and dry as possible to prevent diaper rash. Almost every child gets a diaper rash at some point. Once it starts, however, you must stay on top of it. Change your baby's diaper frequently and wash the diaper area well. Apply petroleum jelly or a cream with zinc oxide in it to keep the wetness and waste off your baby's skin and protect him from further irritation. For a period of time each day, let him lie on an unfastened diaper to expose the area to air. Do not apply any ointment at this time. If you are using cloth diapers, try to not use plastic pants. If you cannot cure a diaper rash yourself after approximately a week, call your baby's doctor. Suspect a yeast infection if the rash becomes bright red and raw, covers a large area, and is surrounded by red dots. You will need a special prescription cream from your doctor to cure a yeast infection diaper rash. Check your baby's mouth for thrush as well if you suspect a yeast infection. These two yeast infections often occur together. See chapter 2 under Rashes for more information.

Drooling Rash

Many babies have a rash on the chin or cheeks that can come and go. This may be due to contact with food and acid that have been spit up from the stomach. If you notice this, carefully rinse your baby's face with a wet washcloth after feedings. Also try placing an absorbent cloth diaper under your baby's face during naps.

Cradle Cap

Cradle cap is a scaly, somewhat greasy, coating on the scalp caused by the normal accumulation of shedding skin cells. Many babies develop this, and it is easily treated. A common treatment is to gently rub mineral or baby oil on your baby's scalp at night and use baby shampoo the next morning. Use a fine-tooth comb, a soft baby brush, or an old soft toothbrush to gently comb your baby's hair. If your baby is prone to cradle cap, you may want to give him more frequent or even daily shampoos until the problem clears up. You want to prevent the buildup of scabs. Some babies may have cradle cap until they are two or three years old.

SLEEPING

No two babies have the same sleeping patterns or the same sleep requirements. Some babies sleep easily; others do not. Some babies sleep for long stretches of time, and some seem to catnap throughout the day. Many babies make a lot of noise when they sleep from breathing and moving. This is normal. Be sure to keep your baby's face clear of all bedclothes, stuffed animals, etc., to prevent smothering. It is recommended that a baby sleep on her back or on her side. Recent research suggests that the side or back sleeping position may be also helpful in preventing *SIDS (Sudden Infant Death Syndrome)*. You can support her on her side with a blanket or cloth diaper rolled tightly and placed at her back. Many newborns seem to sleep better bundled in a receiving blanket or firmly swaddled as is frequently done in the newborn nursery. This may remind your baby of his prebirth environment. Some babies like a blanket rolled and placed near the back of the head to provide a feeling of security. Always tuck your baby in snugly.

Most babies wake at different intervals throughout the day and night for feeding during the first three months of life. Many parents share the job of night feeding so that they can get a little more sleep. For breast-fed babies, this may a good time to let the father give a relief bottle, though it is usually recommended that a relief bottle not be introduced until after three weeks of full-time nursing. If you feel your milk is fully established, you may start relief bottles sooner. After a feeding, place your baby in the side position for sleep so if she spits up, there will be no risk of choking.

After approximately three months, babies usually begin to take more breast milk or formula and sleep for longer periods of time. Usually the parents work to make the longer periods of sleep occur at night. This is done by waking your baby to offer more feedings at regular intervals during the day and letting the baby sleep until she wakes at night. Give night feedings in dim light so that the baby will realize they are different from daytime feedings. You might also find that it helps to keep a low level of noise in the house during daytime and also have it quieter at night. Establish a *sleep routine* early on. You might give your baby a bath, clean pajamas, a good night feeding, and then tuck him in with a lullaby or just a quiet story about your day. Most babies will settle into a pattern after three months, though there will be some who don't. It is important for the mother to sleep while the baby sleeps whenever possible so that she doesn't get overtired.

SPITTING UP

Some newborn babies spit up a great deal. It is very common for babies to spit up one to two mouthfuls of stomach contents. This often begins in the first weeks of life. It may be called "regurgitation," "reflux," "gastroesophageal reflux (GE reflux)," or "chalasia." It is usually caused by a weak valve at the upper end of the stomach. Spitting up usually improves with age and is mostly an inconvenience for the parents. These babies usually respond well to careful attention paid to feeding techniques. Keep your baby in an upright position during feeding and for at least a half hour after feeding. It may be helpful to place him in an upright infant seat after feeding. Also feed your baby more frequently with smaller amounts and burp him often. Avoid pressure on the abdomen after eating including pressure caused by tight diapers. As long as your baby continues to grow and gain weight, spitting up is not a long-term problem. Call your baby's doctor if there is any blood in the spit-up material, your baby is projectile vomiting, or the spitting up causes your baby to choke or cough.

TAKING YOUR BABY OUTDOORS

You can take your baby outdoors at any age; you already took him outside when you left the hospital. Babies can usually be taken outdoors regularly as soon as they are able to regulate their body temperature. This is usually after three days and/or a weight of seven pounds. They must, of course, be dressed properly for the season. Dress your baby with as many layers as an adult would wear for the temperature outdoors. Extra care must be taken in very cold and very hot climates. In winter, be sure your baby wears a hat to prevent excess heat loss. In summer, be sure that your baby is not over-dressed; he wants to stay comfortable in the heat, too. The skin of a baby, however, is more sensitive to the sun than that of an older child or adult. Keep direct sun exposure to a minimum—no more than fifteen minutes at a time. Protect your baby's skin from sunburn with long, loose-fitting clothes and a sunbonnet. Sunscreen or suntan lotions are not recommended for newborn babies. Keeping your baby in the shade is best.

Crowds should probably be avoided during your newborn baby's first month of life. Also try to avoid close contact with anyone who has a contagious illness throughout your baby's first year of life.

TEETH

Very occasionally a baby will be born with a tooth. Most of these are prematurely erupted normal teeth. Rarely, it is an extra tooth without any root. An X ray may be needed to determine which type it is. An extra tooth will probably be removed by a pediatric dentist. A premature normal tooth will be removed only if it becomes loose, because of a danger of possible choking.

THRUSH

Thrush is an infection caused by a yeast that grows rapidly in the mouth. It appears as white, irregularly shaped patches that coat the inside of the mouth and sometimes the tongue. It cannot be washed away or wiped off easily. Thrush is common in babies under six months of age. Sometimes your baby will get thrush when he has been taking antibiotics. It also occurs sometimes with a diaper rash. Talk to your baby's doctor if you think he has thrush. You will need a prescription medicine called Nystatin to clear up the yeast infection.

TONGUE-TIED

The normal tongue in newborns has a short, tight band that connects it to the floor of the mouth. This band normally stretches with time, movement, and growth. Babies with a true tongue-tie are rare.

WEIGHT GAIN

Babies often lose eight to twelve ounces in the first few days after birth, or 6 to 10 percent of their birth weight during the first week. Most of this is from fluids and should not be cause for worry. After that, they usually embark on a pattern of steady weight gain that will be monitored by your baby's doctor in conjunction with his growth in length. A baby will usually double his weight by five to six months of age and triple his birth weight by one year of age. The doctor will chart the baby's weight, length, and head circumference on special growth charts at each visit. He is watching for a steady growth pattern rather than a particular height or weight by a certain age. Babies and children grow in different patterns, and you'll soon be able to predict your baby's pattern.

CHAPTER SEVEN

Behavior and Developmental Issues

One of parenting's greatest challenges is helping our children to become social human beings. We want them to be kind, considerate, polite, well adjusted, competent, independent, and a host of other complementary qualities. These require work and guidance; unfortunately there is not a simple formula we can plug into. Growing up is a very complicated process. This section offers simple tips on a wide range of topics. Take the advice and adapt it to your own circumstances and cultural preferences.

Make sure you and your partner agree on basic strategies for child rearing, or at least always present a united front. Use time apart from your child to develop your strategies and work out compromises when necessary.

Pick your battles. You can't win all the time, and neither can your child. Always be willing to listen carefully and be ready to compromise occasionally. Make safety your number-one concern and never compromise on this issue. Repeat the phrase "No, that's not safe," a million times and mean it.

Set high standards. Don't be afraid to let your child see that you are disappointed in his behavior. Set a good example. For instance, demand that your child always sit in a car seat in the car until she weighs more than forty pounds and at that point uses a seat belt—just as you do. Wear a bike helmet when you go cycling with your child. Love your child; laugh with her; have a lot of fun and be safe.

ATTENTION-SEEKING

Children like attention. Especially between the ages of one and three, it's a normal part of their ego development. They perform for adults and repeat behaviors that draw further attention—both good and bad. With this in mind it's important to always praise good behavior and, when possible, ignore bad behavior. (You can't ignore bad behavior if it places your child in danger, but it is important to *ignore annoying behaviors*.)

Distract your child if she is getting into a routine that you recognize will lead to bad behavior; in this way you set her up for success. Don't place her in a situation she can't handle. If you don't want her to have candy, don't take her to a candy store. Don't let her get so tired or hungry that a "tantrum" is unavoidable. And remember, if you are overtired, any abnormal behavior will probably annoy you more. If attention-seeking behavior is getting to you, talk to your pediatrician for guidance.

BED-WETTING

Children become toilet trained for daytime usually between the ages of two and three. Most children become dry at night by about four years of age. A child is not officially a bed-wetter while he is still training his bladder to last for ten to twelve hours of night-time sleep. A normal percentage of children do not become dry at night until age seven or later. A return to bed-wetting after a child has achieved bladder control may be a sign that something else is occurring. Possible explanations for bed-wetting include:

- Possibility of a bladder or urinary tract infection.
- Increased tension or anxiety associated with a big event such as a new baby.
- Anatomical reason for incontinence (this is more common in girls).
- In rare cases, a sign of diabetes when accompanied by increased thirst and frequency of urination.

If your child does wet the bed, try to be patient and calm. It helps to use a half rubber sheet under a top sheet for quick nighttime bed changes, limit fluids after dinner, and make sure she empties her bladder before bedtime. Some parents like to carry their child to the toilet and sit her on it just before they themselves go to bed. Your child will instinctively empty her bladder and avoid a nighttime accident; many children don't even wake up for this toilet routine. A nighttime toilet routine does not cure bed-wetting or constitute toilet training; but it does keep the sheets dry!

When your child does have an accident at night, follow these tips:

- Stay calm.
- Do not punish or ridicule.
- Assure your child it was not her fault.
- Quickly change her clothes and sheets and settle her back to sleep.

Make sure that there is not a medical reason for bed-wetting such as a urinary tract infection or constipation. A urinary tract infection usually causes both daytime and nighttime accidents because of loss of bladder control, while constipation causes pressure on the bladder that prevents full emptying of the bladder.

If you have a family history of bed-wetters, let your child know this. Usually time is the best cure for bed-wetting: your child will outgrow this habit. There are some commercially available *bed pad alarms* that go off with moisture, and these may prove helpful *for children older than age five.*

BITING

Children bite for different reasons depending on their age. Babies bite when they are teething and also simply for a tactile experience. A child who bites in anger or frustration usually outgrows this as she learns to use words to express herself. You need to have a zero tolerance policy for biting. Immediately after a child bites, say "No biting!" in a serious voice. Try giving the child something she can bite such as a teething ring or zwieback cookie. You may also have to remove the child from the area and give her a "time-out." Sometimes pinching a child's nose while she is biting will force her to release the victim.

BREATH-HOLDING SPELLS

Some children, particularly between the ages of six months and three years, are able to hold their breath long enough to actually pass out. This is usually preceded by an upsetting event such as falling down, being angry or frustrated, or being frightened. Breath-holding out of anger in a temper tantrum, and turning blue but not passing out, is common. In this case, a reflex will kick in and your child will start to breathe normally.

Breath-holding spells are harmless and usually stop by themselves. They seem to last longer than they really do. If your child has breath-holding spells, look at a watch with a second hand and time the spell. You will be surprised how quickly they pass, usually less than sixty seconds.

If your child has breath-holding spells and passes out:

- Remain calm and have your child lie flat to increase blood flow to the brain.
- Don't try giving him anything to drink or eat because he may choke.
- After the attack is over, give your child a hug and then continue acting normally.

A relaxed attitude about breath-holding is best. Most attacks from falls or sudden fright can't be prevented. However, if your child is having daily attacks he probably has learned how to trigger them himself. Talk to your child's doctor about setting up a behavior plan to deal with these daily attacks and for an evaluation to make sure there is no physiological cause for them.

CHILDPROOFING YOUR HOUSE

By the time your child is six months old, you should "childproof" your house. This means making it safe for infants and young children by removing possible hazards. One of the best ways to survey your house is to get down on your hands and knees and see each room from your child's perspective. Crawl around and look at all the interesting holes, objects, and dangling items that you could eat, pull, or poke. A quick checklist for childproofing would include:

- Cover all electrical outlets with plug guards.
- Put safety latches or locks on all cabinets and drawers with potentially dangerous items like cleaning products, alcohol, and medicines.
- Keep all cords, knives, and scissors out of reach of small children.
- Make sure there is nothing your child can pull down like electrical cords, appliances, tablecloths when items are on the table, pots, etc.
- Put gates on all stairs and install window guards on all windows above the first floor to prevent dangerous falls.
- Keep doors to bathrooms and off-limits rooms closed tightly.
- Set the hot water temperature in your home below 120°F to avoid scalding burns.
- Keep small objects, sharp toys, rubber balloons, and plastic bags away from babies to prevent choking.
- If you own a gun, keep it unloaded and locked up. Lock up bullets in a separate location.

Some rooms in your house may have to be declared "off limits" to your children. This might include laundry areas, workshops, and storage areas. Be especially alert in the kitchen. This is a room where you probably spend a lot of time, and it is loaded with hazards like cleaning materials, sharp objects, electrical outlets, small appliances, big appliances that a baby can crawl into, fire hazards, dangling tablecloths, and hot food and drinks. It is also a busy place that may sometimes get quite hectic. The bathroom is another key area. Often there are medicines, cleaning supplies, and water in the toilet bowl (a severe drowning hazard). There may also be hot tap water that could easily burn a baby's sensitive skin. All over the house, look for small items that could choke your baby. Make sure that televisions, stereo components, VCRs, and other heavy appliances are anchored so that they won't easily topple on a child.

When you take your child to other places, watch him extra carefully, as these locations may not be childproof. A large number of accidental medicine poisonings happen to children who take their grandparents' prescription medicines. Make sure your child is always supervised by a trusted adult and put the Poison Control Center number next to your telephone. Many injuries can be prevented if you know where the dangers are and work to avoid them. The Consumer Product Safety Commission can answer your concerns regarding the safety of specific products. Their toll-free telephone number is 1-800-638-2772.

DEVELOPMENTAL MILESTONES

Developmental milestones are a series of guidelines set up by pediatric specialists over the years to measure how your child is progressing as compared to the average child of the same age range. As babies and children grow and mature, their behaviors become more complex. This maturation process can be observed as they master a series of developmental milestones that have been assigned to a loosely structured "normal age range."

The exact time your child learns something new is not as important as the general trend of continued accomplishments.

The normal range represents typical ages at which certain behaviors are usually observed. If you see a wide deviation between an expected developmental behavior for a certain age range and your own child, discuss this with your child's doctor. A healthy child may exceed the "normal range" in some areas, fall below in others, and still be "normal." Pediatric professionals look at the general progression of your child at each of these expected stepping stones. Deviations may signify a particular strength or weakness in your child, or they may signify a need for further investigation and intervention. We have developed a quick reference guide for developmental milestones. This Guide to Children's Development in Table 7.1 covers a typical child from newborn to age five. It is not abnormal if your child does not perform a task at exactly the stated age, though any great deviation should be discussed with your child's doctor.

Table 7.1

Guide to Children's Development

Age	Activity/Ability
Newborn	Active when awake with random uncoordinated movements.
	Needs careful positioning at all times to keep face clear of toys, blankets, etc., to prevent smothering.
	Sleeps in naps of two to four hours; wakes to be fed, changed, and nurtured.
	Responds to sudden noise—startle reflex.
	Likes to be held closely, stroked, and rocked.
1 month	Head flops back when lifted to sitting position. Continue to position carefully.
	Settling-in period; a more contented baby. Continue nurturing.
2 months	Almost no head lag when pulled to sitting position.
	Begins to establish sleeping pattern.
	Follows objects with head and eyes.
	Cries appropriately and comforts easily.
	Responds to parents'/caretakers' voice, touch, and presence.
	Smiles readily; vocalizes when talked to.
4 months	Can hold head steady. Sits supported with straight back.
	Watches own hand movements. Plays with fingers.
	Turns head toward sounds.
	Spontaneous smile. Anticipates being picked up and held.
	Recognizes feeding bottle and/or breast.
6 months	Can roll over from front to back.
	Reaches for objects with both hands; can transfer objects from one hand to the other.
	Responds to name; recognizes familiar voices.
	Cries and fusses more selectively, usually for a reason.
	Anticipates events in daily routine.
	Differentiates between familiar and strange people.

Age	Activity/Ability
9 months	Has improved strength and control (as central nervous system matures). Sits unsupported when placed in position. Drinks from a cup; holds bottle. Crawls or some other form of locomotion; may pull to stand up. Plays peek-a-boo and waves good-bye. Shows fear of strangers. Imitates simple sounds like "da-da."
12 months	Uses more smooth and coordinated movements. Stands, walks with help, may take independent steps. Likes to help with dressing and household chores. Can throw ball overhand. Picks up small blocks and tries to stack them. Likes to look at picture books and help turn pages. Understands simple instructions and "no." Loves an audience; repeats performances that are laughed at.
15 months	Walks unsteadily with feet wide apart. Tries to feed self with fingers and spoon. Likes to scribble/write. Has endless energy and curiosity about the environment. Likes to be read to; points to objects he desires. Follows simple directions. Stays drier longer as bladder gets bigger.
18 months	Needs to use large muscles. Walks up stairs holding an adult hand. Can carry or pull toy when walking. Likes to climb. Feeds self with spoon and controls drinking cup. Builds towers of two or three blocks. Likes regular, routine schedule for daily activities, naps, and bed. Small vocabulary; understands more words than he uses. Says "no" as a means of showing power. Has short attention span and a quick temper; wants everything done immediately.

Table 7.1 (*continued*)

Age	Activity/Ability
2 years	Improved coordination and agility. Climbs and runs more smoothly; jumps and kicks ball. Holds crayon steady and makes a circular scribble. Understands three hundred or more words and uses at least fifty words. Tries short sentences. Begins to use language to express needs. Do not expect your toddler to share or play cooperatively with other children. Plays in parallel alongside other children, not with them. Likes to pretend.
2½ years	Lots of energy. Likes large riding toys. Monitor safety. Bargains for behavior. Give simple commands; don't try to reason. Tries to cut with scissors and likes puzzles. Often ritualistic and rigid; likes everything in proper place and done in a certain way. Routine very important. Plays games like hide-and-seek to use memory skills.
3 years	Increase in agility and hand-eye coordination. Feeds self well. Can stand on one foot and ride a tricycle using pedals. Understands a thousand words; asks "what" questions. Less ritualistic; tries to please adults. Beginning to share; may be good time to start nursery school. Usually keeps dry in daytime.
4 years	Can dress and undress most clothes. Draws a stick person with a head and legs. Knows primary colors. Plays in a shifting loose group with toys and much imagination. Behavior alternates between aggressive and cooperative. Usually keeps dry at night.
5 years	More calm time. Likes to be instructed and get permission. Draws a stick person with arms, legs, and detailed face. Prints letters and numbers; cuts with scissors. Skips with alternating feet; jumps rope alone. Prefers companionship of peers and plays cooperatively. Speaks in sentences (no baby talk); defines words in terms of use. Understands more than two thousand words. Knows full name, address, phone number, and letters of the alphabet.

DISCIPLINE BASICS

All children need reasonable and consistent limits. The goal of all discipline is to keep your child safe from danger and teach an understanding of right and wrong. Discipline is for teaching your child. It takes time and patience, and it is essential in helping your child to develop his character.

You can begin the foundation of discipline when your baby is six months old. As he begins to crawl he must learn the meaning of the word "no" for his own safety. If your baby is approaching danger, you need to say in a very serious and firm voice, "No! That is not safe." And then you can tell him what he may do. Always try to phrase rules positively when there isn't an imminent danger to your child. From approximately six months to two years of age, most of your rules and limits will center on safety.

- Make sure you create a safe and secure environment for your baby.
- Remove things from their reach that are not safe.
- Distract your baby with toys and safe activities.
- Never shake or hit your baby in frustration.

Every family has its own standards of behavior. Behavior that would not be tolerated in one family may be tolerated in another. As a parent, you need to be clear why certain rules are important to you—for example, for reasons of safety, culture, or consideration of the rights and feelings of others. You also need to think about how you will enforce your rules and what you will do when your child does not obey them. Whenever possible, state the rule in a positive way and make sure the punishment or sanction for not following the rule is timely and appropriate. For children between two and five years of age, we recommend these three basic rules for a positive discipline plan.

- Make sure you can always see my eyes. (Don't run away unsupervised or get into something you shouldn't.)
- Be kind to others. (Don't hit or hurt others.)
- Respect property. (Don't break things.)

Children want the approval of their parents, and you need to articulate the limits of acceptable behavior for your child. Sometimes this is referred to as *limit setting*. Children feel more secure when they are given expectations and limits for their behavior and when those expectations are enforced. When you make expectations clear and simple to your child, he will work to meet them.

Ten key principles for positive discipline when enforcing your family's basic rules

1. *Always be consistent and present a united front.* This means that all rules and expectations must be clear; parents and all caretakers must agree on the rules and on any penalties for deviations. Any sorting out of family rules should be done away from your child so that she always sees her caretakers in agreement.

2. *Communicate the rules clearly.* It's a good idea to start with only a few important rules for really important safety and behavior standards and work on enforcing them. Your expectations must always be clear and the rules should be clearly defined. *Don't make exceptions to the rules.* If you think you will need to make an exception, don't list it as a rule.

3. *Know your own limits.* Every child quickly learns how to push his parent's buttons, and your child will be very skillful at pushing yours to his advantage. Remember that this is not defiance—it is normal, instinctual behavior.

4. *Remain unemotional when dealing with bad behavior.* Children perform for their parents. When you react, in good or bad ways, they will repeat that behavior to get a "rise" out of you.

5. *Pick your battles.* Don't worry about small, unimportant, or annoying behaviors. Save your reaction for major issues concerning safety and truly egregious behavior. Avoid constant criticism by establishing only rules that are fair and attainable for your child's age.

6. *Say what you mean.* Don't threaten, and always carry out what you say you will do. It helps to have a plan organized with all your child's caretakers so that any rule breaking is handled with consistency.

7. *Set your child up for success.* Remove him from negative situations, and distract him if he looks like he may get into trouble. Don't tempt him with an opportunity to misbehave.

8. *Always remember that the behavior is bad—not the child.* "Hitting other children is bad" is better than "Sam is bad." As your child gets older and starts attending school, you can begin to help him understand that the actions are bad, and, he is responsible for his actions. Most important, never let your child think you don't love him because he has done something wrong. Make sure he knows that while you don't like the behavior, you will always love him.

9. *Make sure the punishment fits the crime* and is delivered in a timely fashion. For the most effective learning of a toddler and preschool child, any consequences of bad behavior should follow the behavior. A young child does not have a sense of time to understand delayed punishment or to connect it to misbehavior. There should be a logical punishment for the infraction, and it

should help teach your child what he did wrong. For example if Sam (age three) hits Ryan, take Sam home and explain if he can't behave, he can't play with Ryan. At home give him three minutes in isolation and tell him it's his punishment for hitting Ryan. This tried-and-true punishment is called a "time-out" and involves removing your child from a situation for a set amount of time. We recommend one minute for each year of age, so that a four year old will get a four minute time-out.

10. *Always treat your child with respect.* Be the kind of person you expect your child to be. This teaches her to respect others. As your child gets older, you can invite her to participate in the decision-making process to determine a punishment for breaking a rule.

It's normal for a child to occasionally misbehave and test limits; it's also normal for this to upset you. Be sure to take a break from parenting periodically and spend time with your significant other and friends. Finally and most importantly, remember to always praise your child for good behavior and tell her frequently that you love her.

HYPERACTIVITY

Hyperactivity refers to excessively restless physical and mental activity in a child. This excessively high behavior level may contribute to behavior problems. A hyperactive child has a short attention span, is prone to temper tantrums, exhibits seemingly boundless energy, and requires little sleep. These behaviors require parental patience and understanding. Unfortunately, there is no real standard of activity level in children, and some "hyperactive" children may be simply very active at one end of the spectrum of normal behavior. Some parents feel that candy or sugar may cause hyperactivity. There is no research to prove this theory. However, there is research that caffeine, which is present in chocolate and many soda drinks, does cause some jitteriness and hyperactivity. There are some cases when a child has *attention deficit hyperactivity disorder— ADHD*. In order to have this diagnosis, a child must meet certain criteria set by the American Psychiatric Foundation in *The Diagnostic and Statistical Manual of Mental Disorders*. These criteria must include at least six symptoms of inattention for at least six months, or six symptoms of hyperactivity-impulsive behavior for at least six months. A diagnosis of inattention and hyperactive-impulsive disorder is not usually made until a child begins attending school, though evidence of the behaviors may be present earlier.

JEALOUSY

Jealousy is a normal reaction which most children feel at one time or another. It is usually brought on by a feeling of insecurity or fear of loss of a parent's love, and often becomes more evident about the time of an arrival of a new baby. Jealousy can become a problem if it is mismanaged. It's important, therefore, that you always treat the *cause* of the jealousy—not the jealousy itself. Some good guidelines to follow are:

- Always show your child respect and treat him as an individual.
- Take care to give special attention evenly to each child.
- Never select a "favorite" among your children, and never compare your child to a sibling, cousin, or other child.
- Always acknowledge his good attributes.
- Continue to praise your child for good behavior with both words and actions.

The most important things you can give each of your children are both your individualized attention and individualized time.

LANGUAGE DEVELOPMENT

Language involves both talking and listening for understanding. Children learn to talk when they are constantly exposed to the sound of voices, a process that originates prior to birth. Newborn and very young babies associate the sounds of their parents' voices with comfort and security, and babies as young as two months of age start to make a variety of noises that mimic these sounds. The two most important things that you can do to help your baby's language development are to talk to, and read to, your baby.

In the second half of his first year your baby will recognize his own name and start to make some distinguishable sounds like "da-da" and "ma-ma." When your child says a sound close to a word, repeat it back to him. Name objects you use and explain to him what you are doing. For example, "I am putting on your jacket." It is okay—in fact, it is preferable—to use two languages in your home. Babies do not get confused and can easily develop a bilingual vocabulary.

After twelve months of age a child's vocabulary starts to expand, and he may say a few recognizable words. At this point, his understanding of language *(receptive language)* is much better than his ability to speak *(expressive language)*. Your eighteen-month-old uses ten to twenty words and a lot of gestures and pointing to communicate his needs. He probably also likes to sing. By the end of her second year, your child will be able to communicate most of her thoughts and needs. She understands simple commands and speaks in sentences of two to three words; she understands approximately three hundred words at this point. A three-year-old asks a lot of "what" questions to learn more about everything. His sentences are three to four words long, and he understands close to one thousand words now. A four-year-old also can name most primary colors and follow a command, even when the object is not present. (This is the beginning of abstract understanding.) She knows and understands around fifteen hundred words and uses four- to six-word sentences. Your five-year-old knows his full name and age, as well as his full address and phone number. He uses most speech sounds correctly, knows two thousand words, and can use six- to eight-word complex sentences. See Table 7.1, "Guide to Children's Development."

To help your child's language development here are a few tips:

- Sing and talk to your baby as much as possible.
- Look directly at your child so that your expressions and tone of voice give her clues to what you are saying.
- Read to your child.
- Arrange opportunities for your child to play with other children, to help develop communication skills.
- Encourage your child to use his words to communicate what he wants, even if his words are not grammatically correct.

Delayed speech development may be the result of a number of issues including normal late development, a lot of early childhood illness, a lack of adult stimulus, and emotional stress. It also could be a result of a hearing problem, especially if your child has had a large number of ear infections. Talk to your doctor if you have any concerns.

MANNERS

Set a good example in social situations. Always be polite when addressing your child and expect them to return the behavior. Patiently wait for "please," "thank you," and "excuse me," until they become a habit. Talk to your child about your expectations. For example, "We are going to church. I know it is hard, but I need you to be quiet." You can also help your child to succeed by bringing quiet activities she enjoys that are used only in special circumstances such as attending church. Fabric squares can be entertaining and quiet, and cloth picture and activity books are also useful. Teach your child to whisper, and teach her the differences between "inside voices" and "outdoor voices." Sit near the back of any public meeting, theater, etc., so that you can slip out if noise becomes an issue. *Always reward good behavior.*

NAIL-BITING

Nail-biting is a comfort habit that often develops in preschool and school-aged children. It may be copied from other children, or it may be a sign of anxiety, stress, or nervous tension. Nail-biting may cause a little pain when the nails are bitten very low; generally it causes no health risk—it only looks ugly. If the nail-biting is related to stress, you must determine the cause in order to end it. With children under the age of five, it may be another sibling, starting nursery school, or general nervousness about friends.

You can try distracting your child or keeping her hands busy elsewhere. It also is helpful to keep her nails trimmed and smooth. The bitter tasting liquids available to discourage nail-biting usually don't work, and they may only make your child resentful.

NIGHTMARES AND NIGHT TERRORS

All children partially awaken after dreams, and most can put themselves back to sleep with no problems. Nightmares (scary dreams) are normal for infants after approximately six months of age and common by four years of age. When a baby has a nightmare, he will cry until someone comes to comfort him; toddlers and preschoolers may awaken and run into their parents' room for comfort. Separation anxiety, nursery school or day care phobia, arrival of a new sibling, fear of the dark, and exposure to violent television shows or movies are the most common causes of nightmares in young children. A high fever can also cause a sleep disturbance. When your child has a nightmare, help her back to bed and reassure her that everything is okay, then talk about the nightmare the following day. There may be a new fear surfacing that you can help your child deal with. Suggest that she draw a picture of the bad dream to help you understand. You can also encourage your child to create a happy ending for the drawing. If lack of sleep becomes a problem, talk to your doctor about prescribing a mild sedative to break the pattern of nightmares and sleeplessness.

Night terrors are less frequent. With these, your child seems to be in a trancelike state, not quite awake and not quite asleep. Lead your child back to bed and try to soothe her back to sleep. Protect her from injuring herself. Usually occurring within two hours of falling asleep, night terrors are self-limiting (they run their course). The problem usually disappears completely as your child gets older.

PACIFIERS

Sucking is actually a self-comforting behavior for babies, causing them to relax or soothe themselves and go back to sleep when awakened. Many newborn nurseries even provide pacifiers for new babies.

You have control over whether or not to start your baby on a pacifier. If you decide to use one and find a pacifier that he likes, buy a good supply. Always use a one-piece commercial pacifier. Homemade ones can be pulled apart and cause your baby to choke. Rinse the pacifier under hot, running tap water after your baby uses it or when it gets dropped. If it is dropped in a particularly dirty area, throw it out. Replace pacifiers regularly with a clean, new one—especially after every illness. When your child starts to grow teeth, inspect the pacifier regularly to make sure there are no loose pieces. Don't dip the pacifier in any liquids or sugar. Once your baby is six to eight months old, you may want to limit pacifier use to his crib, car seat, and stroller. It also may be useful to take some with you on an airplane to help your child avoid ear pain on takeoffs and landings. *Never tie a pacifier on a string around your baby's neck* as it can become caught and strangle your baby. If you want to attach it to your baby's clothing, special pacifier clips are available in the baby department of most drugstores and supermarkets.

Have a plan to help your child get rid of his pacifier. Many dentists recommend giving it up before the age of two. This can coincide with your child's first visit to the dentist. (Many dentists can help by giving instructions to your child that it is time to give up the pacifier.) Some children will give up the pacifier cold turkey, but more often it is a difficult process. You can help your child with gentle weaning if necessary by gradually taking away places where he may use the pacifier. Make sure the final surrender of the pacifier is during a relatively stress-free time for your child when no other new situation is being introduced. Many parents are successful in helping a child give up a pacifier around a birthday or major holiday. Other happy events can prove a valuable distraction. Some parents introduce the "pacifier fairy" as a prelude to the "tooth fairy." Use whatever system works best for your family situation.

PLAY

Play is the work of a child and how she really learns about her environment. Children need all kinds of play: quiet play, group play, and real high-energy play. Early effort on your part to teach your child how to play quietly by herself will pay off every year as she grows. The type of play your child engages in will change as she develops more fine and gross motor skills as well as cognitive and language skills. Play can also help her advance through development by creatively challenging her abilities.

Your child does not need expensive toys to play with. Many babies are more fascinated by the wrapping paper or box a toy comes in than the toy itself. Fun and learning will often be generated by whatever materials are available. Pots and pans, measuring spoons, and other nonbreakable kitchen items make for great fun for babies and toddlers. Take your cues from your child. It's also a good idea to show him early on that television exaggerates how a toy operates and that toy commercials are often unrealistic. Have fun with your child and do silly things like reading a book under the dining room table or blowing bubbles in the bathtub. Be patient with your child if she doesn't seem to want to play with other children. Real sharing and cooperative playing can only begin at around the age of three. A sampling of play activities and abilities for young children is contained in Table 7.2.

This table offers a few suggestions for play activities that may be appropriate for your child's age and abilities. Every child develops at his own pace, so pick activities that best suit your child's individual preferences and skill levels. Reading with your child is a great activity that can start with a little baby and continue throughout childhood. Music and singing are also fun and stimulating for your growing child. Always pick activities that you enjoy because chances are that if you are having fun with your child they are having fun, too.

RESPONSIBILITY

Your child is ready for responsibility at as young as six months of age when she begins to sit up and hold her own cup or bottle. Her first responsibilities are to learn to do some things for herself. Responsibility increases gradually as your baby grows and develops new skills. Once your child is walking, have her help pick up and put away her toys at intervals during the day when you are ready to move on to a new activity. Children love to help. One of your child's first skills will probably be feeding herself. Between the ages of one and two, she will learn to undress herself, and between the ages of three and four to dress herself. Use these opportunities to also teach her to put her clothes in the hamper.

You also teach her to be responsible for her own actions by learning the limits of "no." Children respond well to limits but they must be consistent. We always like to frame rules around safety. "I love you and want you to be safe." The word "no" often sounds better when framed with "No, that is not safe." Teach your child that when you say "no," you mean "no." If she repeats the action anyway, there has to be a consequence. Usually what works best for a young child is a "time-out." Basically you remove her from the situation to a time-out place for a short period of time. Many parents use one minute for each year to determine how long to leave a child in time-out. Remember that time passes much more slowly for children, and in this case a little can mean a lot.

Table 7.2

Play Activities and Abilities for Young Children	
Age	**Activity/Ability**
Newborn	Sensory stimulation, soft music.
	Rocking, stroking, singing, and talking to your baby.
1–3 months	Continue sensory stimulation.
	Add mobiles and simple rattles.
	Read to your baby.
	Sing and tell stories.
4 months	Increase socialization. Sit him in an infant seat to watch and participate in his environment.
	Can hold rattle and shake it.
	Continue reading and singing.
6 months	Stimulate communication by telling her what you are doing and naming objects around her.
	Give her small toys to transfer from one hand to the other.
	Let her bang pots and pans.
9 months	Provide a safe environment to explore as locomotion increases.
	Play peek-a-boo.
	Likes to drop and throw toys.
12 months	Play ball. Let her stack one block on top of another.
	Invite her participation in reading by having her turn the page.
	She can make a mark with a crayon.
	Begin art.
15 months	Plays patty-cake.
	Likes to scribble.
	Can stack two blocks.

Table 7.2 (*continued*)

Age	Activity/ Ability
18 months	Uses a pull toy or push toy. Doll strollers and little wagons are good.
	Give her a picture book and let her "read" on her own.
	Builds towers of three or more blocks.
	Can wind up a toy after being shown how.
2 years	Able to climb, run, jump, and kick a ball.
	Can hold a crayon and make steady strokes.
	Engages in "parallel play" (side by side with another child with no interaction and no common goal).
	Not able to share, especially toys.
2½ years	Can wait for his turn in play.
	Likes large riding toys including tricycle (though unable to pedal). Jumps with two feet.
	Encourage quiet activities like puzzles and picture books.
	Play hide-and-seek to encourage memory skills.
3 years	Able to pedal tricycle.
	Repeats songs and rhymes.
	Likes to "make believe."
	Enjoys role-playing and likes dolls, trucks, blocks, and housekeeping toys.
	Can begin to share and begins to play cooperatively.
4 years	Plays in shifting loose groups with toys.
	Can catch a big ball and learns to pump on a swing.
	Likes matching games.
	Uses imagination and lots of pretend games.
5 years	More coordinated and more social interaction.
	Enjoys peer interaction and participation in simple games like freeze tag and pickle.
	Can jump rope and use skates, sleds, and scooters.
	Longer attention span so can begin modified team sports.
	Can color within lines and use scissors.

SCHOOL READINESS

The decision to send a child to nursery school is a personal one, determined by preference, finances, availability of playmates, and other individual factors. Those in favor of nursery school feel that it prepares children for kindergarten and helps them to relate to adults other than their parents. It also gives stay-at-home caretakers a break from at least one child, which many feel helps to make them better parents. Some nursery schools also function as a day care center with an extended day, and this may be a desirable option for some working parents. Others feel that they can provide the same educational and learning experience at home and they would rather keep their young child with them as long as they are able. If you choose the latter, we recommend that you and your child join a play group to enhance his social skills. Both choices are good ones, and you have to decide what works best for your family.

When your child is around the age of five, you need to decide when your child is ready for kindergarten. Many schools have an age cutoff. An example would be that your child must be age five by September 1 or December 31. This can give you general information about the age of the children in the class; it's a good idea to have your child in a class with kids who are within his same age group. Children at age five have variable academic skills, physical and coordination skills, and social skills; by about the third grade most have caught up and are on the same level. In addition to age there are some key skills necessary for your child to be able to successfully start school. These include the ability to:

- Spend time away from home and his primary caretaker.
- Interact with adults other than parents.
- Listen and follow directions for tasks and behaviors.
- Use language skills to express ideas and needs.
- Focus on a single activity for at least fifteen minutes.

SHARING

Sharing is an extremely hard task for young children, and nearly impossible for any child under the age of three. Don't expect your young child to share or play cooperatively as this is more of an adult value and usually outside of a baby's ability. When another child is over for a play-date make sure that there are enough toys for two. Warn your child ahead of time that when Sarah comes over, we are going to let her play with some of your toys. Be vigilant and prepared to distract both children as need be. Never let your child hit another child for a toy. It is your responsibility to avoid particularly difficult situations. For example, if your child has an especially favorite toy, put it away in a closet before Sarah visits. At around age three you can begin to work on the concept of sharing, but set your expectations low. The easiest task to start with is taking turns, and this skill will be needed for kindergarten and nursery school. You can encourage children in these activities through simple games that emphasize how much fun it is to play with another child.

SIBLING RIVALRY

During the first five years, most sibling rivalry centers around the arrival of another child. Almost 80 percent of children grow up with at least one brother or sister, and it is normal for the older child to sometimes feel displaced, frustrated, and unloved. An additional complication is that the arrival of a second child often occurs around the stressful ages of two and three. Make sure that the arrival of a new baby does not interfere with the special time you spend with your older child. Be sure to include him in as many activities as possible. Before the baby is born, give your child his baby (doll) to play with. Take him with you to a doctor's visit and let him listen to the baby's heart, if possible. If this is a time for "changing beds," make sure he is firmly settled in his new bed long before the baby arrives so that the new baby does not "take his bed." Try to take down the crib for a few months before you set it up again. After you have the baby, let your older child come visit you in the hospital. Give your older child a special present from his new sibling, and spend some time each day exclusively with him. Always be fair about the attention you give each child. Never show favoritism.

Some of the following methods will help you to dispel any feelings of sibling rivalry:

- As your children get older, teach them to be loyal to each other and to use words to settle disputes.
- Emphasize the strength of your family and the importance of working together.
- Give praise for cooperative behaviors.
- On each child's birthday have the siblings give a compliment to each other.
- Try to teach children constructive ways of expressing feelings of competition with a sibling and show your confidence in their ability to get along.
- Always protect each child's personal possessions, privacy, and friendships.
- Use limit-setting techniques to monitor acceptable behaviors with each other.
- As they get older, encourage your children to settle their own disagreements. Do not permit hitting, name calling, or destroying each other's toys or other possessions.

SLEEPING PATTERNS

Children have a wide variety of sleeping patterns. About 10 to 15 percent of children ages four months to two years wake up at least once during the night. Normal sleep for your child may not be normal sleep for a neighbor's child. As long as your baby or child is healthy and happy when she is awake, she is normal and there is no cause for alarm.

Newborn sleeping patterns

Most newborn babies sleep sixteen to twenty hours a day in two- to three-hour periods. Most often they wake up because they are hungry or wet. Gradually, as your baby takes more formula or breast milk at each feeding, he will sleep for longer time periods and be awake for longer time periods. You can help your baby to sleep more at night by making a clear difference between going to sleep for daytime naps and settling down for a big sleep at night. Take extra care to get your baby ready for bed at night. *It's never too early to start a bedtime routine.* You may start by singing to your baby at night and gradually evolving the routine into a bedtime story. You can feed her at bedtime, but don't let her hold or keep the bottle. If she needs to suck, give her a pacifier. After she has been fed, burped, and changed into clean diapers and clothes, darken the room and "tuck her in" securely. Make sure she is warm enough. Keep any middle-of-the-night feedings as brief, quiet, and nonstimulating as possible in order to keep your baby in a sleepy state. By four months of age, most full-term babies without any special medical problems do not need any calories during the night.

Sleeping pattern for ages six months to twelve months

By around six months of age, your baby will need less sleep, usually ten to sixteen hours per twenty-four-hour period. Between the ages of six to nine months, he will settle into two daytime naps per day—one in the morning and one in the afternoon. At this point, he will still fall asleep when he needs to. That starts to change at around nine months of age. Your baby is now able to keep himself awake more and is often reluctant to leave the excitement of his family for sleep. It is now very important to have a bedtime routine to get your child ready for bed and willing to leave the rest of the family to go to sleep. Bedtime routines should be pleasant and help your baby to slow down and get ready for sleep. A nice supper, followed by a warm bath, then maybe a special snack, visit to the toilet, a story, and a good "tuck in" is an example of a potential bedtime routine. Some children also rely on a comfort item like a special blanket or stuffed animal to snuggle with when the parent leaves the room. You may want to use a night light as another comfort measure for your child.

Sleeping pattern for the one- to two-year-old

As your child approaches his first birthday, he probably still needs an average of ten to twelve hours of sleep at night. His daytime naps will gradually decrease, however. You may sometimes have to wake him during the day in order to ensure that he will be able to go to sleep again at night. This becomes particularly important when your toddler reaches that awkward phase when one nap is not enough and two naps are too much. Getting overtired is a very common toddler problem during this time. You might help the transition by providing one nap and one rest period during which you help your toddler do quiet activities alone and also with you. Most of the quiet activities will be with you, but you can encourage brief periods of five to ten minutes when your child can do something on his own, like a few puzzles or a quiet book look.

Sleeping pattern for the two- to five-year-old

By the time your child falls into the two- to five-year-old bracket, you probably have figured out whether he is a good sleeper or a problem sleeper. Be thankful for a good sleeper. But don't despair if he's not. There are some practical approaches you can take to promote sleep and rest. Many children actually spend more time *in* bed than actually *sleeping* in bed so you want to make it attractive. Usually between two and three years of age, most children are ready for a big bed, and it's worth going to some extra trouble to make this transition special. Some options you can consider to make his bed special include: particular sheets and bed quilts, special snugly toys, picture books, a reading light, a bedside table with special puzzles, or other reasonably neat toys to play with in bed.

Problem sleepers

For problem sleepers, the bedtime routine is more important than ever. Your young toddler or preschooler needs plenty of notice when bedtime is coming up. You must turn down the activity level and have a series of quieter nighttime activities. Don't start a long game, story, or television show if there is not time to finish it before bedtime. Reading a bedtime story with your child in bed is a tried-and-true end to a perfect day. Do not allow your child to get out of bed after the bedtime story, and during toilet training be relaxed about nighttime accidents. Get a nice half-sheet that is made of plastic or rubber and cover it with a regular sheet. This makes it easy to do a quick bed change, if necessary, in the middle of the night.

If your child refuses to go to sleep and cries when put to bed for the night even after the usual bedtime routine, you can try a "withdrawal" approach. There are two different ways to approach withdrawal: gradual and sudden. Whichever one you choose, you will need total consistency from both parents and all caretakers and babysitters in order to make progress.

Gradual withdrawal method

- Put your child to bed after the bedtime ritual and say goodnight.
- Leave the room and tell him you will be back in ten minutes.
- Return in ten minutes, say goodnight again, and say that you will return in twenty minutes.
- Keep coming back every twenty minutes and repeat the routine of saying goodnight and that you will be back in twenty minutes until he falls asleep.

This may take four or more hours the first night, but it should gradually decrease.

Sudden withdrawal method

- Put your child to bed after the bedtime ritual and say goodnight.
- Leave the room and do not go back even when your child starts to cry.
- Be prepared for your child to cry for one to two hours.
- Do not reenter his room.

The first few nights will be extremely difficult, but the crying should decrease with each successive night. After one to two weeks, your child should go to sleep without a fuss. *Crying will not hurt your child*, though this method is very difficult for any parent to endure.

Your child may *talk and laugh in her sleep*. As long as she is calm, there is no need to wake her. She is probably dreaming. Some children also wake up early in the morning. If you are not ready to get up and get going, the best thing to do is to start your child on an early morning routine of entertaining himself with the special toys and cuddly items you have left on his bed and bedside table. A music box or child tape player can be very useful to help entertain your early bird.

SLEEPWALKING

Many children go through a short phase of sleepwalking. Your child may get out of bed as part of a dream and wander around with his eyes open; however, he won't see you or understand you. The best thing to do is to guide him safely back to bed without waking him. If you notice your child is starting to sleepwalk, make sure you have a gate at the top or bottom of any stairs in your home so that he can't injure himself by falling. Most cases of sleepwalking pass on their own. If your child's sleepwalking is associated with nightmares or is becoming a problem due to safety, you might speak with his doctor to help sort out the cause of this behavior. Sometimes your child may be referred to a child psychologist to sort out the problem.

TELEVISION AND MOVIES

Television and movies are all basically passive activities that replace important learning from self-initiated activities. Children under the age of five are unable to distinguish between fantasy and reality, thus television can have a tremendous influence on your child. Many shows on television are violent and very scary for young children, and they can be the source of sleep problems. Children under the age of five also relate to characters on television as role models and may see the aggressive behavior portrayed as appropriate behavior for them.

Do not be tempted to use the television as a babysitter. Try to limit your child's viewing to special television shows and videotapes produced specifically for his age group. We prefer children's television shows that tell a story or have a theme, as they encourage a child to follow a story and develop his attention span. Television also takes the place of more active playtime for children. Tired children sleep better, and active children will eat better.

Theatrical movies are not really appropriate for most young children under the age of three. The dark environment may prove scary, and, quite frankly, most movies just last too long for a young child to sit through. The only exception is if you are taking your newborn to a movie you want to see because you know your baby will sleep in your lap or in a baby sling. Once your child is around three years old, you can start taking her to a cartoon-like movie. Be aware, however, that the dark room and big screen may still be scary even if the movie itself is appropriate. You should start by renting a full-length cartoon video and see how your preschooler reacts while watching it. Make sure that you always know what movies and television shows your child is watching. Become familiar with the television and movie rating systems so that you won't be caught off guard. Discuss any movie or television show that upsets your child. If he has seen something that disturbs him, have him draw a picture of the scary part and then create a happy ending.

TOILET TRAINING TIPS

When you are ready to start toilet training, dress your child in clothing that is easy to remove. And so for this very reason, we like to recommend toilet training in warmer weather when less clothing is needed. Start a potty chair or toilet schedule. Put your child on it when she wakes up in the morning, before and after meals, before and after naps, and as part of her bedtime routine. Praise and reward your child for all successes including the use of child training pants as soon as he starts to use the toilet. We have successfully used a chart with a new sticker every time the child succeeds. Always be patient and matter-of-fact about accidents, making certain to call them accidents and not failures. Quickly change your child's clothes (as soon as it is convenient) and assure her that she will do better next time. *Never punish your child for an accident.*

Disposable diapers are so good today that often children don't feel wet. At night-time, we think it's a good idea to use disposable training pants or pull-ups until your child is dry at night for at least two weeks.

Toilet training can be slow. Unfortunately, too many parents start toilet training before the child is ready and think the whole process lasts six months. *Let your child set the pace.* There is no one universal "right age" to begin toilet training. Be patient. Problems occur when parents feel that training is not happening fast enough. Toilet training can also be complicated if your child attends a nursery school or day care since it's very difficult to implement a good toilet training regime in a group setting. Be flexible and work with your child's school or day care to design an optimal program. You will probably have to bend more and adapt your ideas to their philosophy. It also may take a little bit longer. If you are meeting with excess resistance to toilet training from your child, or if constipation becomes a problem, the time may not be right. In these cases, talk to your child's doctor for more specific help.

TRADITIONS

Just as your child flourishes with routines for bed and activities of everyday life, he will flourish participating in family traditions. Some traditions go back generations, and others are begun when a new family is established. A tradition can be as simple as a special family dinner once a week or as complex as a special holiday celebration. Start with a few simple ones like your child's birthday and a few major holidays. Keep the celebration simple so that you can repeat it. For example, for your child's birthday tell him it's his special day and you are having a special family meal for him. As your child gets older, he can pick his favorite meal. You can also do the same for your own birthday and the birthdays of other family members. Keep telling your child that "this is how our family celebrates birthdays." If you practice an organized religion, there may be traditions affiliated with religious holy days. These may have a little more ritual in them and involve more of your extended family and/or involvement in a religious community group. Traditions give your child a sense of belonging to a special group—your family. Finally, be flexible in your traditions. When you outgrow one, store it in memory and let it go.

WHINING

There's no doubt about it, whining is extremely annoying. Usually, however, it is a sign of fatigue or hunger. Step back and take a look. Has her sleep been disrupted? Is your routine different? Have you missed giving her a meal? Are you scheduling her for too many activities? Adults are much better adapted to "going with the flow." Children can get "out of sync" easily and don't quite know what is wrong. Just as sometimes they can't wait to go the bathroom, they can't wait to eat or sleep, etc. Everyone needs a little time to mellow out or be bored.

Appendix A

Your Child's Health Record

Name: _____   Phone: _____

Address: _____

_____

Birthdate: _____   Sex: _____

Parent/Guardian: _____

Immunizations

	Date	Date	Date	Date	Date	Date
DPT						
OPV						
MMR						
Hib						
HB (Hepatitis B)						
Chicken pox						

History—Including medical, developmental, or allergic issues

Toilet trained: _____

Allergies: _____

Lab Tests

	Date	Date	Date	Date	Date	Date
Urinalysis						
Hematocrit						
Lead test						
Other						

Physical Exam

Date: _____

Birthdate: _____   Sex: _____

Height: _____   Weight: _____   B.P.: _____

Tuberculosis Skin Test (PPD): _____   Date: _____   Result: _____

Exam was normal, unless abnormalities are listed below:

Physician Signature: _____   Date: _____

The parents, by their signature, deny any significant health problems have occurred since the date of the physical examination.

Parent Signature: _____   Date: _____

Appendix B

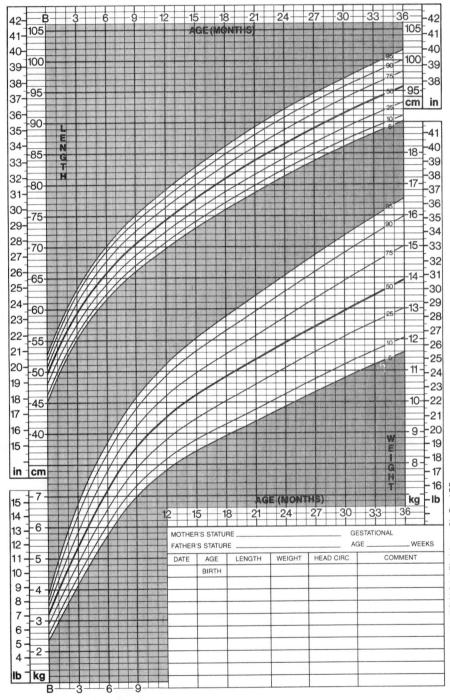

GIRLS: BIRTH TO 36 MONTHS
PHYSICAL GROWTH
NCHS PERCENTILES*

NAME_____ RECORD #_____

* Adapted from: Hamill PVV, Drizd TA, Johnson CL, Reed RB, Roche AF, Moore WM: Physical growth: National Center for Health Statistics percentiles. AM J CLIN NUTR 32:607-629, 1979. Data from the Fels Longitudinal Study, Wright State University School of Medicine, Yellow Springs, Ohio.

© 1982 Ross Laboratories

MOTHER'S STATURE _____ GESTATIONAL
FATHER'S STATURE _____ AGE _____ WEEKS

DATE	AGE	LENGTH	WEIGHT	HEAD CIRC.	COMMENT
	BIRTH				

GIRLS: BIRTH TO 36 MONTHS
PHYSICAL GROWTH
NCHS PERCENTILES*

NAME _____ RECORD # _____

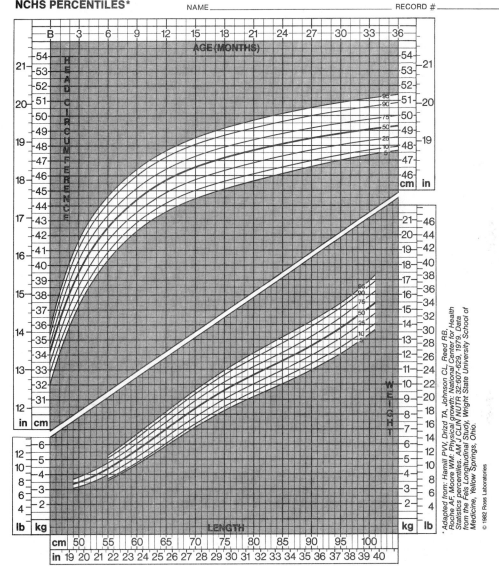

* Adapted from: Hamill PVV, Drizd TA, Johnson CL, Reed RB, Roche AF, Moore WM: Physical growth: National Center for Health Statistics percentiles. AM J CLIN NUTR 32:607-629, 1979. Data from the Fels Longitudinal Study, Wright State University School of Medicine, Yellow Springs, Ohio.

© 1982 Ross Laboratories

DATE	AGE	LENGTH	WEIGHT	HEAD CIRC.	COMMENT

SIMILAC® WITH IRON
Infant Formula

ISOMIL®
Soy Protein Formula with Iron

Reprinted with permission
of Ross Laboratories

BOYS: BIRTH TO 36 MONTHS
PHYSICAL GROWTH
NCHS PERCENTILES*

NAME _____ RECORD # _____

AGE (MONTHS)

LENGTH

WEIGHT

MOTHER'S STATURE _____ GESTATIONAL
FATHER'S STATURE _____ AGE _____ WEEKS

DATE	AGE	LENGTH	WEIGHT	HEAD CIRC.	COMMENT
	BIRTH				

*Adapted from: Hamill PVV, Drizd TA, Johnson CL, Reed RB,
Roche AF, Moore WM: Physical growth: National Center for Health
Statistics percentiles. AM J CLIN NUTR 32:607–629, 1979. Data
from the Fels Longitudinal Study, Wright State University School of
Medicine, Yellow Springs, Ohio.

© 1982 Ross Laboratories

BOYS: BIRTH TO 36 MONTHS
PHYSICAL GROWTH
NCHS PERCENTILES*

NAME _____ RECORD # _____

MOTHER'S STATURE _____ GESTATIONAL

FATHER'S STATURE _____ AGE _____ WEEKS

DATE	AGE	LENGTH	WEIGHT	HEAD CIRC.	COMMENT
	BIRTH				

*Adapted from: Hamill PVV, Drizd TA, Johnson CL, Reed RB, Roche AF, Moore WM: Physical growth: National Center for Health Statistics percentiles. AM J CLIN NUTR 32:607-629, 1979. Data from the Fels Longitudinal Study, Wright State University School of Medicine, Yellow Springs, Ohio.

© 1982 Ross Laboratories

GIRLS: 2 TO 18 YEARS
PHYSICAL GROWTH
NCHS PERCENTILES*

NAME _____ RECORD # _____

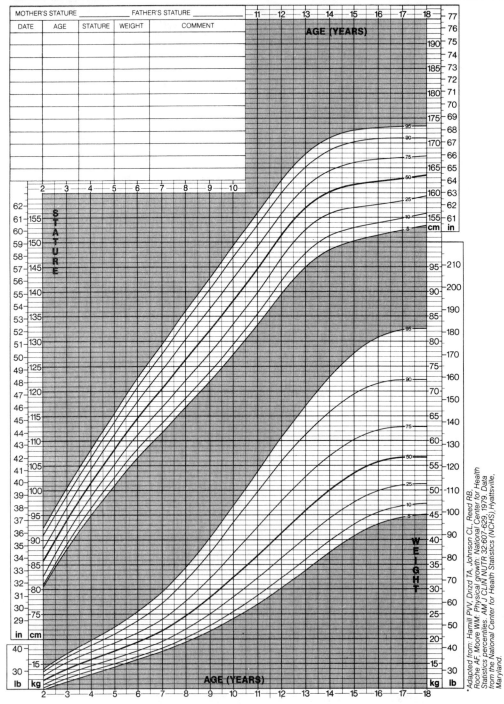

*Adapted from: Hamill PVV, Drizd TA, Johnson CL, Reed RB, Roche AF, Moore WM: Physical growth: National Center for Health Statistics percentiles. AM J CLIN NUTR 32:607-629, 1979. Data from the National Center for Health Statistics (NCHS), Hyattsville, Maryland.

GIRLS: PREPUBESCENT
PHYSICAL GROWTH
NCHS PERCENTILES*

NAME _____ RECORD # _____

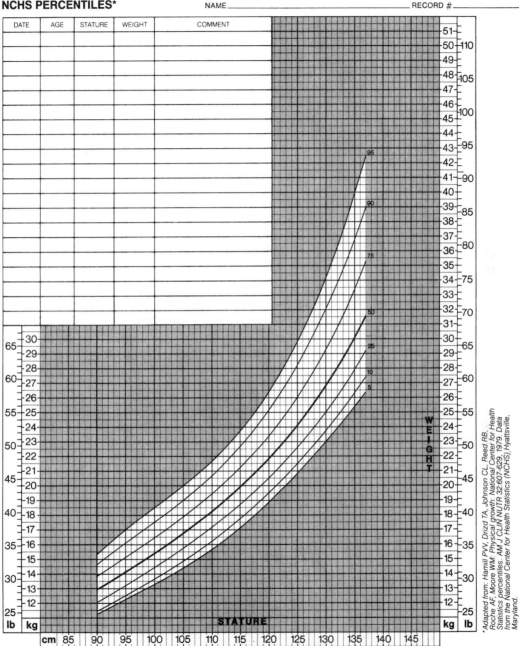

DATE	AGE	STATURE	WEIGHT	COMMENT

STATURE

*Adapted from: Hamill PVV, Drizd TA, Johnson CL, Reed RB, Roche AF, Moore WM. Physical growth: National Center for Health Statistics percentiles. AM J CLIN NUTR 32:607-629, 1979. Data from the National Center for Health Statistics (NCHS), Hyattsville, Maryland.

© 1982 Ross Laboratories

SIMILAC® WITH IRON
Infant Formula

ISOMIL®
Soy Protein Formula with Iron

BOYS: 2 TO 18 YEARS
PHYSICAL GROWTH
NCHS PERCENTILES*

NAME_____ RECORD #_____

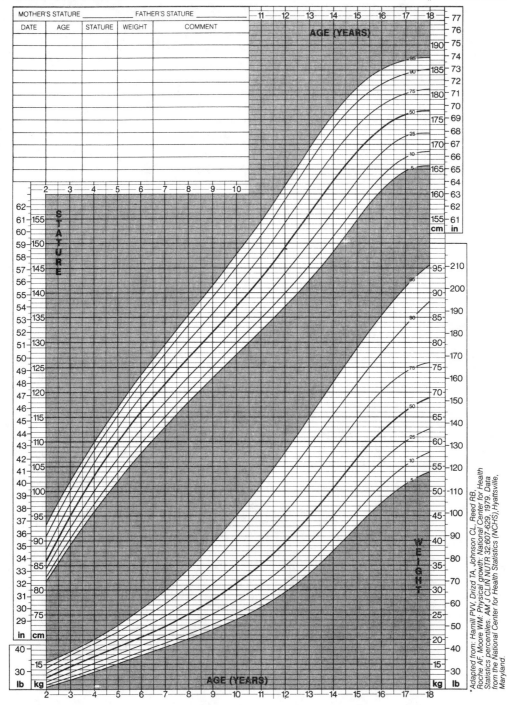

MOTHER'S STATURE_____ FATHER'S STATURE_____

DATE	AGE	STATURE	WEIGHT	COMMENT

AGE (YEARS)

STATURE

WEIGHT

AGE (YEARS)

* Adapted from: Hamill PVV, Drizd TA, Johnson CL, Reed RB, Roche AF, Moore WM: Physical growth: National Center for Health Statistics percentiles. AM J CLIN NUTR 32:607-629, 1979. Data from the National Center for Health Statistics (NCHS), Hyattsville, Maryland.

BOYS: PREPUBESCENT
PHYSICAL GROWTH
NCHS PERCENTILES*

NAME_____ RECORD #_____

DATE	AGE	STATURE	WEIGHT	COMMENT

95
90
75
50
25
10
5

WEIGHT

STATURE

cm 85 90 95 100 105 110 115 120 125 130 135 140 145

in 34 35 36 37 38 39 40 41 42 43 44 45 46 47 48 49 50 51 52 53 54 55 56 57 58

*Adapted from: Hamill PVV, Drizd TA, Johnson CL, Reed RB, Roche AF, Moore WM.: Physical growth: National Center for Health Statistics percentiles. AM J CLIN NUTR 32:607-629, 1979. Data from the National Center for Health Statistics (NCHS), Hyattsville, Maryland.

© 1982 Ross Laboratories

SIMILAC® WITH IRON
Infant Formula

ISOMIL®
Soy Protein Formula with Iron

Reprinted with permission
of Ross Laboratories

Appendix C

Routine Immunization Schedule

Vaccine*	Hep-B	DTP	OPV	Hib	MMR	Varicella	Td
For	Hepatitis-B	Diphtheria Tetanus Pertussis	Polio	Haemo- philus influenza-B	Measles Mumps Rubella	Chicken pox	Tetanus Diphtheria
Birth	1st dose						
1 month	2nd dose						
2 months		1st dose	1st dose	1st dose			
4 months		2nd dose	2nd dose	2nd dose			
6 months		3rd dose	3rd dose	3rd dose			
12–18 months		4th dose		4th dose	1st dose	1st dose	
4–5 yrs		5th dose	4th dose		2nd dose		

* These are general recommendations for childhood immunizations started at birth. The exact schedule for your child may vary slightly due to your child's doctor's preferences and your child's specific medical status. Children who are not immunized as infants will have a special schedule developed by their doctor.

Appendix D

Dosage Charts for Common Over-the-Counter Medicines

Acetaminophen

Brand Names: Liquiprin, Tempra, Tylenol
Exact dose: five to seven mg per pound per dose; can be given every 4–6 hours
Recommendation:

Average Weight	Average Age	Dose Range	Practical Available Dose
Less than 10 lbs	Birth–6 months	25–50 mg	0.4 ml infant dropper (40 mg)
10–20 lbs	6–12 months	50–100 mg	0.8 ml infant dropper (80 mg)
20–30 lbs	1–2 years	100–150 mg	1.2 ml infant dropper (120 mg)
30–40 lbs	3–4 years	150–200 mg	5 ml or 1 tsp of the elixir (160 mg) or 2 chewable tablets (160 mg)
40–50 lbs	4–5 years	200–250 mg	7.5 ml or 1½ tsp of elixir (240 mg) or 1½ chewable tablets (240 mg)

Be sure to use the preparation most appropriate for your child's age. Most brands of acetaminophen come in infant drops with a calibrated medicine dropper for 0.4 ml and 0.8 ml (40 mg = 0.4 ml), a liquid elixir (160 mg = 1 tsp = 5 ml), chewable tablets (1 tablet = 80 mg), and junior caplets (1 tablet = 160 mg). It also comes in suppositories of 80 mg and 120 mg.

Ibuprofen

Brand Names: Children's Advil, Children's Motrin
Exact dose: 3–5 mg per pound per dose; can be given every 6–8 hours.
Recommendation:

Average Weight	Average Age	Dose Range	Practical Available Dose
Less than 10 lbs	Birth–6 months	15–30 mg	0.625 ml infant dropper (25 mg)
10–20 lbs	6–12 months	30–60 mg	1.25 ml infant dropper (50 mg)
20–30 lbs	1–2 years	60–90 mg	1.875 ml infant dropper (75 mg)
30–40 lbs	3–4 years	90–120 mg	5 ml or 1 tsp of suspension (100 mg) or 2 chewable tablets (100 mg)
40–50 lbs	4–5 years	120–150 mg	7.5 ml or 1½ tsp suspension (150 mg) or 3 chewable tablets (150 mg)

Be sure to use the preparation most appropriate for your child's age. Most brands of ibuprofen come in infant drops with a calibrated medicine dropper for 0.625 ml (25 mg) and 1.25 ml (50 mg), a liquid suspension (5 ml = 1 tsp = 100 mg), chewable tablets (1 tablet = 50 mg), and junior caplets (1 caplet = 100 mg).

Dextromethorphan

Brand Names: Benylin DM Pediatric Cough Formula, Cremacoat-1, Delsym, Pediacare-1,
St. Joseph Cough Syrup for Children
Exact Dose: 0.25 mg per pound; can be given every 6–8 hours.
DO NOT GIVE TO CHILDREN UNDER AGE 1, UNLESS DIRECTED BY YOUR DOCTOR.
Recommendation:

Average Weight	Average Age	Dose Range	Practical Available Dose
20–30 lbs	1–2 years	5–7.5 mg	5 ml or 1 tsp (5 mg) of elixir
30–40 lbs	3–4 years	7.5–10 mg	7.5 ml or 1½ tsp (7.5 mg) of elixir
40–50 lbs	4–5 years	10–12.5 mg	10 ml or 2 tsp (10 mg) of elixir

Most brands of dextromethorphan come in a liquid elixir (5 ml = 1 tsp = 5 mg). Some come in a liquid elixir of 5 ml = 1 tsp = 7.5 mg. Read the label carefully to be sure that you give the right amount. This table is based on 5 mg per 5 ml or 1 tsp.

Diphenhydramine*

Brand Names: Benadryl, Benylin Cough Syrup
Exact Dose: 0.5 mg per pound per dose; can be given every 6–8 hours.
DO NOT GIVE TO CHILDREN UNDER AGE 1, UNLESS DIRECTED BY YOUR DOCTOR.
Recommendation:

Average Weight	Average Age	Dose Range	Practical Available Dose
20–30 lbs	1–2 years	10–15 mg	5 ml or 1 tsp (12.5 mg) of elixir
30–40 lbs	3–4 years	15–20 mg	7.5 ml or 1½ tsp (18.75 mg) of elixir
40–50 lbs	4–5 years	20–25 mg	10 ml or 2 tsp (25 mg) of elixir or 2 chewable tablets (25 mg)

Be sure to use the preparation most appropriate for your child's age. Most brands of diphenhydramine come in a liquid elixir (5 ml = 1 tsp = 12.5 mg) and/or a chewable tablet (1 tablet = 12.5 mg).

* Remember that diphenhydramine has a strong sedative affect. Use a lower dose if your child is too sleepy. Do not give more than 25 mg per dose unless directed by your child's doctor.

Guaifenesin

Brand names: Cremacoat-2, Glycotuss, Robitussin
Exact Dose: 1.5–2 mg per pound per dose; Can be given every 6 hours.
DO NOT GIVE TO CHILDREN UNDER AGE 2, UNLESS DIRECTED BY YOUR DOCTOR.
Recommendation:

Average Weight	Average Age	Dose Range	Practical Available Dose
30–40 lbs	3–4 years	45–80 mg	2.5 ml or ½ tsp (50 mg) of elixir
40–50 lbs	4–5 years	60–100 mg	5 ml or 1 tsp (100 mg) of elixir

Most preparations of just guaifenesin have 100 mg = 5 ml = 1 tsp. Read the labels carefully to make sure the one you choose is in the same concentration as shown on this dosage table. Many cough preparations have mixed both dextromethorphan (cough suppressant) and guafenesin (cough expectorant). Check with your doctor to ascertain the correct dose for these mixed preparations if she recommends one for your child.

Selected Glossary

Abscess: Lump nodule that contains pus.

Adenoiditis: An infection of the adenoid tissue itself that causes it to become enlarged and inflamed. If it becomes severe it can interfere with breathing, particularly when your child is sleeping; may also cause swelling and blockage of the eustachian tubes that can interfere with your child's hearing.

Adenoids: Lymph tissue located at the upper back part of the throat, near the eustachian tubes and the nasal passages. They help filter bacteria and other infections that are in the mouth.

AIDS (Acquired Immune Deficiency Syndrome): Deterioration of the body's immune system caused by the HIV virus. Most children contract the virus from their mother before they are born. The first symptom of AIDS in a baby is an unusual increase in the frequency and severity of infections and failure to thrive. Pregnant women with HIV should consult their doctor for medicines to prevent transmission to their unborn babies.

Allergic reaction: Abnormal response of the immune system to some substance that produces a variety of symptoms such as itching, hives, or other rash; runny nose; headache; and diarrhea. Severe allergic reaction may cause wheezing, difficulty breathing, and shock.

Analgesic: Pain-relieving medicine.

Anesthesia: The temporary loss of sensation caused by a medicine to relieve pain. General anesthesia will make your child unconscious; the medicines are given via inhalation by a specialist called an anesthesiologist. Local anesthesia is given by injection under the skin and/or a topical liquid medicine or cream applied on the skin surface.

Antibiotic: General category of medicine used to treat a specific bacterial infection.

Antibody: Substance produced by the plasma called immunoglobulin to provide protection against most common infections.

Antihistamine: Medication that decreases the symptoms that are caused by allergens. (These substances cause a histamine release in the body.) When taken orally, they tend to make your child sleepy. We do not recommend giving antihistamines in a cream or lotion (unless recommended by your doctor) because you cannot measure how much of the medicine your child actually absorbs.

Antiseptic: Inhibits growth of germs/microorganisms.

Aortic stenosis: Abnormally narrow heart valve between the left ventricle and the aorta, the main artery carrying blood away from the heart.

Apnea: A very brief pause or stopping of breathing. It often occurs during sleep and is accompanied by a falling heart rate and bluish lips, nails, and skin. Apnea tends to occur in premature, small babies, born before thirty-four weeks' gestation and babies with respiratory or lung disease. Both of these groups exhibit decreased lung capacity and irregular breathing. Anything that blocks an infant's airway may also cause apnea. Occasionally babies born after thirty-four weeks develop "late apnea" at the age of six weeks or older. Late apnea may lead to **sudden infant death syndrome (SIDS)**.

Appendicitis: Inflammation of the appendix that causes pain in the abdominal area. Signs and symptoms usually include a constant pain around the belly button that moves to the right lower abdomen, fever of 101°F taken rectally, and loss of appetite associated with nausea and/or vomiting.

Arrhythmia: Any change or variation in the rhythm of a normal heartbeat. It is measured by the rate and quality of the heartbeat. Arrhythmias are common in children and usually do not require treatment. **Bradycardia** refers to a very slow heartbeat, and **tachycardia** refers to a very fast heartbeat.

Range of Normal Heart Rates	
Age	Beats per minute
Newborn	110–150
Toddler	85–125
Preschool	75–115

Some arrhythmias occur when the heart does not beat in a regular pattern.

Arthritis: Inflammation of a joint, usually accompanied by pain, swelling, tenderness, and stiffness. May be caused by an injury or infection in the joint.

Aseptic: Absence of germs.

Asphyxia: Reduction or absence of the ability to get oxygen and lose carbon dioxide as part of breathing.

Atopic: Out of place; malpositioned.

Autism: Developmental disorder that includes a pattern of behavior of social withdrawal by a child. The child usually has an accompanying deficit in the development and use of language, possible hearing abnormality, and rigid restriction to daily routines and behavioral rituals.

Bacterial infection: Infection caused by one of many possible bacteria (one-cell organisms). Treated with antibiotics that inhibit the growth of bacteria or destroy them.

Benign: Refers to tumors that are not cancerous or spreading to other body tissues. Opposite of **malignant**.

Biliary Atresia: Severe defect in the network of ducts that carry bile away from the liver. Becomes apparent three to six weeks after birth when the liver becomes enlarged and the baby becomes jaundiced.

Birthmark: Visible skin mark present from birth or noted shortly after birth; due to either an abnormality of the skin's blood vessels or the skin's pigment.

Botulism: Poison caused by a toxin from certain bacteria that multiplies rapidly in a vacuum—such as improperly canned foods. Can be fatal.

Bronchodilator: Special medicine that opens up and relaxes the air passages (bronchi) in the lungs. It is often used for treating asthma. Bronchodilators come in a form that can be taken orally and a different form that can inhaled through an inhaler or nebulizer.

Bruxism: Habit of grinding or clenching teeth together, usually during sleep. Can cause local discomfort or headache. Frequently occurs during the process of losing baby teeth when a child has an imperfect fit between the upper and lower teeth (malocclusion) or between remaining primary teeth and new permanent teeth.

Cancer: General name for a large variety of diseases that involve uncontrollable and abnormal growth of cells. Cancers are often referred to as **tumors**. A tumor is **malignant** when there is uncontrolled growth of the abnormal cells that spread to nearby tissue. A tumor is called **benign** or noncancerous when the growth is confined to a specific area and does not invade and destroy healthy tissue. A **primary cancer** or tumor describes the kind of cell or tissue where the abnormal growth starts. When a cancer spreads to other cells or tissues, it is said to **metastasize**. Leukemia is the most common kind of cancer in children. Doctors who specialize in the treatment of cancer are called **oncologists**.

Celiac disease: Sensitivity to gluten, the protein found in wheat and rye. It doesn't appear until gluten is introduced into the diet, usually after the age of six months. Undigested gluten irritates the small bowel and interferes with normal digestion. The common symptoms of celiac disease include abdominal distention, foul-smelling diarrhea, and loss of appetite. It often leads to failure to gain weight. Gluten is found in many common foods including baby foods, breads, pastries, and many prepared meats and packaged foods. It is often a filler in many processed foods.

Centers for Disease Control (CDC): U.S. government agency that provides investigation, identification, prevention, and control of diseases.

Cerebral palsy: Includes a range of conditions caused by a malfunction in those areas of the brain responsible for movement. This neurological disorder, which involves posture and movement, is not progressive. A child with mild cerebral palsy may just be awkward, while a more severe case may be seriously physically handicapped. It may also be associated with epilepsy as well as vision, speech, and intellectual difficulties. The United Cerebral Palsy Association is a good source for information and referrals regarding this disorder.

Chalasia: Relaxation of sphincters. It causes spitting up when the lower end of the esophagus sphincter is not strong enough to close. It leads to passive reflux of the stomach contents back up into the esophagus, causing vomiting.

Chest physical therapy: Chest PT. Noninvasive group of therapies to mobilize lung secretions. Can be done at home. Includes percussion, manual vibration, and postural drainage.

Cleft lip and cleft palate: Cleft lip is a congenitally split upper lip; it is commonly called a hare lip. A cleft palate is a congenital split in the roof of the mouth or palate. These birth defects can occur separately or together and are usually observed at birth. Surgery can correct both of these conditions. A cleft lip repair is usually done when a baby is one to three months old; cleft palate repair is usually done when the baby is eight to twelve months old. Prior to surgery, adequate nutrition is the main concern. A special syringe called a cleft lip feeder or a Breck feeder can be used to feed these babies.

Clubfoot: Birth defect involving malformation of the anklebones and foot bones, usually noticed at birth. Treatment usually starts within a few days to obtain optimum results. The foot is manipulated into proper position, and a series of casts (called serial casting) are applied to hold the foot in place. For the first three months, these casts are usually changed weekly. After three months, it is determined whether surgery would also be helpful.

Colon: Last portion of the large intestine before the rectum.

Coma: State of unconsciousness from which a person cannot be roused. A child who is unconscious needs emergency medical attention.

Compress: Cloth or container used to apply heat or cold to the body.

Concussion: Very brief loss of consciousness secondary to an injury to the head.

Congenital: Present at birth.

Congenital heart disease: Used to describe a grouping of inherited heart diseases and anatomical anomalies of the heart a baby is born with. **Atrial Septal Defect (ASD)** is a common non-life-threatening heart defect. The septum is the wall that divides the right and left chambers of the heart. The atria are the top chambers of the heart. An ASD is a defect or hole in the wall (septum) that divides the right and left atria. Many septal defects are small and will close on their own during the first two years of life. Larger ones may need surgery. **Ventricular Septal Defect (VSD)** is a defect or hole between the two ventricle chambers of the heart. The ventricles are the lower chambers of the heart. A small VSD may close on its own during the first year or two of life. Larger holes may need surgery to close them. **Coarctation of the Aorta** is a narrowing of the main artery that carries blood away from the heart—the aorta. It causes high blood pressure. Surgery is necessary to correct this anatomical problem. **Patent Ductus Arteriosus** involves a continued opening of the ductus arteriosus, a special channel in the fetus that passes blood from the pulmonary artery to the aorta, bypassing the unused fetal lungs. After birth, this special channel usually closes within two weeks. When it does not close, it is called a patent ductus arteriosus. Surgery is then needed to close it. **Tetralogy of Fallot** is an uncommon but serious heart defect that a baby may be born with. It is a combination of four different structural problems. They include: VSD (a hole between the lower right and left chambers of the heart), Pulmonary Stenosis (narrowing of the pulmonary heart valve that causes decreased flow of blood to the lungs), Misplacement of the aorta (the main artery that sends blood though the body), and Enlargement of the right ventricle. This defect interferes with blood flow to the lungs and thus decreases the amount of oxygen-carrying blood circulating through the body. This is a major cause of **"blue babies."** **Transposition of the Great Arteries** is a very serious defect. The two great arteries are the pulmonary artery that takes blood to the lungs to get oxygen, and the aorta that takes oxygen-rich blood into circulation throughout the body. In this congenital heart defect, these great arteries are reversed, and oxygen-rich blood cannot be circulated through the body. Immediate surgery is needed to correct the problem.

Congestive Heart Failure (CHF): Heart condition in which the heart is unable to pump enough blood to supply the body with needed oxygen and nutrients.

Contusion: Skin injury that does not break the skin but involves swelling, discoloration, and pain.

CPR: Cardiopulmonary resuscitation. It is used to try to revive a child whose breathing and heartbeat have stopped.

Cross-eyes: See **Strabismus**.

Cyanosis: Inadequate oxygen in the blood. Signs and symptoms include bluish skin, lips, and nail beds.

Cystic fibrosis: Inherited disease that causes breathing and digestive difficulties. There is no cure for cystic fibrosis; treatment is aimed at controlling the symptoms.

Dermatitis: Irritation or inflammation of the skin characterized by a rash, itching, redness, swelling, or any other skin lesions. Remove the cause of the irritation, and you will cure the dermatitis.

Dermis: Second layer of skin including all the small blood vessels, nerves, and hair follicles.

Diabetes mellitus: Disease that involves a problem with carbohydrate (glucose) metabolism. It is a serious lifelong illness. Children with diabetes are said to have Type I Diabetes or *Juvenile Diabetes*. This is also *Insulin Dependent Diabetes*. Children with diabetes usually need to take insulin to help regulate the amount of glucose (sugar) in the blood.

Diphtheria: Serious contagious bacterial infection with a potent toxin that causes severe inflammation of the throat and also affects the respiratory system, nerves, muscles, and heart. Children are routinely immunized against diphtheria by their DTP vaccination. Every child should receive this immunization at approximately two months, four months, six months, eighteen months, and between four and six years of age prior to entering kindergarten. Once fully immunized, a child will not contract this very serious illness.

Down Syndrome: Congenital disorder caused by a chromosome abnormality. Chromosomes carry a person's genes. Ninety-five percent of children with Down syndrome usually have forty-seven instead of forty-six chromosomes in the cells of the body; this is called Trisomy 21. The rest have what is called translocation of chromosomes. Down syndrome is associated with other birth defects including congenital heart disease. Children with Down syndrome benefit from early intervention programs and special education.

Dyspnea: Shortness of breath.

Electrocardiogram: Record of the electrical activity of the heart as it beats. Also known as EKG or ECG.

Electrolytes: Special minerals in the blood, tissue fluids, and cells. They include sodium, potassium, calcium, magnesium, and chloride.

Emollient: Soothing and softening. Often used to describe a cream with or without medicine added.

Encephalitis: Very serious illness that involves inflammation of the brain. It can be caused by a virus or bacterial infection. Rarely, encephalitis may occur as a reaction to a pertussis (whooping cough) vaccination. The symptoms include stiff neck (or inability to touch your chin to your chest), fever, headache, projectile vomiting, sleepiness or confusion, lack of coordination, and convulsions. Encephalitis is a serious life-threatening illness that requires immediate medical attention.

Encopresis: Condition associated with constipation when hard, dry stools accumulate in the lower part of the bowel and loose, watery stools trickle out past it. The first sign is frequent soiling of bowel material in your child's underpants after he has been toilet trained.

Enuresis: Lack of bladder control. When it occus only at night, it is called nocturnal enuresis.

Epidermis: Top layer of skin. It is the area that is usually injured in a sunburn, cut, or scrape.

Epiglottis: Tissue flap that closes over the windpipe (trachea) when food is swallowed to keep it from going down into the lungs.

Epiglottitis: Infection of the flap of tissue that closes over the windpipe when food is swallowed. The flap and the surrounding area swell, and there are problems with breathing and swallowing. It is very serious because blockage of the airway can occur due to swelling.

Epistaxis: Nosebleed. Usually used to describe a particularly large nosebleed.

Erythema: Generalized redness of the skin.

Failure to thrive: Used to describe an infant or child who does not grow physically and falls below the growth curve for his age and starts to lose weight rather than gain it. It can also be associated with developmental delays.

Febrile: Having a fever or elevated body temperature. A child is considered to have a fever when his rectal temperature reads 100.6°F.

Febrile convulsion: Seizure that occurs when a child has a rapidly rising body temperature, often associated with a viral infection. Febrile seizures usually occur between the ages of six months and four years and, in general, do not have any long-term effects. It is thought that the tendency to have a febrile seizure runs in families.

Fontanelle: Soft spot in a baby's head that lies between the cranial bones in the skull. The posterior fontanelle at the back of the baby's head usually closes by age two to four months, and the front or anterior fontanelle closes before the end of the second year.

Gamma globulin: Part of the blood that carries antibodies to fight disease. It is sometimes given to a person who has been exposed to a certain disease in the hopes of preventing him from getting it or at least to lessen its impact.

Gastrointestinal: Having to do with the stomach and the intestines. Abbreviated GI.

Generic: Word used to describe medicines sold under a chemical or descriptive name rather than a brand name. Acetaminophen is the generic name for Tylenol. Generic medicines often cost less than brand medicines but contain essentially the same drug.

Genito-urinary: Pertaining to the genitals and urinary tract organs. Commonly abbreviated GU.

Gestation: Length of time from conception to birth.

Giardiasis: Infestation of the intestinal tract by the microorganism *giardia lamblia*. It may cause diarrhea and abdominal pain. It is easily spread and often occurs in day care centers and nursery schools.

Glaucoma: Eye disorder caused by an increase in pressure in the eye. If not treated, the pressure can damage the optic nerve and blood vessels in the eye and can result in blindness. Children most often suffer from infantile glaucoma. This may be present at birth or develop early in life.

Heart murmur: Extra heart sound made by the heart as blood is pumped through the body.

Hematocrit: Measurement of the percentage of red blood cells in the blood. It is done with a blood sample. A normal hematocrit for a child is between 33 and 42 percent. A normal hematocrit for a newborn is between 44 and 77 percent.

Hematoma: Bruise or collection of blood trapped in tissues of the skin or other organ.

Hemoglobin: Measurement of the part of the blood that carries oxygen taken from a blood sample. Normal hemoglobin for a child is 11–14 gm/dl.

Haemophilus influenza-B: Bacterial infection not related to influenza. Similar to a cold, it is carried in the upper respiratory tract. Can be serious, particularly in babies and small children and can lead to meningitis, epiglottitis, and pneumonia. Children can be protected against this with the Hib vaccination given at two, four, six, and twelve to eighteen months.

Hemorrhage: Severe loss of blood from a blood vessel. Can be internal (when blood passes into the tissues surrounding a ruptured blood vessel) or external (when the blood escapes from the body).

Hepatitis: Serious liver inflammation that causes destruction of the liver cells, most often caused by a virus. Vaccinations are available for Hepatitis A, the most contagious, and Hepatitis B, the most serious. Routine immunization for Hepatitis B for children is available in most states. You should consider having your child immunized against Hepatitis A if you do a lot of traveling, particularly to areas outside the U.S. and western Europe.

Herpes viruses: Group of three different viruses. Herpes simplex I causes cold sores. Herpes simplex II causes venereal disease. *Herpes zoster* causes shingles.

Hydrocephalus: Condition that results from an excess accumulation of cerebral spinal fluid within the cavities of a baby's brain. It usually results in a swelling of the head. Hydrocephalus is often treated with the placement of a shunt that enables the extra fluid to drain from the brain into another part of the body.

Hypertension: High blood pressure. It can exist as a disease or may be a symptom of another illness. A child's blood pressure is usually measured at his regular checkups starting at age three.

Hyperthermia: Circumstance in which the body temperature exceeds the normal range; it usually means a very high fever. Also known as **hyperpyrexia**.

Hypoglycemia: Low blood sugar. Symptoms include extreme tiredness, restlessness, irritability, weakness, seizures, or coma.

Hypothermia: Circumstance in which the body temperature falls dramatically below the normal range to approximately 93°F or 35°C. It is usually associated with prolonged exposure to cold.

Imperforate anus: Congenital condition that is usually a result of a defect of the lower colon or rectum so that a baby does not have an external rectal opening. It literally means "absent anus." It can be surgically corrected but not prevented.

Incubation: Time between exposure to a disease when the infectious agent enters the body to the start of symptoms in someone who may contract the disease.

Inflammation: Symptom of injury or infection that usually involves swelling, redness, and pain. It is often indicated by the suffix "-itis" at the end of a word. For example, appendicitis is an infection of the appendix.

Intussusception: Condition in which a part of the intestine loops or telescopes through another part of the intestine and becomes stuck. It then causes an intestinal obstruction resulting in sharp abdominal pain. The intestine must be pushed back to its normal position. This requires medical intervention either through a special X-ray procedure or surgery.

Jaundice: Yellow discoloration of the skin, mucous membranes, and sclera (white part of the eyes) caused by a greater-than-normal amount of bilirubin (a by-product of the liver) in the circulating blood. Can be caused by a disease of the liver, gall bladder, biliary system, or blood.

Kawasaki disease: Rare illness that affects children usually under five years of age. It causes fever, rash, swelling of hands and feet, conjunctivitis, increased redness of the tongue and mucous membranes in the mouth, and swollen lymph nodes in the neck. It is thought to be caused by a virus but doesn't seem to be contagious. It may affect the blood vessels of the heart.

Laceration: Torn, jagged cut in the skin.

Lactose intolerance: Difficulty digesting cow's milk caused by a deficiency of the enzyme lactase. Lactase helps to digest the sugar in milk (lactose). Lack of it causes diarrhea and vomiting whenever something with lactose in it is eaten. This condition is inherited. Some individuals will develop it later in life.

Laryngitis: Inflammation of the larynx or voice box, caused by a virus or bacteria. Common symptoms include a hoarse voice, dry or barking cough, and sometimes a fever. It can be serious in young children because a swollen voice box can block a small airway and cause breathing difficulty and croup. It is usually accompanied by a mild cold or sore throat and lasts about two weeks.

Lead poisoning: Illness caused by swallowing or breathing of substances containing lead. It is very dangerous, particularly in children under five years of age. Children are most often affected by lead dust and lead paint in older homes. Lead dust can get on children's hands and toys, and from there into their mouths. It can cause permanent damage to a child's brain and kidneys at a certain blood level.

Leukemia: Most common type of childhood cancer involving both the bone marrow and the circulating blood. It causes the rapid growth of immature white blood cells that prevent the normal growth of red blood cells. This results in both an increased susceptibility to infection (because of a lack of normal white blood cells) and anemia (because of a lack of red blood cells). Leukemia also prevents the growth of platelets, which causes problems with normal blood clotting. Possible symptoms of leukemia include increased tiredness, paleness, anemia, increased infections, a tendency to bruise easily, increased nosebleeds, limb pain, and a purplish red rash on the body that doesn't disappear with pressure.

Malignant: Describes a tumor with an uncontrolled growth of abnormal cells that spreads to nearby tissue.

Measles: Infectious disease caused by a particular virus; starts with cold-like symptoms for three or four days, and then a rash usually starts behind the ears and eventually spreads all over the body. Sometimes the eyes are red and watery, and sometimes there are small white spots inside the cheeks (Koplik's spots). The fever is high, and your child feels very sick during the first two days when the rash is spreading. Complications from measles include otitis media (earache), pneumonia, and encephalitis. Measles and its possible complication should be prevented with immunization through the MMR vaccination. This is usually given at fifteen months, with a booster at approximately five years.

Meckel's diverticulum: Condition in which an abnormal finger-like outpouching occurs in the small intestine. It occurs when a duct necessary during the first month of fetal development does not disappear. This may cause twisting, an obstruction, or bleeding at some point. Symptoms include sudden, painless rectal bleeding or blood in a bowel movement. Surgery is required to repair this if the diverticulum becomes inflamed or bleeds.

Melanoma: Malignant, darkly pigmented skin mole often associated with excessive sun exposure.

Metabolism: Complex chemical process used by the body to break down food, utilize oxygen, build tissue, and evacuate waste products.

Molluscum contagiosum: Viral skin infection that appears as a raised, waxy, pimple-like rash. It is quite contagious and is spread by direct contact or through contact with clothing or towels used by an infected person.

Mumps: Infectious disease caused by a particular virus that affects the salivary glands, principally the parotid glands that are located under the ear lobes. It usually starts with swelling under the ear and pushes the ear up, thus changing the shape of your child's face. There may also be a fever. An older child may complain of pain around his ear or the side of his throat, and he may feel generally sick. The swelling usually lasts three or four days but can last as long as ten days. Complications from mumps include encephalitis or meningitis. Mumps and any possible complications from the disease should be prevented with immunization through the MMR vaccination. This is given at fifteen months, with a booster at approximately five years.

Muscular dystrophy: Term given to group of congenital disorders characterized by a gradual weakening and wasting of the muscle fibers. Early possible symptoms include late development in ability to sit, walk, and run; difficulty getting upright and climbing stairs; poor balance; waddling gait or toe walking; and overdeveloped-looking muscles.

The most common form of the disease in children is called **Duchenne muscular dystrophy**, which affects boys only.

Neonate: Stage of life from birth to one month; newborn.

Neonatologist: Doctor who specializes in the care of newborn babies from birth to one month.

Nephritis: Inflammation of the kidney caused by an infection or result of sensitivity to a medicine.

Osteomyelitis: Rare, bacterial infection of the bone characterized by extreme pain and tenderness over a red, swollen area of skin over a bone.

Pedialyte: Brand name of a solution of electrolytes including water, minerals, and sugar that can be given orally to prevent dehydration during an illness involving vomiting and diarrhea.

Pediatric Nurse Practitioner (PNP): Registered nurse with advanced training and/or education in the care of pediatrics who is able to provide primary care for children in an outpatient, hospital, or community setting.

Pertussis: Whooping cough. Begins similar to a regular cold with a mild, dry cough. During the second week the cough becomes more intense with eight to ten coughs in one breath, sometimes followed by vomiting. The "whoop" is the crowing sound a child makes trying to get her breath back after a coughing spell. Whooping cough usually lasts one month, but it can go on for as long as three months. It can be very serious in babies and children under five years of age. Medical treatment with antibiotics and respiratory management is required. Children should be protected against whooping cough by immunization against it with the DPT vaccination. The "P" stands for "pertussis."

Petechiae: Small purple-reddish spots on the skin that do not blanch when pressed.

PKU (phenylketonuria): Inherited metabolic disorder that can lead to mental retardation if a special diet isn't followed. A special blood test is done at birth to check for this disorder.

Poison Control Center: Network of facilities that provides information on all aspects of poisoning, poison substances, and how to treat them. Usually has a local or toll-free number in the U.S. Keeps records of all occurrences of poisoning to help educate the public.

Poliomyelitis (Polio): Serious viral infection of the gray matter of the spinal cord. In major cases muscle paralysis occurs, including paralysis of the breathing muscles. This disease can be prevented in children with a polio vaccination. There are two types of polio vaccine available. The oral polio vaccine is the most common type administered in the U.S. today. The OPV, oral polio vaccine or Sabin vaccine, is an attenuated live polio virus (type 1, 2, or 3) given four times: at ages two, four, and eighteen months, and again at about age five. The IPV, inactivated polio vaccine or Salk vaccine, is an injection given to children who are unable to take the live virus.

Postural drainage: Use of position to help drain secretions from different areas of the lungs.

Prophalactic: Preventive.

Pruritus: Itching.

Pulmonary: Pertaining to the lungs and respiratory system.

Pulmonary stenosis: Abnormally narrow heart valve between the right ventricle chamber of the heart and the pulmonary artery: the main artery that takes blood to the lungs. Any narrowing of this artery slows blood flow. If it is severe, surgery can be performed.

Purulent: Producing or containing pus.

Pyloric Stenosis: Obstruction at the lower end of the stomach near the pyloric valve. The most telltale symptom is projectile vomiting (persistent forceful vomiting) after feeding. It usually begins in infants two to three weeks old.

Reflux: Abnormal backward flow or return of fluid.

Regurgitation: Return of swallowed food into the mouth.

Respiratory Distress Syndrome (RDS): Failure of the lungs to expand with air because of the absence of an essential substance called surfactant. Also known as Hyaline Membrane Disease. It is usually the result of premature birth because the lungs have not achieved full development. The incidence of RDS is very high in babies born before the twentieth-week gestation. At birth, these babies have shallow, fast breathing and a blue skin color. They usually require artificial respiration in an intensive care unit.

Respiratory Syncytial Virus (RSV): RSV is a highly contagious viral infection that begins with cold-like symptoms. In babies under the age of one, it can be very serious and progresses rapidly from a runny nose to wheezing and difficulty breathing. The symptoms that should prompt you to call your doctor immediately include: wheezing, fever greater than 101°F taken rectally, more than sixty breaths per minute for children under the age of two years (forty breaths per minute for children over the age of two years), inability to suck and breathe at the same time, pale color, difficulty sleeping but lethargic, extremely runny nose, and loss of appetite. RSV appears every October, peaks in January and February, and disappears in the spring. Babies and younger children are more susceptible to more serious illness with RSV.

Retinoblastoma: Retinoblastoma is the most common eye cancer in children. It is most often malignant and affects the rear portion of the eye which receives the light rays, the retina. It usually affects just one eye, and the predominant symptom is a whitish cast on the pupil.

Reye's syndrome: Reye's syndrome is a very serious (possibly fatal), noncontagious illness, characterized by brain dysfunction and liver failure. Sometimes there are also problems with the pancreas, heart, kidney, spleen, and lymph nodes. Reye's syndrome usually begins two to seven days after a viral infection, particularly influenza type A and B, and chicken pox. Symptoms include forceful vomiting, sleepiness, hallucinations, delirium, and aggressive, uncooperative behavior. Onset of the disease has also been linked to the use of aspirin with a viral illness, though aspirin has not been involved in every case.

Rheumatic fever: Serious illness that affects the heart and joints. It is associated with certain types of streptococcal infections. Symptoms include fever and joint pain and sometimes a sore throat or swollen joints. It is rare in children under two years of age and most often affects children ages five to fifteen.

Rhinitis: Inflammation of the mucous membranes in the nose; often causes a runny nose.

Rickets: Rickets is a childhood disorder in which the bones become soft and deformed because of a deficiency of Vitamin D, calcium, or phosphate.

Rocky Mountain Spotted Fever: Infectious disease spread by wood ticks and dog ticks. A child becomes ill one to eight days following a tick bite in an infected area. Symptoms include fever and a characteristic purple or rose red rash that spreads from the torso to the wrists and palms of the hands, and to the ankles and soles of the feet.

Rubella: Rubella, also known as the **German measles** or three-day measles, is a viral infection characterized by a low fever and runny nose followed in one to two days by a rash of small, red, slightly raised spots. It also usually gives a child swollen neck glands, and joint pain and swelling. The rash usually begins on the face, then spreads to the rest of the body and lasts around three days. Most children are vaccinated against rubella with the MMR vaccination. Any possible complication should be prevented with immunization through the MMR vaccination. This is usually given at fifteen months of age with a booster shot at approximately five years of age. If an unimmunized pregnant woman is exposed to active rubella, especially in the first trimester, there is risk of a birth defect to the developing fetus (blindness, deafness, and heart disease).

Scabies: Skin infestation by mites, characterized by severe itching and a reddish rash, usually between the fingers, toes, palms, and soles of the feet. Can be treated with an over-the-counter anti-mite lotion or cream. Ask your doctor for a specific product.

Seborrheic dermatitis: Chronic skin condition of red, scaly, irregularly shaped patches of skin. It is commonly found behind the skin folds of the ear, on the face, and on the scalp. Looks similar to psoriasis. Affected skin surfaces can be treated with a corticosteroid cream for the skin, prescribed by your doctor. If the scalp area is involved, use a special medicated shampoo such as Neutrogena Therapeutic T-Gel Shampoo.

Sepsis: Infection in which bacteria are found in the bloodstream. Can be very serious in neonates.

Shingles: Painful rash caused by the *herpes zoster* virus. The rash starts as a cluster of red pimples that blister and then crust over. It follows the path of nerves and is very painful.

Shock: Serious disorder of blood circulation caused by serious illness or injury. Symptoms of shock include weakness; cool, clammy, and pale skin; excessive thirst; weak pulse; dizziness; and difficulty breathing. **Traumatic shock** is caused by a serious injury. **Anaphylactic shock** is caused by a severe allergic reaction to a certain substance. With anaphylactic shock, the child may also have hives, swelling of the eyes, skin, tongue, or throat. **Insulin shock** is caused by too high a level of insulin, usually when administered to a diabetic.

Sinusitis: Sinusitis is an inflammation and infection of the lining of the sinuses. It often follows a cold and usually affects older children. Symptoms include: fever, opaque or discolored nasal discharge, mouth breathing, morning cough, and fatigue.

Spasm: Sudden onset of involuntary muscle movement.

Spina bifida: Failure of one or more of the vertebrae in a fetus's spine to join properly during the first month of fetal development. The mild form is called *spina bifida occulta*. The only symptom of this form at birth may be a small dimple or birthmark on the lower spine at the site of the defect. The more severe form has a *meningomyelocele*. The spinal cord and its nerves are exposed at a point on the baby's spine. Some of the spinal fluid may leak. Spinal nerves do not develop past the opening, so nerves needed for walking and bladder and bowel control may be incomplete. A newborn with an exposed spinal cord and nerves requires surgery to close the spine soon after birth. If the circulation of cerebral spinal fluid is blocked, fluid accumulates in the baby's brain causing his head to enlarge. This is called **hydrocephalus.** Babies with hydrocephalus may require a shunt operation in which a plastic tube (shunt) is inserted to allow excess fluid from the brain to drain to some other part of the body such as the bloodstream.

Spurious diarrhea: Name given to false diarrhea. Usually seen with severe constipation when stool or feces leak around the blockage.

Sterile: Without germs.

Steri-strip: Commercial term for thin "butterfly" tape used to help close a small, deep cut that gapes open a little.

Strabismus: Strabismus is the medical term for **cross-eyes**. This means that a child cannot focus both eyes on the same object at the same time. A child with cross-eyes may begin to favor one eye without realizing it; this allows the child to have normal vision in the preferred eye. A condition called **lazy eye** develops in the eye not being used and it loses some of its ability to see. For infants under six months of age, some wandering of the eye is normal; a baby learns to focus and control eye muscles between the ages of three to six months. If you have any questions about your baby's eyes, bring it to the attention of her doctor at the next visit.

Sudden Infant Death Syndrome (SIDS): Also known as **crib death**, this refers to the sudden, inexplicable death of a healthy baby between three weeks and seven months of age. There is no medical explanation; the baby is simply found dead in the crib. It is currently thought that putting a baby to sleep in the crib on his side or back for the first seven months will help prevent this phenomenon. Call the National Sudden Infant Death Syndrome Alliance at 1-800-221-SIDS for the most up-to-date information.

Suppository: Medicine made to be given by insertion into the rectum or vagina.

Sutures: Surgical stitches to close a gaping wound.

Tetanus: Serious but rare bacterial infection (caused by the bacteria *clostridium tetani*) found in dirt, gravel, and rusty metal. It enters the body through a cut and makes a poison in the bloodstream that causes the muscles to go into spasm. The jaw muscles are usually the first ones affected; the common name for this illness is **lockjaw**. Tetanus is entirely preventable if your child has received his tetanus immunization through his DPT shots and maintains tetanus booster shots every ten years for the rest of his life.

Tonsils: Tonsils are lymph tissue located in the throat near the base of the tongue. With your adenoids, they serve as a defense against infection by filtering bacteria and other infections that are in the mouth. **Tonsillitis** is an infection and inflammation of the tonsils themselves. It is very common in young children and only presents a problem if it interferes with breathing or swallowing. Children usually outgrow their susceptibility to tonsillitis. **Tonsillectomy** is the surgical removal of the tonsils. In the past this was done when a child had a large number of strep throat infections. It was determined, however, that removing the tonsils did not lessen the severity or number of these illnesses. Today a tonsillectomy is performed only if there is a pronounced problem with breathing or swallowing.

Tracheoesophageal Fistula (TEF): TEF is a rare abnormal connection between the trachea, windpipe, and esophagus (food pipe). It is commonly detected during one of your baby's first feedings when he spits up any liquid swallowed. Pneumonia is a very serious complication. Surgery is needed to correct the problem as soon as possible. Even after surgery, however, these babies will have lifelong problems with swallowing and will have to learn special techniques.

Tuberculosis (TB): Tuberculosis is a chronic infectious disease caused by the tubercle bacillus; it is unusually resistant to ordinary antibiotics. The infection is spread through the air when a person with active TB coughs. It usually affects the lungs, called pulmonary TB. Early symptoms of TB include extreme fatigue, loss of appetite, headache, and cough. As the disease continues, children will have "night sweats", cough up blood, and experience breathlessness and fever. In its early stages, TB can be mistaken for pneumonia. The BCG vaccine offers some protection and is used routinely in areas where the disease is common. Most children have a TB-screen skin test called a PPD (purified protein derivative) around nine months to one year of age, and every three to four years after that. A few children may fall into a high-risk category and require a yearly PPD skin test.

Ulcerative colitis: Ulcerative colitis is an inflammatory disease of the large intestine or colon. Diarrhea with mucus, pus, or blood is the most common symptom. It usually affects older children after the age of ten.

Undescended testicles: The testicles, a male's reproductive organs, form early in fetal development; however, they remain in the fetus's abdomen until the thirty-second to thirty-sixth week of gestation, and then descend into the scrotum. A testicle that does not reach the scrotum is known as undescended. Your physician will feel for the testicles during your baby's regular physical exam. Surgery can be performed to correct this. Your baby's doctor will discuss the best time to have this corrected.

Uticaria: Hives.

Vaccine: Substance used for inoculation to prevent contagious disease.

Varicella: Chicken pox virus.

Wheal: Elevated white to pinkish circular ridge that is very itchy. A mosquito bite often leaves a wheal.

Wheezing: Sound in chest due to narrowing of the air passages that lead to the lungs, which causes breathing difficulty.

Wilm's tumor: Wilm's tumor is a cancer of the kidneys that commonly affects children under the age of five. The cause is unknown, but the most common sign is a swollen or bloated abdomen. If detected early, the disease can be treated successfully with surgery, radiation, or chemotherapy.

Yeast infection: Infection caused by monilla. Common yeast infections in children include thrush and certain diaper rashes.

Bibliography

American Academy of Pediatrics. *2000 Red Book: Report of the Committee on Infectious Disease*. Edited by G. Peter. 25th ed. Elk Grove Village, Ill.: American Academy of Pediatrics, 2000.

American Academy of Pediatrics. Toilet Training Round Table Participants. "Physiological and Clinical Considerations Regarding Toilet Training: An Updated Review." In *Pediatrics* 103 (6): 1350–1377.

Barkin, Roger M. *Problem-Oriented Pediatric Diagnosis*. Boston: Little, Brown and Company, 1990.

Behrman, R. E., R. M. Kliegman, and H. B. Jenson, eds. *Nelson's Textbook of Pediatrics*. Philadelphia: W. B. Saunders Company, 2000.

Betz, Cecily L., and Linda A. Sowden. *Mosby's Pediatric Nursing Reference*. St. Louis: Mosby Yearbook, 1996.

Boynton, Rose W., Elizabeth S. Dunn, and Geraldine R. Stephens. *Manual of Ambulatory Pediatrics*. Philadelphia: J. P. Lippincott Company, 1994.

Brown, Jeffrey L. *Pediatric Telephone Medicine: Principles, Triage and Advice*. Philadelphia: J. P. Lippincott Company, 1994.

Chow, M. P. Durand *Handbook of Pediatric Primary Care*. 2d ed. Albany: Delmar Publisher, Inc., 1984.

Clemes, Harris, and Reynold Bean. *How to Discipline Children Without Feeling Guilty*. Los Angeles: Price Stern Sloan, 1990.

Erikson, Erik. *Childhood in Society*. New York: W. W. Norton, 1991.

Fraiberg, S. H. *The Magic Years*. New York: Scribner's, 1984.

Johnson, K. K., ed. *The Harriet Lane Handbook: A Manual for Pediatric House Officers*. St. Louis: C. V. Mosby, 1994.

Leach, P. *Your Baby and Child Care*. New York: Alfred A. Knopf, 1997.

Merenstein, Gerald B., David W. Kaplan, and Adam A. Rosenberg. *Handbook of Pediatrics*. Norwalk, Conn.: Appleton and Lange, 1994.

Offit, P. A. and L. M. Bell. *What Every Parent Should Know About Vaccines*. New York: Simon & Schuster, 1998.

Oski, F. A., et al. *Principles and Practice of Pediatrics*. Philadelphia: J. P. Lippincott Company, 1994.

Physician's Desk Reference, 54th ed. Montvale, N. J.: Medical Economics Company, 1999.

Physician's Desk Reference for Non-Prescription Drugs, 19th ed. Montvale: Medical Economics Company, 1998.

Potter, Patricia A., and Anne G. Perry. *Fundamentals of Nursing: Concepts, Process and Practice*. St. Louis: Mosby Yearbook, 1993.

Rosenstein, Beryl J., and Patricia D. Fosarelli. *Pediatric Pearls: The Handbook of Practical Pediatrics*. St. Louis: C. V. Mosby, 1993.

Schiff, D., and S. P. Shelov. American Academy of Pediatrics: *The Official Complete Home Reference Guide to Your Child's Symptoms*. New York: Villard, 1997.

Schmidt, Burton. *Instructions for Pediatric Patients*. Philadelphia: W. B. Saunders Company, 1992.

———. *Pediatric Telephone Advice*. Boston: Little, Brown and Company, 1999.

Stedman's Medical Dictionary. 26th ed. Baltimore: Williams and Wilkins, 1995.

Taber's Cyclopedic Medical Dictionary. Philadelphia: F. A. Davis Company, 1997.

Index

breast pumps, 241

breath-holding spells, 253

breathing
  checking in emergency situation, 210, 211
  of newborns, 228

breathing problems. *See also* allergies; asthma;
  bronchiolitis; bronchitis; croup; pneumonia
    rescue breathing, 211, 212
    stopped breathing, calling emergency med-
      ical help for, 209

breathing stress test, 118

broken bones, 77–78, 186–188
  calling help for, 210

bronchioles, inflammation of, 116–118

bronchiolitis, 30, 116–118

bronchitis, 118–121

bronchodilator, 291

burns, 188–191
  preventing, 191
  when to call for emergency medical help, 210

burping baby, 230–231

C

caffeine, 261

Caladryl lotion, about, 123, 165

calamine lotion, 18, 123, 165

Candida albicans, 174

cancer, 291

candy, 261

canker sores, 121–122

carbon monoxide poisoning, 71, 215

cardiopulmonary resuscitation (CPR), 211–213

car safety, 231–232

car seats, 231–232

celiac disease, 41, 63, 291

chalasia, 90, 248–249, 292

checkups, well-baby/child, 3–8
  procedures, by age, 5–7

chest compression, in CPR, 211, 212

chest physical therapy, 292

chicken pox, 122–125, 286

rash, 84

chicken pox vaccine, 7, 74–75, 125

child health fundamentals, 1–35
  administering medicines, 24–29
  body temperature, 13–17
  calling doctor, 33–34
  choosing doctor, 1–3
  dealing with infectious illnesses, 29–33
  diet, 8–10
  dressing sick child, 34–35
  exercise and physical activity, 12–13
  fluid intake, 10–12
  medical exams, 34
  medical supplies, 17–19
  over-the-counter remedies, 19–24
  return to school after illness, 35
  well-baby/child checkups, 3–8

childproofing house, 93, 253–255

child rearing strategies, 251–276
  discipline basics, 259–261

Children's Development, Guide to, 256–258

chocolate, 261

choking, 53, 54, 55–56, 216–217

circulation, checking in emergency situation,
  210, 211

circumcision, 232

cleft lip, 292

cleft palate, 292

clothes on fire, 217

clubfoot, 292

coarctatin of the aorta, 293

colds, 29, 30, 32, 127–130
  baby's, 233–234
  earaches and, 136

cold sores, 45–46

colic, 125–127, 234

coma, 292

compression bandages, 201

concussion, 219, 292

congenital heart disease, 292–293

congestive heart failure, 293

conjunctivitis, 31, 130–131

hepatitis, 296–297
hepatitis-B vaccine, 5, 7, 74, 286
hernia, 86
herpes simplex virus, 45
hiccoughs (hiccups), 228
hives, 72–73, 84, 104, 108, 214
HMOs, 2–3
honey, and botulism, 144
house fire, 219–220
human bites, 183–184
human papilloma virus, 178
humidifier, cool air, 18, 82, 134, 161
hyaline membrane disease, 301
hydration, 10–12, 39, 68. *See also* dehydration
  constipation and, 47–48, 49
hydrocele, 86–87
hyperactivity, 261
hypothermia, 195, 197

I

ibuprofen, 17, 206, 287
  for fever reduction, 69
  for headaches, 70
ice, applying, 201
illnesses. *See specific illness or problem, e.g.,*
  asthma; chicken pox; rashes
immunizations and vaccinations
  egg allergy and, 73–74, 107
  first, 3
  guidelines for, by age, 5–7, 286
  how they work, 4
  reactions to, 73–76
imperforate anus, 297
impetigo, 31, 85, 152–154
inattention, 261
infants. *See also* babies; newborns
  bathing, 226–227
  bowel movements, 229–230
  colic, 125–127
  diet choices, 8–9
  formulas, 107, 110

jaundice of, 244
  newborn, 223–250
infectious diseases. *See* contagious diseases
inguinal hernia, 86, 87
injuries, 179–207. *See also* emergency
    situations
  bites, animal, 181–182
  bites, human, 183–185
  broken bones, 186–188
  burns, 188–191
  cuts, scrapes, and wounds, 191–193
  facial injuries, 193–195
  first aid basics for, 179–181
  frostbite, 195–197
  penis injury, 197–198
  puncture wounds, 198–200
  sprains, 200–202
  stings, insect, 202–203
  stings, jellyfish, 204–205
  sunburn, 205–206
insect bites, 184–185, 202–203
intussusception, 40
ipecac syrup, 18, 166, 220
  dosage, 166
iron-deficiency anemia, 109, 111
iron supplements, 110, 111

J

jaundice, in infants, 244
jealousy, 262. *See also* sibling rivalry
jellyfish stings, 204–205
jock itch, 168

K

Kawasaki disease, 298
Koplick's spots, 299

L

labels, reading, 106
lacerations, 193

lactose intolerance, 41, 106, 298
language development, 262–263
lanugo, 246
laryngitis, 134, 298
laxatives, 47
lead poisoning, 72, 167
Legg-Calve-Perthes disease, 78
leukemia, 298
lice, 30, 148–152
limb pain, 74–78
limping, 76, 78
lockjaw, 304
lumbar puncture, 158, 159
Lyme disease, 85, 154–159
lymph nodes
  location of, 91, 92
  swollen, 78, 79, 80, 86, 91–92

M

manners, 263
measles vaccine, 4, 74, 75
measurements, 7–8
Meckel's diverticulum, 299
meconium, 229
Medi-Alert bracelet/necklace, 106
medical examinations. *See* exams
medications
  Acyclovir, 125
  allergies to, 107–109
  allergy and rash, 17, 20
  antibiotic creams, topical, 18, 23
  anti-diarrhea, 62
  antifungal creams, topical, 18, 23, 115, 116,
    168
  antihistamines, 55, 66, 103
  anti-itch, 138–139, 140
  anti-seizure, 52
  cough medicine, 18, 21–22, 55, 56
  decongestants, 18, 23
  for diarrhea, 146
  fever-reducing, 17, 23, 69

  for head lice eradication, 149
  to induce vomiting, 18
  non-oral, administering, 29
  oral, administering, 24–27
  over-the-counter remedies, 19–24
  swimmer's ear, 173
  tips on administering, 24–29
medicine allergies, 107–109
melanoma, 229, 299
meningitis, 80, 157–159
migraine headaches, 70
milia, 246
milk allergy, 104, 105
miscarriage, and fifth disease, 141
molluscum contagiosum, 299
Mongolian spots, 229
moro reflex, 245
mouth
  canker sores, 121–122
  cold sores/fever blisters, 45–46
  hand, foot and mouth disease, 146–148
  injuries to, 193–194
  thrush, 174–175
movies 274
mucus, in newborns, 245
mumps vaccine, 4, 74
muscle spasms/cramps, 76, 77, 78
muscle strains, 76, 77, 78
muscular dystrophy, 299–300

N

nail-biting, 264
nasal aspirator, 233, 245
nasal congestion, OTC remedies for, 23
nebulizers, 112, 113
neck pain, 78–80
nevus, congenital, 229
newborns
  acne, 246
  Apgar Score, 224–225
  appearance of, 225–226

S

safety
    car safety, 231–232
    childproofing house, 93, 253–255, 259
    Consumer Product Safety Commission, 255
salmonella, 141
scabies, 303
scarlet fever, 31, 87, 170–171
    rash, 85
scarletina. *See* scarlet fever
scarring, 193
scars, chicken pox, 124
school readiness, 269
scrapes, 191–193
scrotum swelling, 86–87
seborrheic dermatitis, 137
seizures. *See* convulsions or seizures
sharing, concept of, 269–270
shigella, 141
shingles, 124
shock (anaphylaxis), 214
shunt, 303–304
sibling rivalry, 270
SIDS (Sudden Infant Death Syndrome), 248
sight, infant's, 246
sinusitis, 303
skin, newborn, 246–247
skin infections
    applying topical medicines to, 28
    remedies, over-the-counter, 23
sleeping patterns, 271–273
sleeping patterns, babies, 248
sleeping problems, 272–273
sleepwalking, 273
smallpox vaccine, 47
smoke, secondhand, 55
smoke detectors, 220
sore throat, 87–89
spina bifida, 303–304
spinal cord injury, suspected, 221
spinal tap, 158, 159

spitting up (reflux), 89–90, 98, 100, 248–249
splinters, 200
sprains, 200–202
    RICE for, 201
spurious diarrhea, 63, 304
staphlococcus
    boils and, 43
    food poisoning, 141
stethoscope, 34
stiff neck, 80
stings
    insect, 184–185, 201–203
    jellyfish, 204–205
stomachache, *See* abdominal pain; gastro-
    enteritis
stomach flu, 40, 60
stork bite, 229
strabismus, 304
strawberry hemangioma, 229
strep throat, 40, 87, 89, 171
streptococcus infections
    scarlet fever, 40, 87, 89, 170–171
    strep throat, 40, 87, 89
stys, 131
sucking, 264–265
sucking callus, 239
suck-swallow-gag reflex, 245
sudden infant death syndrome, *See* SIDS
sugar in diet, 10, 261
sulfa drugs, reaction to, 109
sunburn, 188, 190, 205–206
    preventing, 206
sun poisoning, 205
supplies to have on hand, 17–19
sutures (stitches), 193
swimmer's ear, 134, 135, 172–173
symptoms, common
    abdominal pain, 37–41
    allergies, 41–43
    boils, 43–45
    cold sores/fever blisters, 45–46
    constipation, 47–49

V